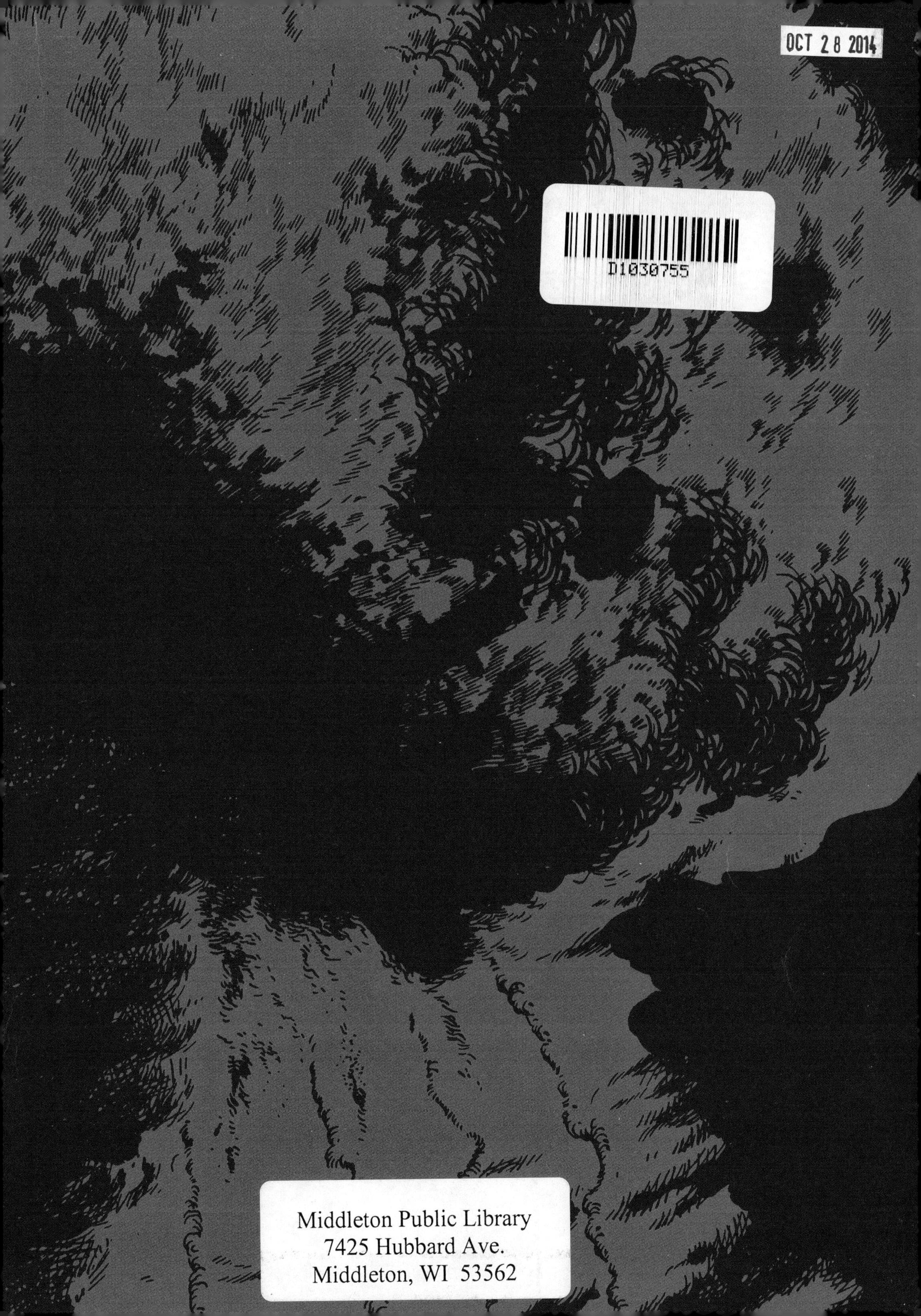

ZEN

PHAS

GRANT MORRISON

E O N E

STEVE**YEOWELL**

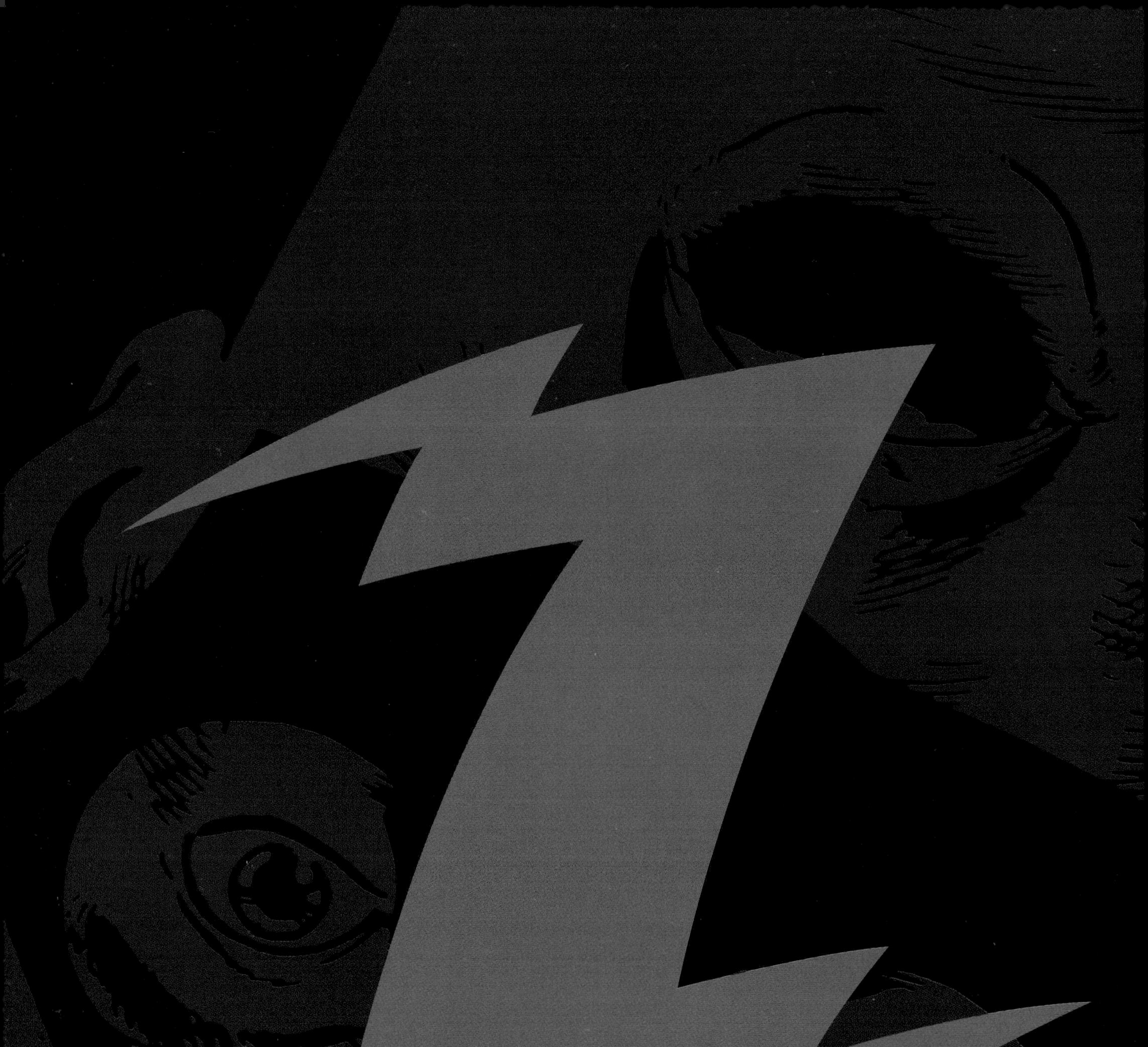

PHASE I

Script: Grant Morrison
Art: Steve Yeowell
Letters: Mark King

Originally published in *2000 AD* Progs 535-550

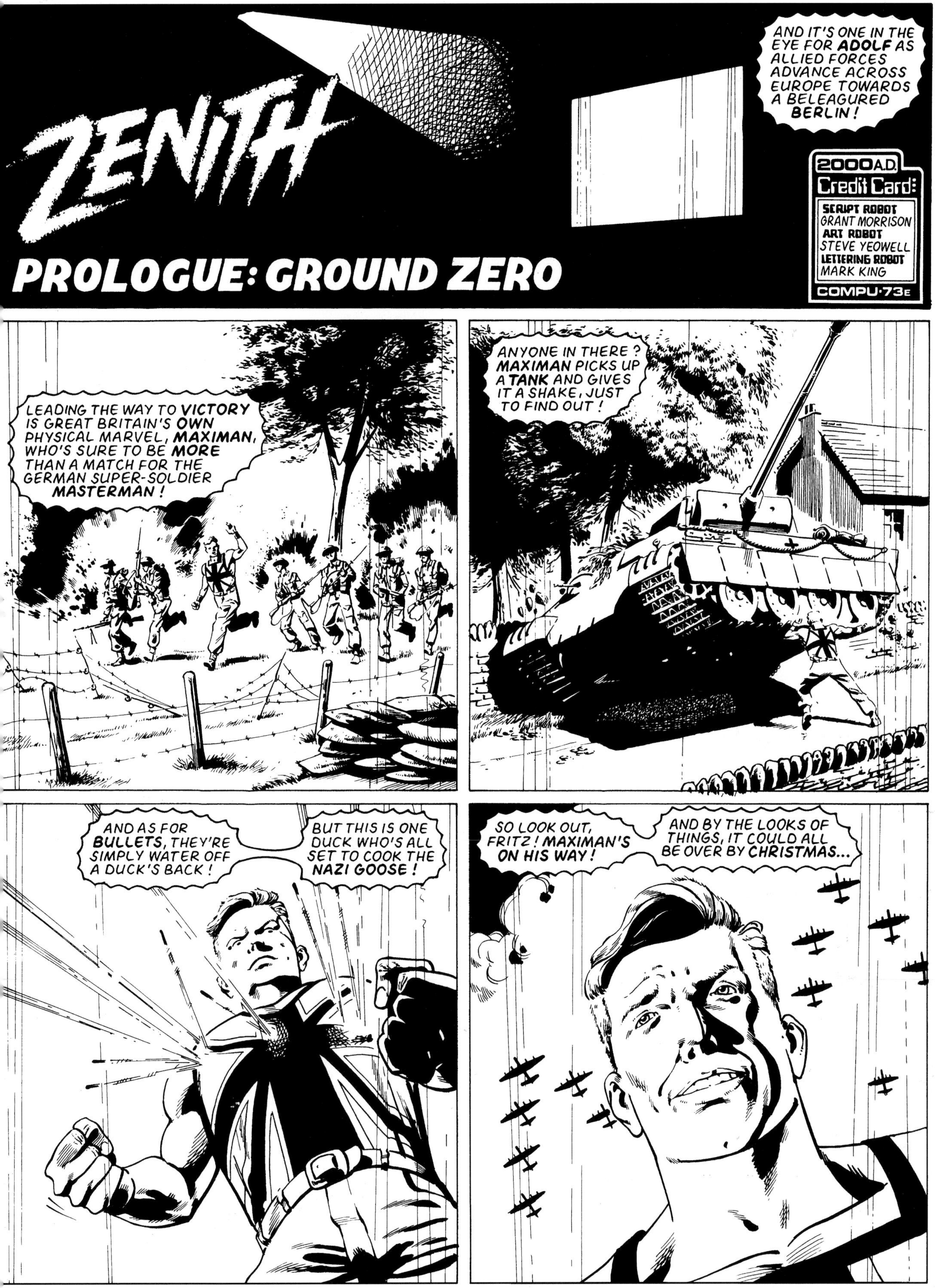
ZENITH
PROLOGUE: GROUND ZERO
AND IT'S ONE IN THE EYE FOR ADOLF AS ALLIED FORCES ADVANCE ACROSS EUROPE TOWARDS A BELEAGURED BERLIN!
2000 A.D. Credit Card: SCRIPT ROBOT GRANT MORRISON ART ROBOT STEVE YEOWELL LETTERING ROBOT MARK KING COMPU·73E
LEADING THE WAY TO VICTORY IS GREAT BRITAIN'S OWN PHYSICAL MARVEL, MAXIMAN, WHO'S SURE TO BE MORE THAN A MATCH FOR THE GERMAN SUPER-SOLDIER MASTERMAN!
ANYONE IN THERE? MAXIMAN PICKS UP A TANK AND GIVES IT A SHAKE, JUST TO FIND OUT!
AND AS FOR BULLETS, THEY'RE SIMPLY WATER OFF A DUCK'S BACK!
BUT THIS IS ONE DUCK WHO'S ALL SET TO COOK THE NAZI GOOSE!
SO LOOK OUT, FRITZ! MAXIMAN'S ON HIS WAY!
AND BY THE LOOKS OF THINGS, IT COULD ALL BE OVER BY CHRISTMAS...

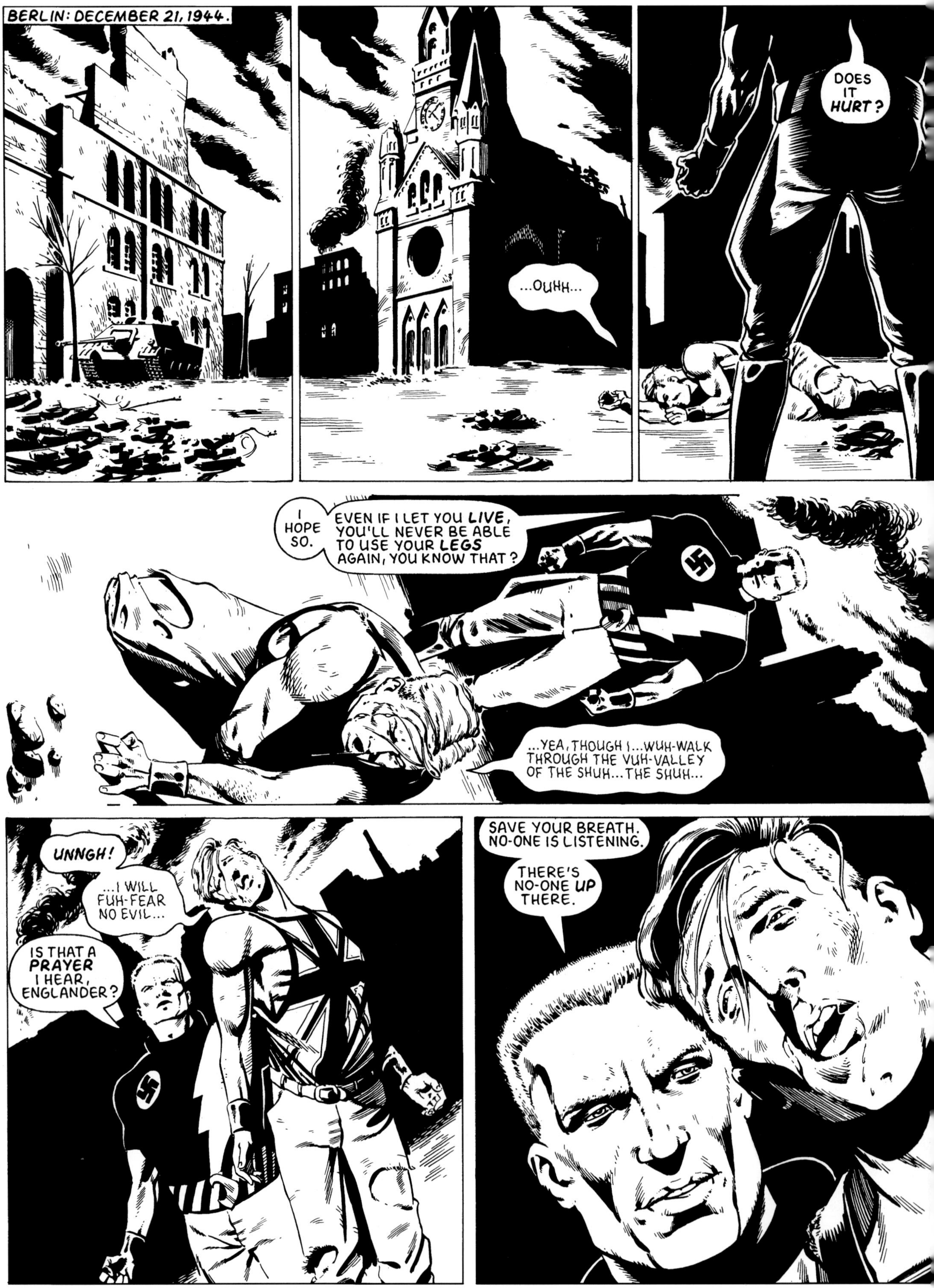
BERLIN: DECEMBER 21, 1944.
...OUHH...
DOES IT HURT?
EVEN IF I LET YOU LIVE, YOU'LL NEVER BE ABLE TO USE YOUR LEGS AGAIN, YOU KNOW THAT?
I HOPE SO.
...YEA, THOUGH I...WUH-WALK THROUGH THE VUH-VALLEY OF THE SHUH...THE SHUH...
UNNGH!
...I WILL FUH-FEAR NO EVIL...
IS THAT A PRAYER I HEAR, ENGLANDER?
SAVE YOUR BREATH. NO-ONE IS LISTENING.
THERE'S NO-ONE UP THERE.

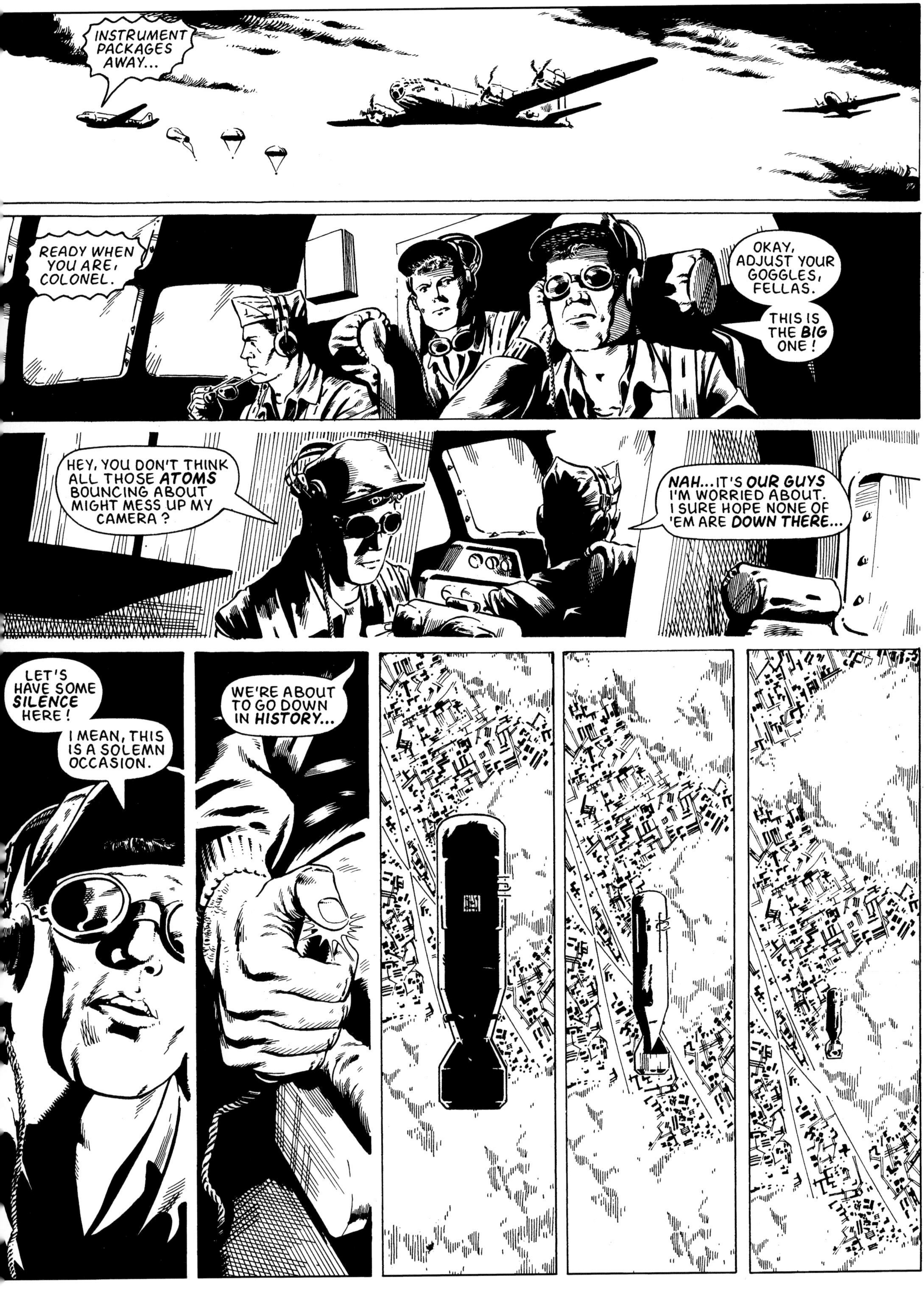

INSTRUMENT PACKAGES AWAY...
READY WHEN YOU ARE, COLONEL.
OKAY, ADJUST YOUR GOGGLES, FELLAS.
THIS IS THE BIG ONE!
HEY, YOU DON'T THINK ALL THOSE ATOMS BOUNCING ABOUT MIGHT MESS UP MY CAMERA?
NAH... IT'S OUR GUYS I'M WORRIED ABOUT. I SURE HOPE NONE OF 'EM ARE DOWN THERE...
LET'S HAVE SOME SILENCE HERE!
I MEAN, THIS IS A SOLEMN OCCASION.
WE'RE ABOUT TO GO DOWN IN HISTORY...

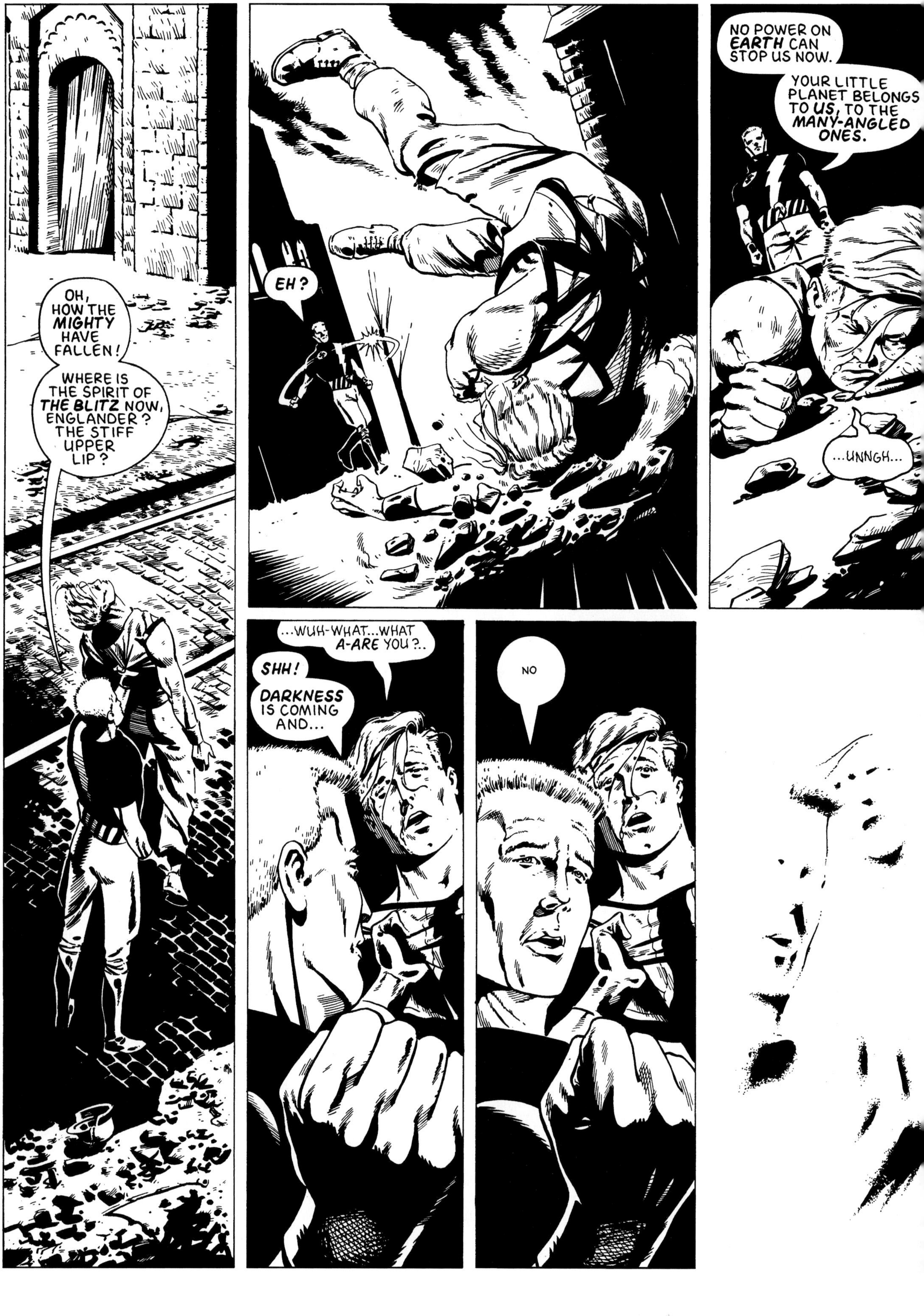
OH, HOW THE MIGHTY HAVE FALLEN!
WHERE IS THE SPIRIT OF THE BLITZ NOW, ENGLANDER? THE STIFF UPPER LIP?
EH?
NO POWER ON EARTH CAN STOP US NOW.
YOUR LITTLE PLANET BELONGS TO US, TO THE MANY-ANGLED ONES.
...UNNGH...
...WUH-WHAT...WHAT A-ARE YOU?..
SHH! DARKNESS IS COMING AND...
NO

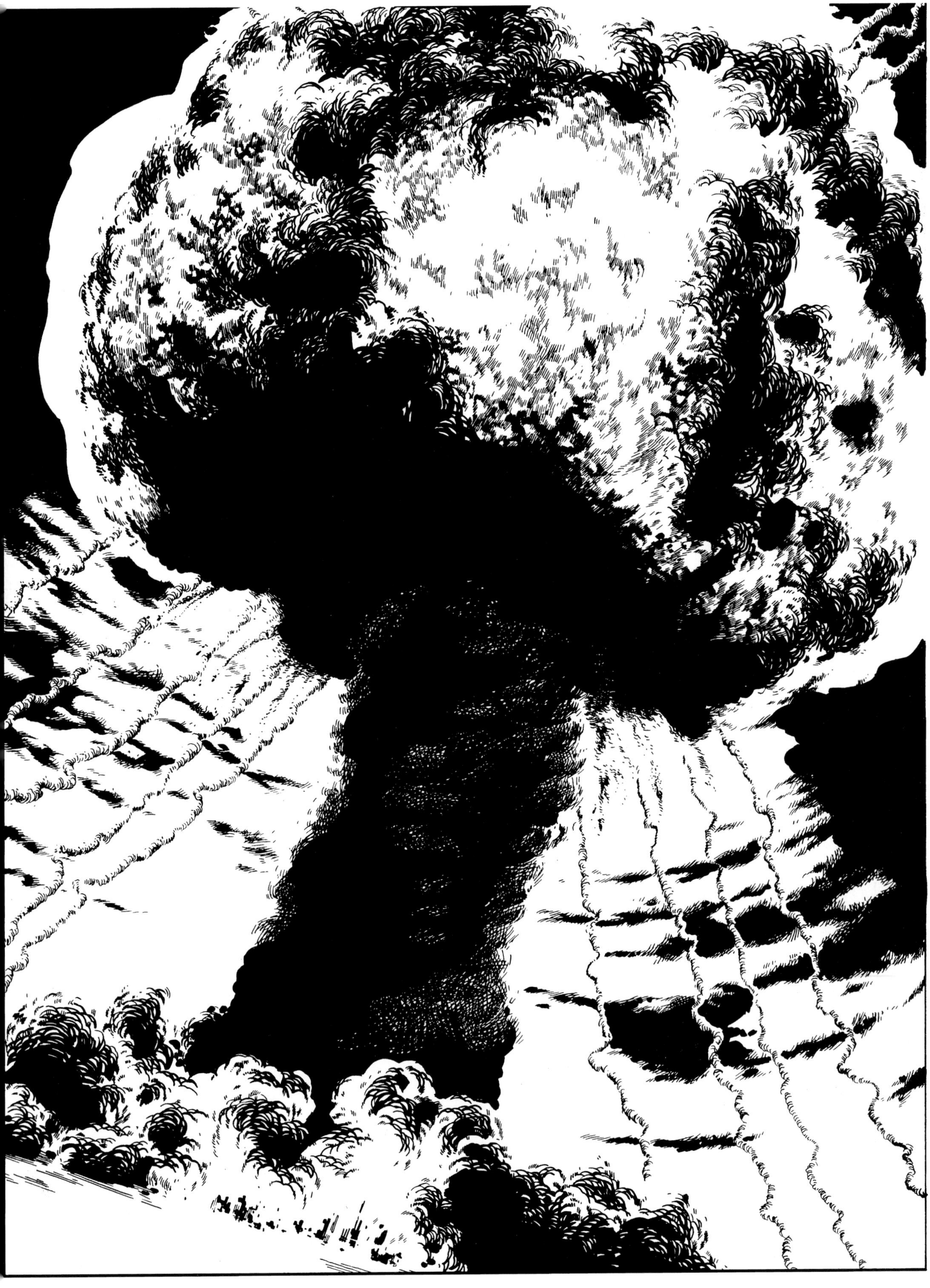

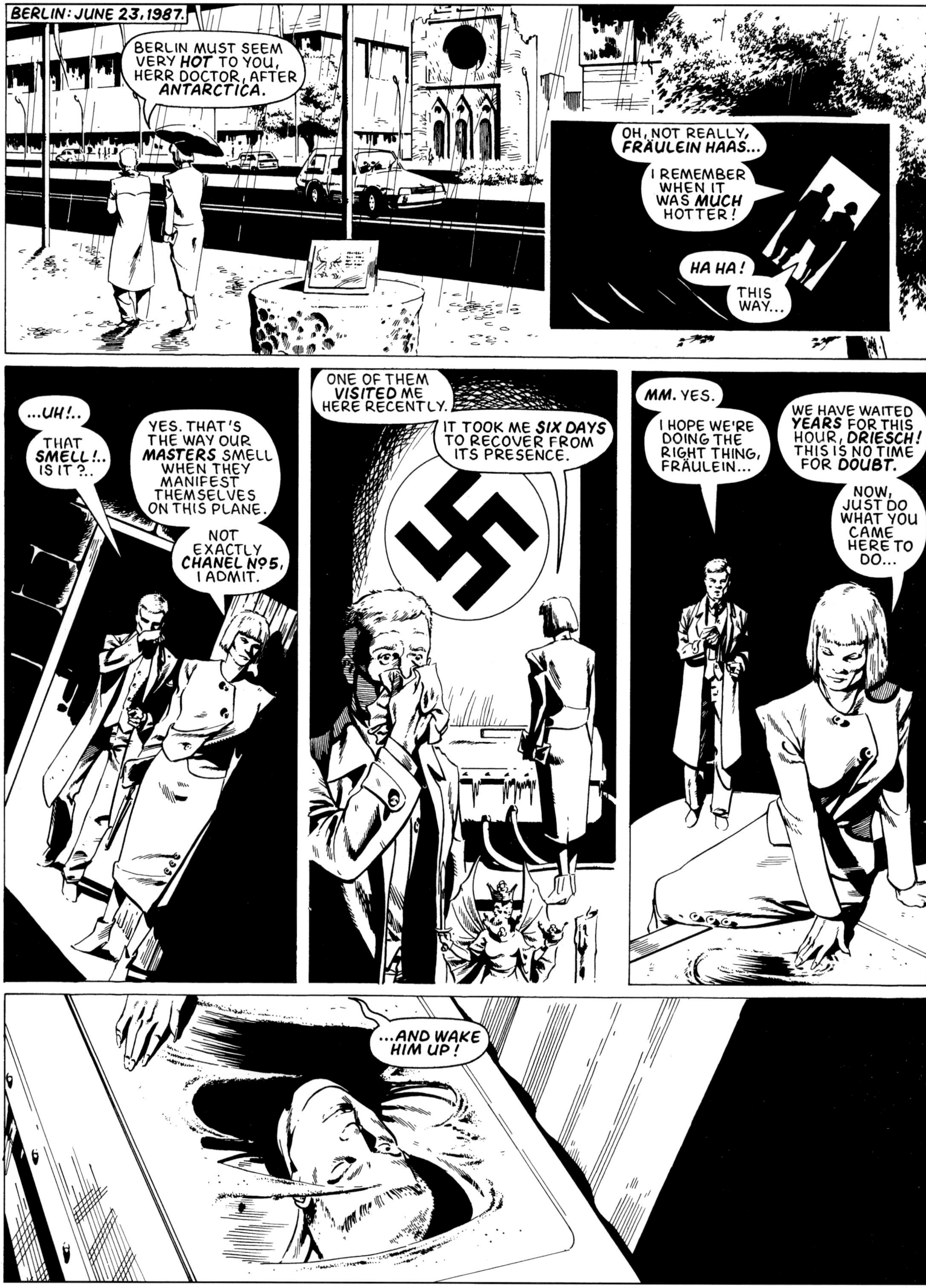
BERLIN: JUNE 23, 1987.
BERLIN MUST SEEM VERY HOT TO YOU, HERR DOCTOR, AFTER ANTARCTICA.
OH, NOT REALLY, FRÄULEIN HAAS...
I REMEMBER WHEN IT WAS MUCH HOTTER!
HA HA!
THIS WAY...
...UH!..
THAT SMELL!.. IS IT?..
YES. THAT'S THE WAY OUR MASTERS SMELL WHEN THEY MANIFEST THEMSELVES ON THIS PLANE.
NOT EXACTLY CHANEL Nº5, I ADMIT.
ONE OF THEM VISITED ME HERE RECENTLY.
IT TOOK ME SIX DAYS TO RECOVER FROM ITS PRESENCE.
MM. YES.
I HOPE WE'RE DOING THE RIGHT THING, FRÄULEIN...
WE HAVE WAITED YEARS FOR THIS HOUR, DRIESCH! THIS IS NO TIME FOR DOUBT.
NOW, JUST DO WHAT YOU CAME HERE TO DO...
...AND WAKE HIM UP!

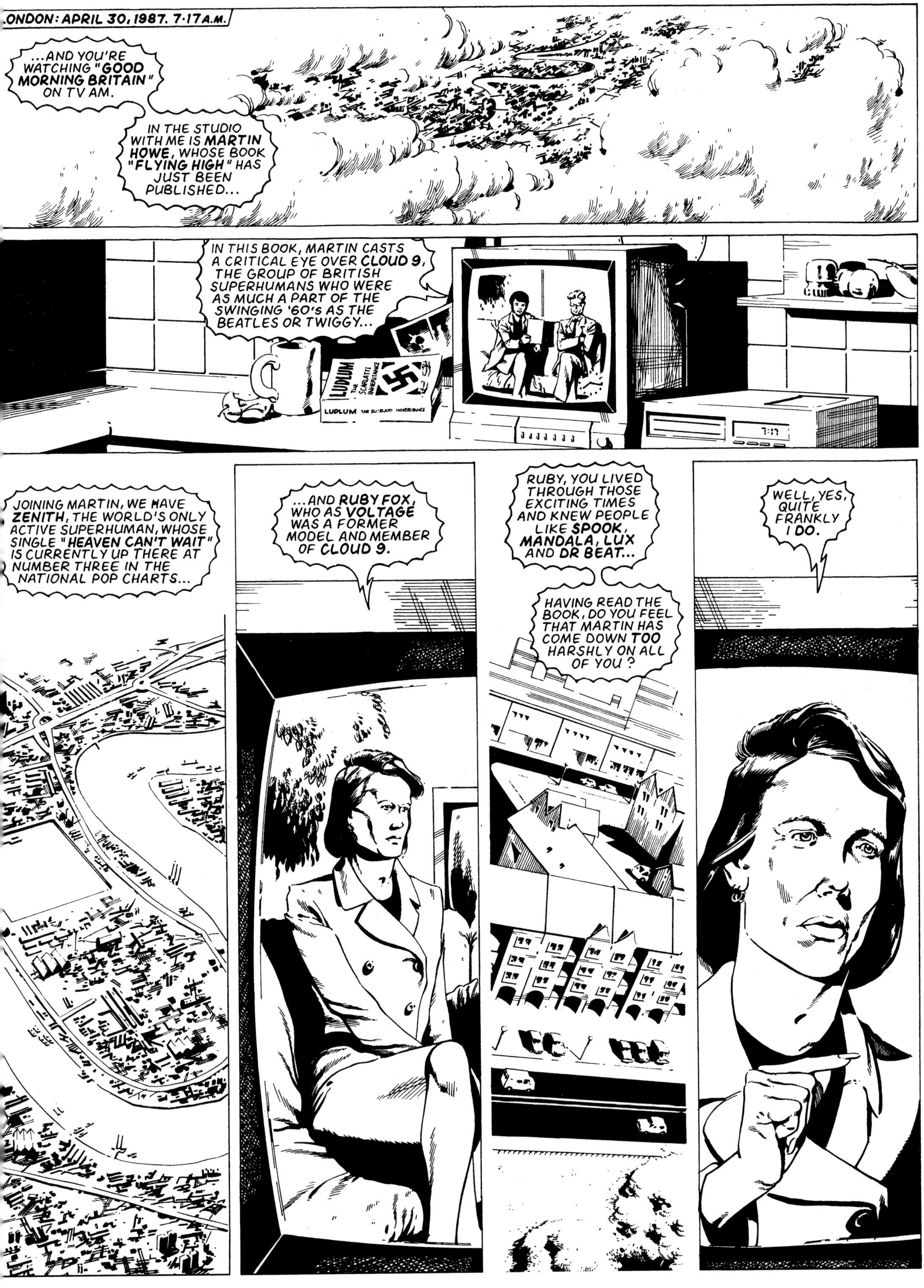

LONDON: APRIL 30, 1987. 7·17 A.M.
...AND YOU'RE WATCHING "GOOD MORNING BRITAIN" ON TV AM.
IN THE STUDIO WITH ME IS MARTIN HOWE, WHOSE BOOK "FLYING HIGH" HAS JUST BEEN PUBLISHED...
IN THIS BOOK, MARTIN CASTS A CRITICAL EYE OVER CLOUD 9, THE GROUP OF BRITISH SUPERHUMANS WHO WERE AS MUCH A PART OF THE SWINGING '60's AS THE BEATLES OR TWIGGY...
LUDLUM THE SCARLATTI INHERITANCE
JOINING MARTIN, WE HAVE ZENITH, THE WORLD'S ONLY ACTIVE SUPERHUMAN, WHOSE SINGLE "HEAVEN CAN'T WAIT" IS CURRENTLY UP THERE AT NUMBER THREE IN THE NATIONAL POP CHARTS...
...AND RUBY FOX, WHO AS VOLTAGE WAS A FORMER MODEL AND MEMBER OF CLOUD 9.
RUBY, YOU LIVED THROUGH THOSE EXCITING TIMES AND KNEW PEOPLE LIKE SPOOK, MANDALA, LUX AND DR BEAT...
HAVING READ THE BOOK, DO YOU FEEL THAT MARTIN HAS COME DOWN TOO HARSHLY ON ALL OF YOU?
WELL, YES, QUITE FRANKLY I DO.

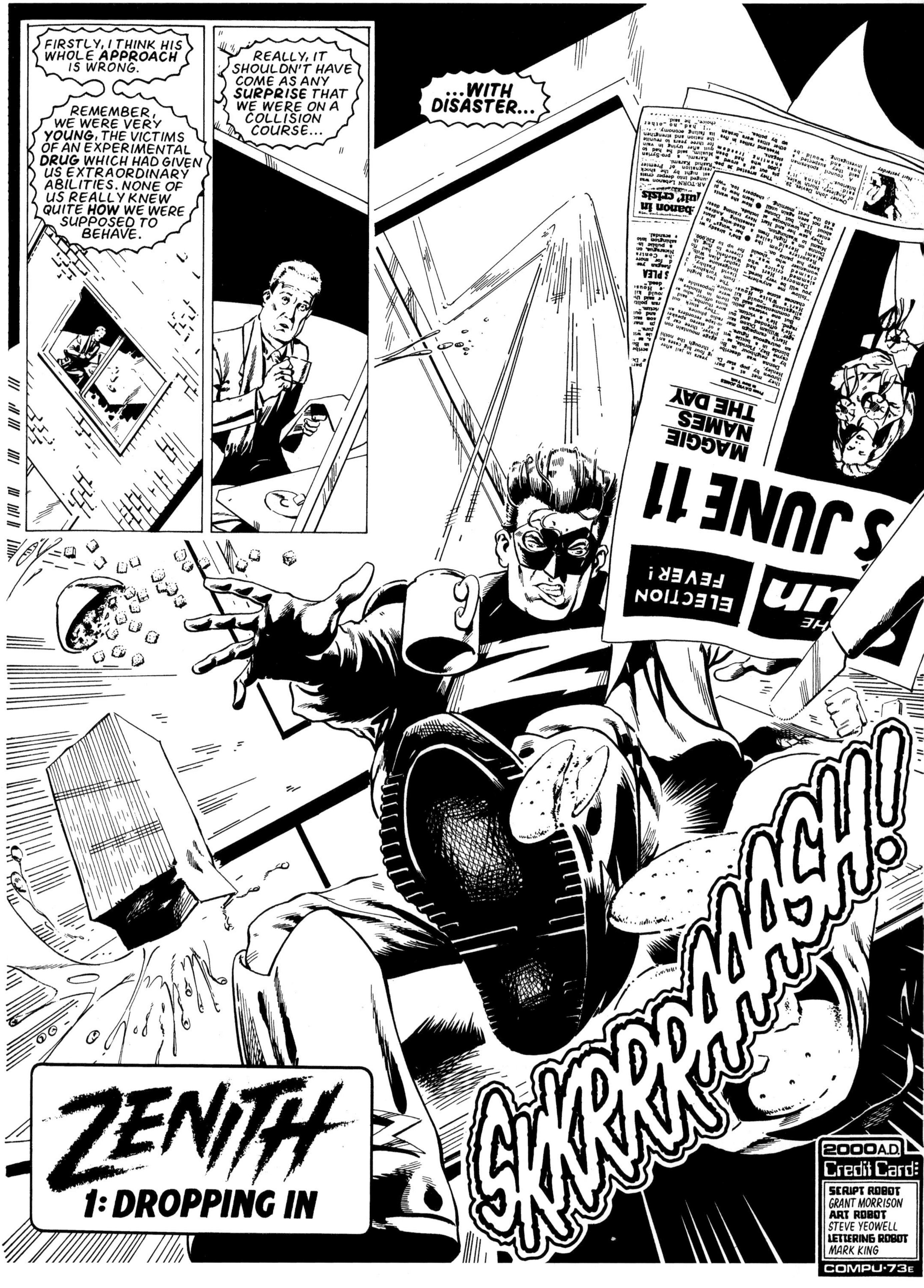
FIRSTLY, I THINK HIS WHOLE APPROACH IS WRONG.
REMEMBER, WE WERE VERY YOUNG, THE VICTIMS OF AN EXPERIMENTAL DRUG WHICH HAD GIVEN US EXTRAORDINARY ABILITIES. NONE OF US REALLY KNEW QUITE HOW WE WERE SUPPOSED TO BEHAVE.
REALLY, IT SHOULDN'T HAVE COME AS ANY SURPRISE THAT WE WERE ON A COLLISION COURSE...
...WITH DISASTER...
ELECTION FEVER!
JUNE 11
MAGGIE NAMES THE DAY
SKRRRAAASH!
ZENITH
1: DROPPING IN
2000 A.D.
Credit Card:
SCRIPT ROBOT
GRANT MORRISON
ART ROBOT
STEVE YEOWELL
LETTERING ROBOT
MARK KING
COMPU-73E

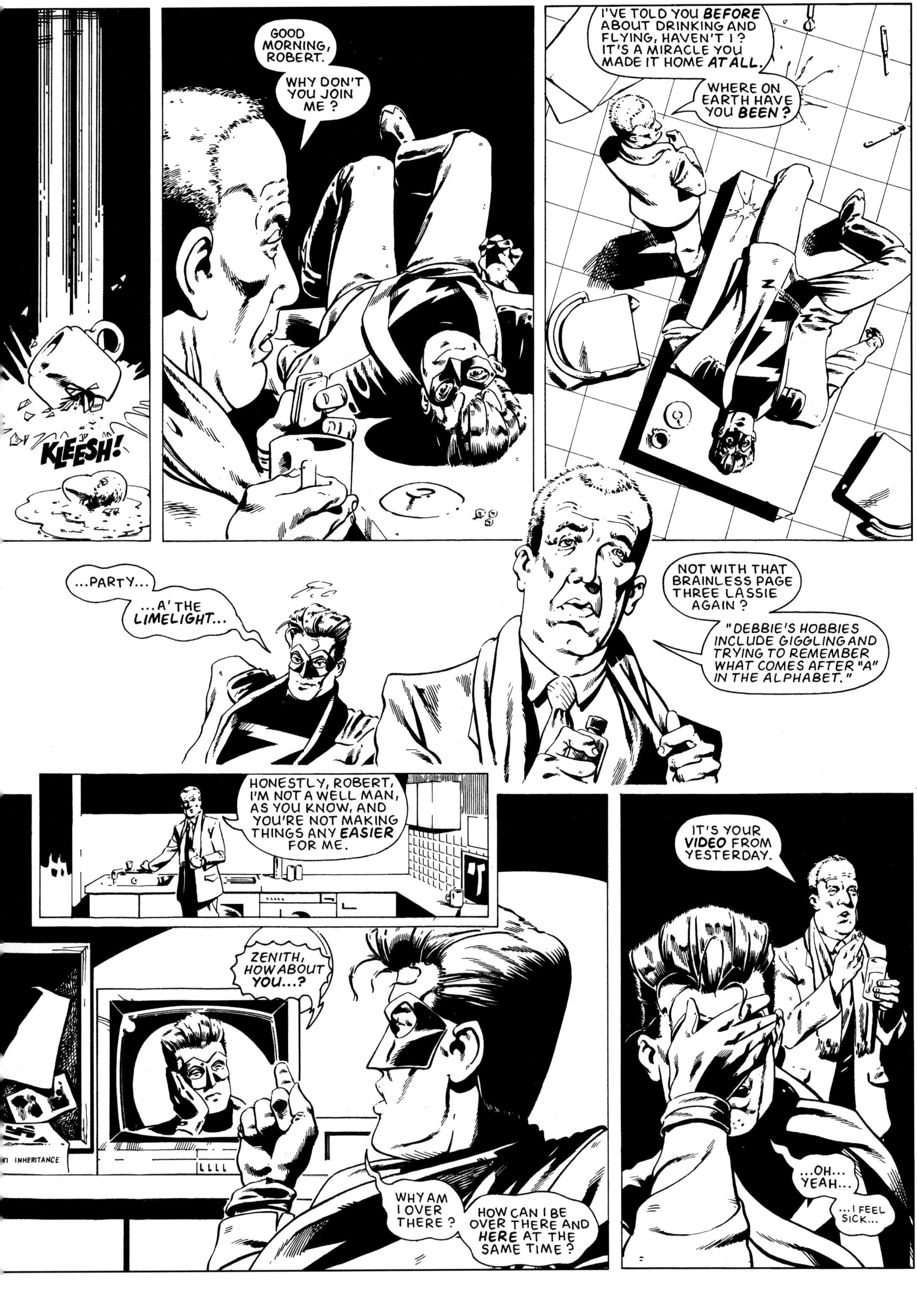
KLEESH!
GOOD MORNING, ROBERT.
WHY DON'T YOU JOIN ME ?
I'VE TOLD YOU BEFORE ABOUT DRINKING AND FLYING, HAVEN'T I ? IT'S A MIRACLE YOU MADE IT HOME AT ALL.
WHERE ON EARTH HAVE YOU BEEN ?
...PARTY...
...A' THE LIMELIGHT...
NOT WITH THAT BRAINLESS PAGE THREE LASSIE AGAIN ?
"DEBBIE'S HOBBIES INCLUDE GIGGLING AND TRYING TO REMEMBER WHAT COMES AFTER "A" IN THE ALPHABET."
HONESTLY, ROBERT, I'M NOT A WELL MAN, AS YOU KNOW, AND YOU'RE NOT MAKING THINGS ANY EASIER FOR ME.
ZENITH, HOW ABOUT YOU...?
INHERITANCE
WHY AM I OVER THERE ?
HOW CAN I BE OVER THERE AND HERE AT THE SAME TIME ?
IT'S YOUR VIDEO FROM YESTERDAY.
...OH... YEAH...
...I FEEL SICK...

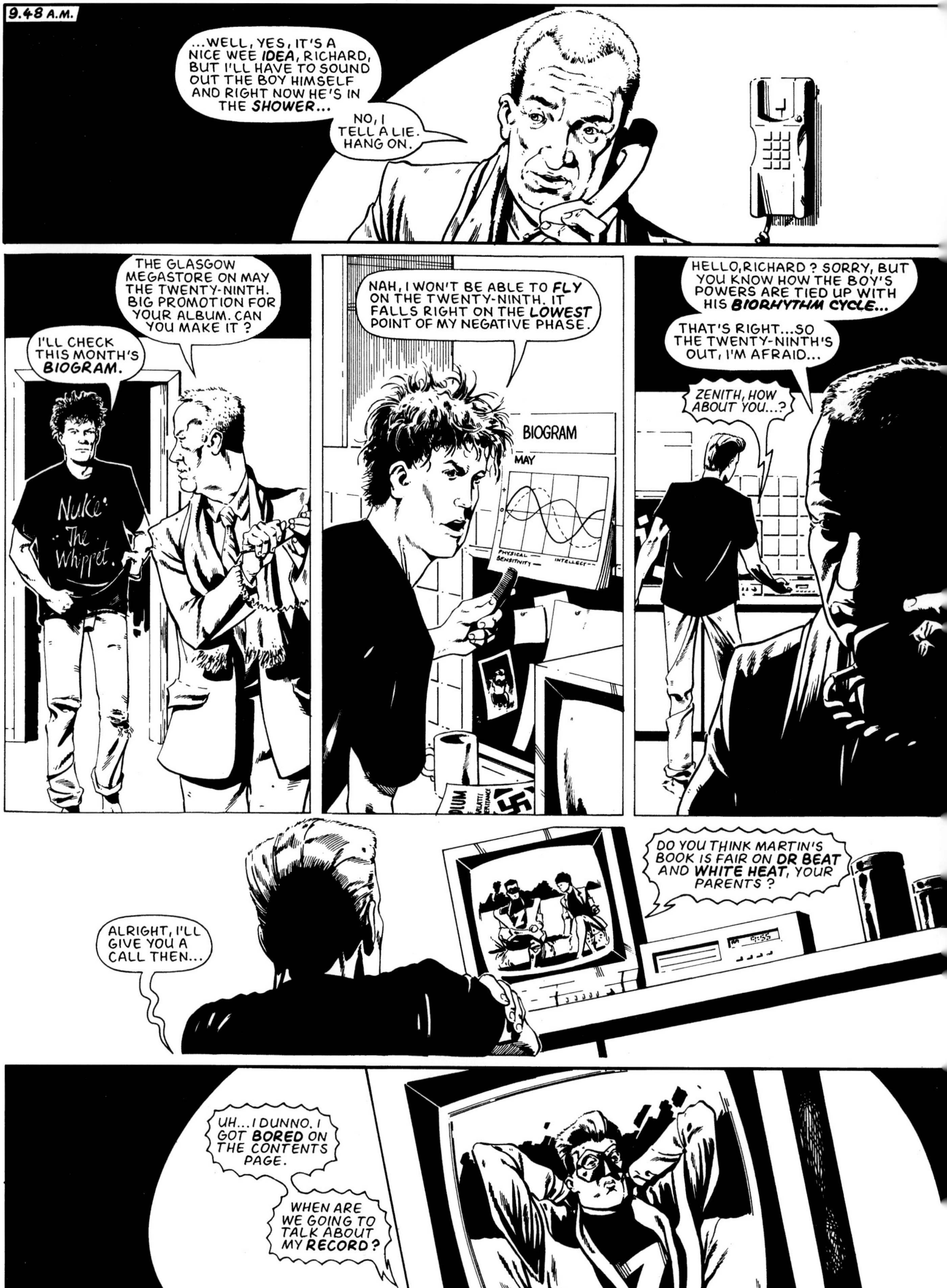
9.48 A.M.
...WELL, YES, IT'S A NICE WEE IDEA, RICHARD, BUT I'LL HAVE TO SOUND OUT THE BOY HIMSELF AND RIGHT NOW HE'S IN THE SHOWER...
NO, I TELL A LIE. HANG ON.
THE GLASGOW MEGASTORE ON MAY THE TWENTY-NINTH. BIG PROMOTION FOR YOUR ALBUM. CAN YOU MAKE IT?
I'LL CHECK THIS MONTH'S BIOGRAM.
Nuke The Whippet.
NAH, I WON'T BE ABLE TO FLY ON THE TWENTY-NINTH. IT FALLS RIGHT ON THE LOWEST POINT OF MY NEGATIVE PHASE.
BIOGRAM
MAY
PHYSICAL
SENSITIVITY
INTELLECT
HELLO, RICHARD? SORRY, BUT YOU KNOW HOW THE BOY'S POWERS ARE TIED UP WITH HIS BIORHYTHM CYCLE...
THAT'S RIGHT...SO THE TWENTY-NINTH'S OUT, I'M AFRAID...
ZENITH, HOW ABOUT YOU...?
ALRIGHT, I'LL GIVE YOU A CALL THEN...
DO YOU THINK MARTIN'S BOOK IS FAIR ON DR BEAT AND WHITE HEAT, YOUR PARENTS?
UH...I DUNNO. I GOT BORED ON THE CONTENTS PAGE.
WHEN ARE WE GOING TO TALK ABOUT MY RECORD?

HAH! *THAT* SHUT THEM UP.

I MEAN, ALL THIS '60's STUFF... WHO *CARES*?

DON'T YOU *KID* YOURSELF! '60's NOSTALGIA IS *MEGABUSINESS* THESE DAYS.

THE BEATLES, DAVID BAILEY, CLOUD 9, DEAR OLD ANDY WARHOL...

BO-*RING!*

WHAT ARE YOU DOING IN MY FLAT ANYWAY?

I'M YOUR *AGENT*, ROBERT. I WORRY ABOUT WHAT YOU'RE DOING TO YOUR *HEALTH*.

ALL THESE PARTIES AND CLUBS AND FIRST NIGHTS...

IT'LL ALL END IN *TEARS*, YOU MARK MY WORDS.

COME *ON*, EDDIE...

I'M NINETEEN, I CAN FLY, I CAN FLATTEN *BALLBEARINGS* BETWEEN MY FINGERS AND I'M PRACTICALLY INVULNERABLE TO DAMAGE.

I MEAN, LET'S FACE IT...

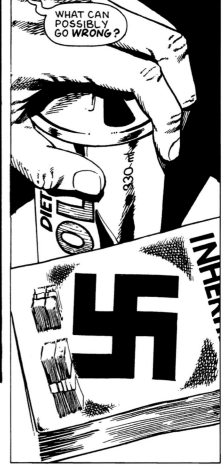

WHAT CAN POSSIBLY GO *WRONG?*

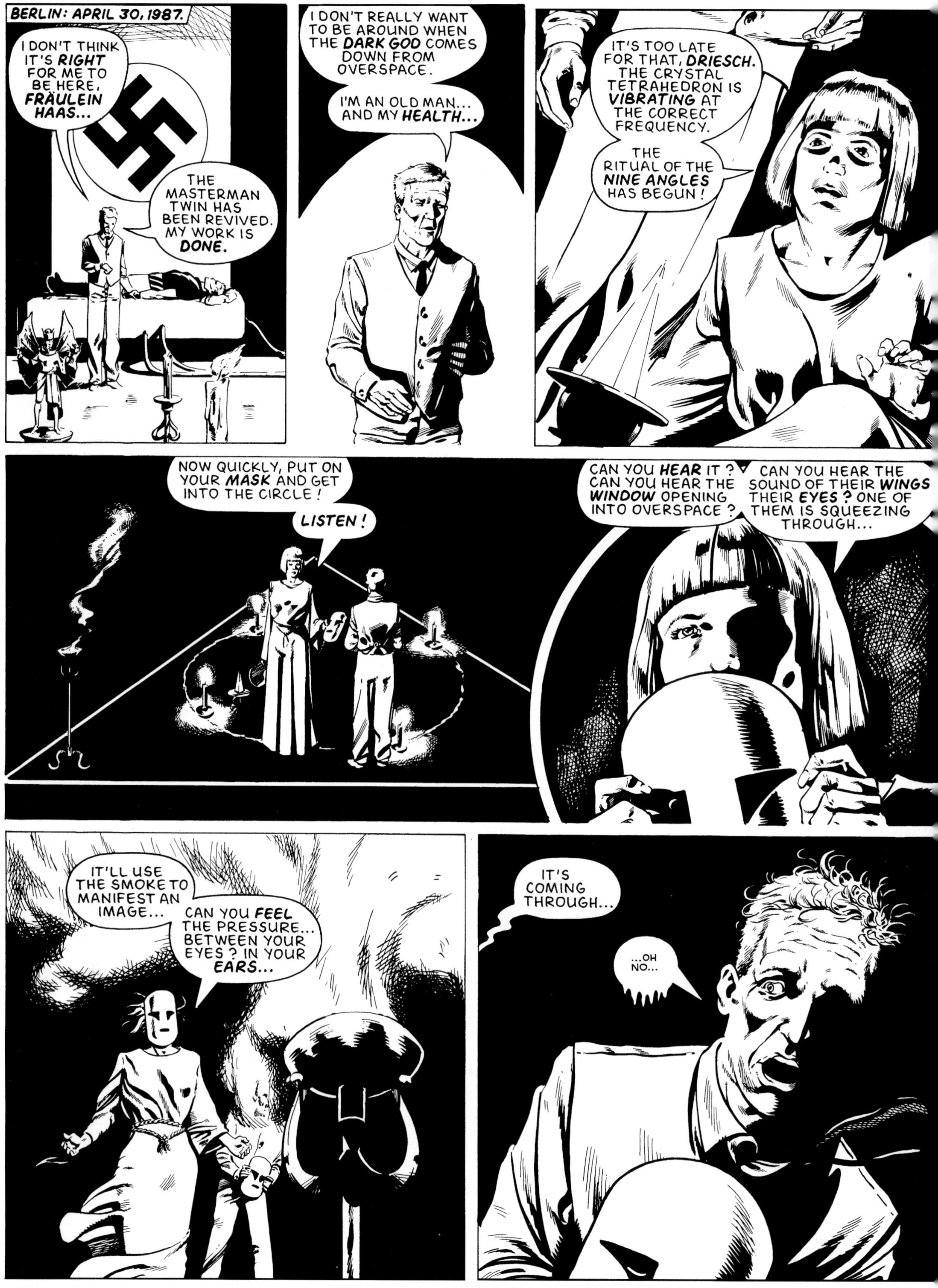
BERLIN: APRIL 30, 1987.
I DON'T THINK IT'S RIGHT FOR ME TO BE HERE, FRÄULEIN HAAS...
THE MASTERMAN TWIN HAS BEEN REVIVED. MY WORK IS DONE.
I DON'T REALLY WANT TO BE AROUND WHEN THE DARK GOD COMES DOWN FROM OVERSPACE.
I'M AN OLD MAN... AND MY HEALTH...
IT'S TOO LATE FOR THAT, DRIESCH. THE CRYSTAL TETRAHEDRON IS VIBRATING AT THE CORRECT FREQUENCY.
THE RITUAL OF THE NINE ANGLES HAS BEGUN!
NOW QUICKLY, PUT ON YOUR MASK AND GET INTO THE CIRCLE!
LISTEN!
CAN YOU HEAR IT? CAN YOU HEAR THE WINDOW OPENING INTO OVERSPACE?
CAN YOU HEAR THE SOUND OF THEIR WINGS THEIR EYES? ONE OF THEM IS SQUEEZING THROUGH...
IT'LL USE THE SMOKE TO MANIFEST AN IMAGE...
CAN YOU FEEL THE PRESSURE... BETWEEN YOUR EYES? IN YOUR EARS...
IT'S COMING THROUGH...
...OH NO...

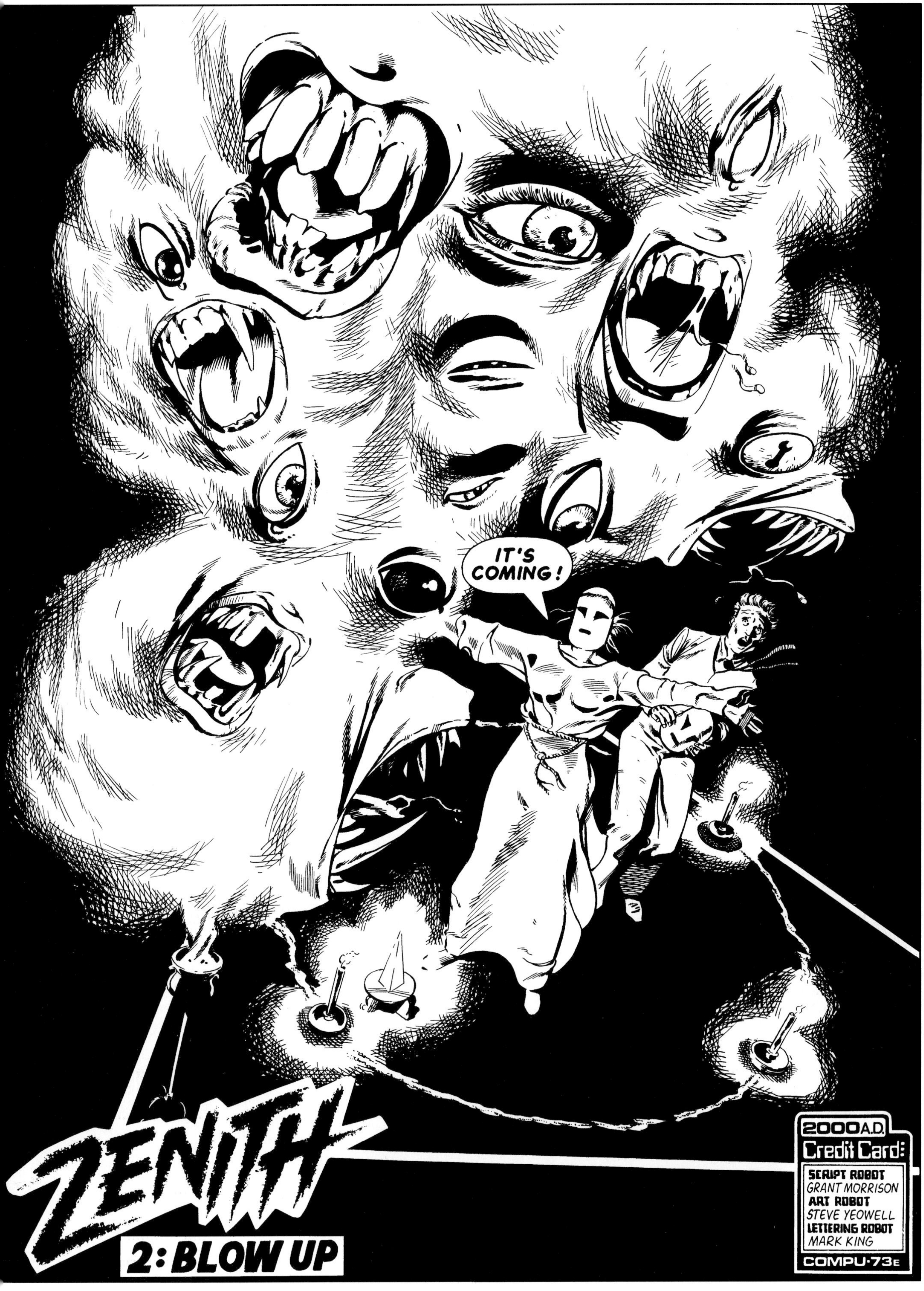
IT'S COMING!
ZENITH
2: BLOW UP
2000 A.D.
Credit Card:
SCRIPT ROBOT
GRANT MORRISON
ART ROBOT
STEVE YEOWELL
LETTERING ROBOT
MARK KING
COMPU-73E

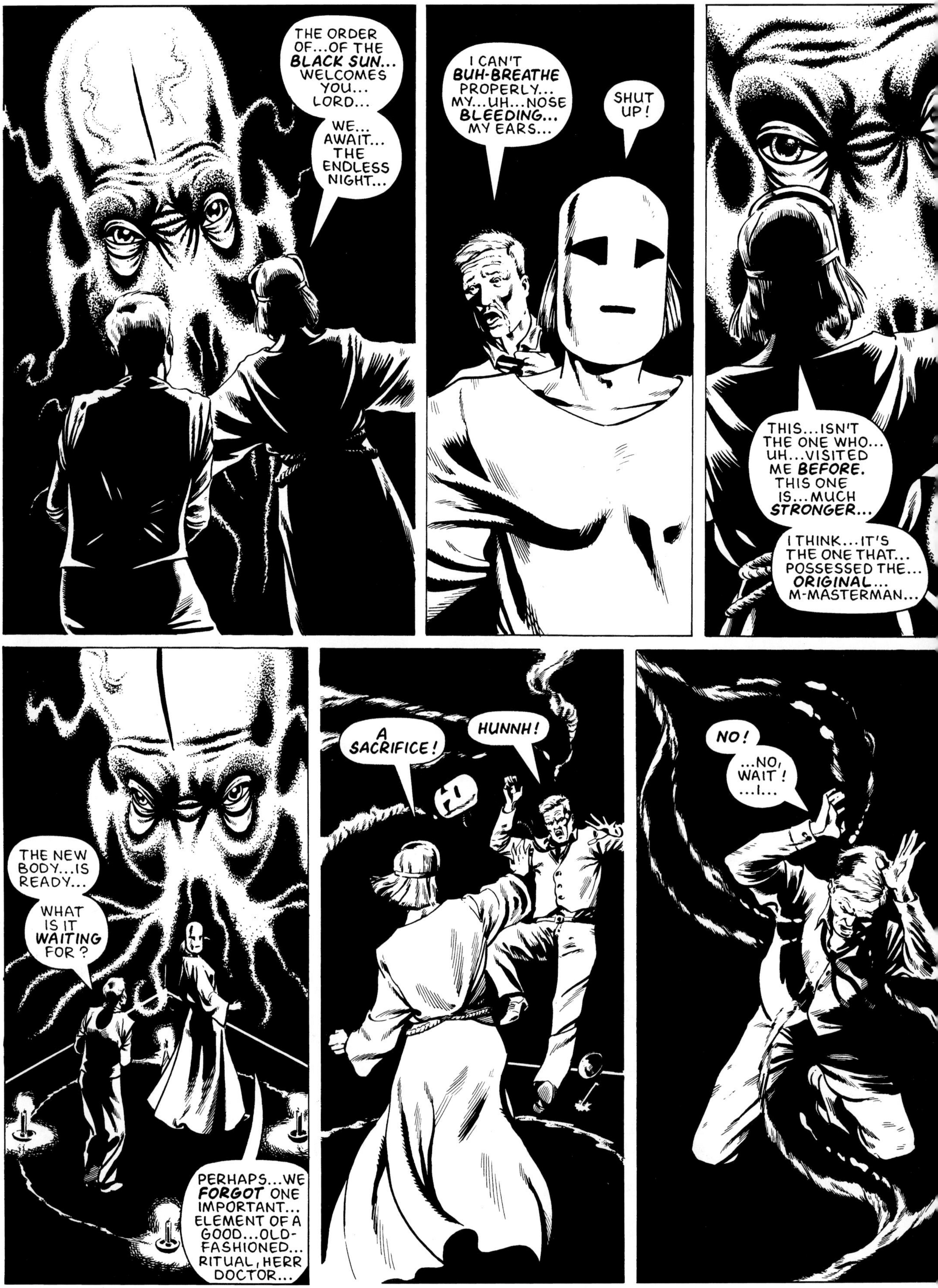
THE ORDER OF...OF THE **BLACK SUN...** WELCOMES YOU... LORD...
WE... AWAIT... THE ENDLESS NIGHT...
I CAN'T **BUH-BREATHE** PROPERLY... MY...UH...NOSE **BLEEDING...** MY EARS...
SHUT UP!
THIS...ISN'T THE ONE WHO... UH...VISITED ME **BEFORE.** THIS ONE IS...MUCH **STRONGER...**
I THINK...IT'S THE ONE THAT... POSSESSED THE... **ORIGINAL...** M-MASTERMAN...
THE NEW BODY...IS READY...
WHAT IS IT **WAITING** FOR?
PERHAPS...WE **FORGOT** ONE IMPORTANT... ELEMENT OF A GOOD...OLD-FASHIONED... RITUAL, HERR DOCTOR...
A SACRIFICE!
HUNNH!
NO!
...NO, WAIT! ...I...

HUH-HELP ME! IT'S INSIDE...
IT'S INSIDE ME!
...PRESSURE...
OH...THE PRESSURE... THE...
...AHH...

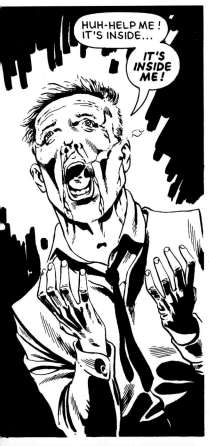

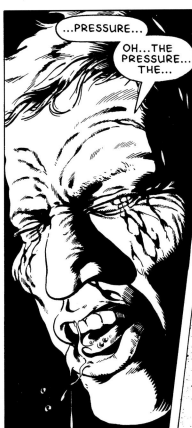

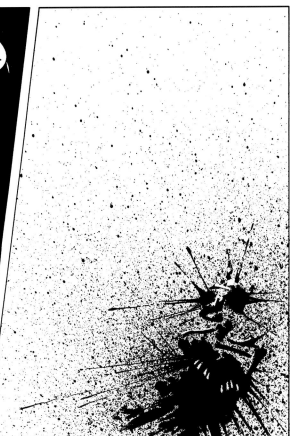

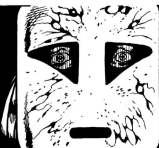

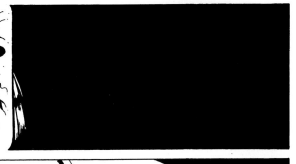

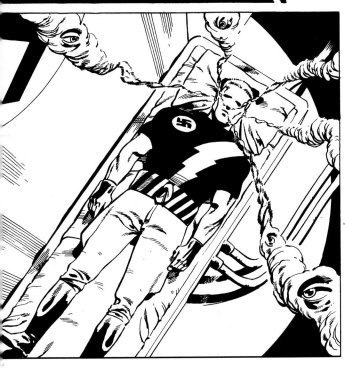

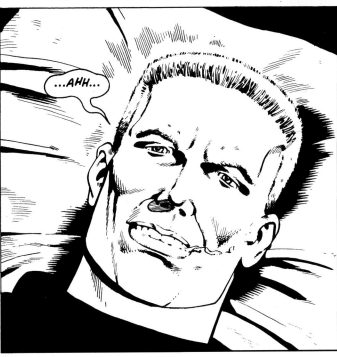

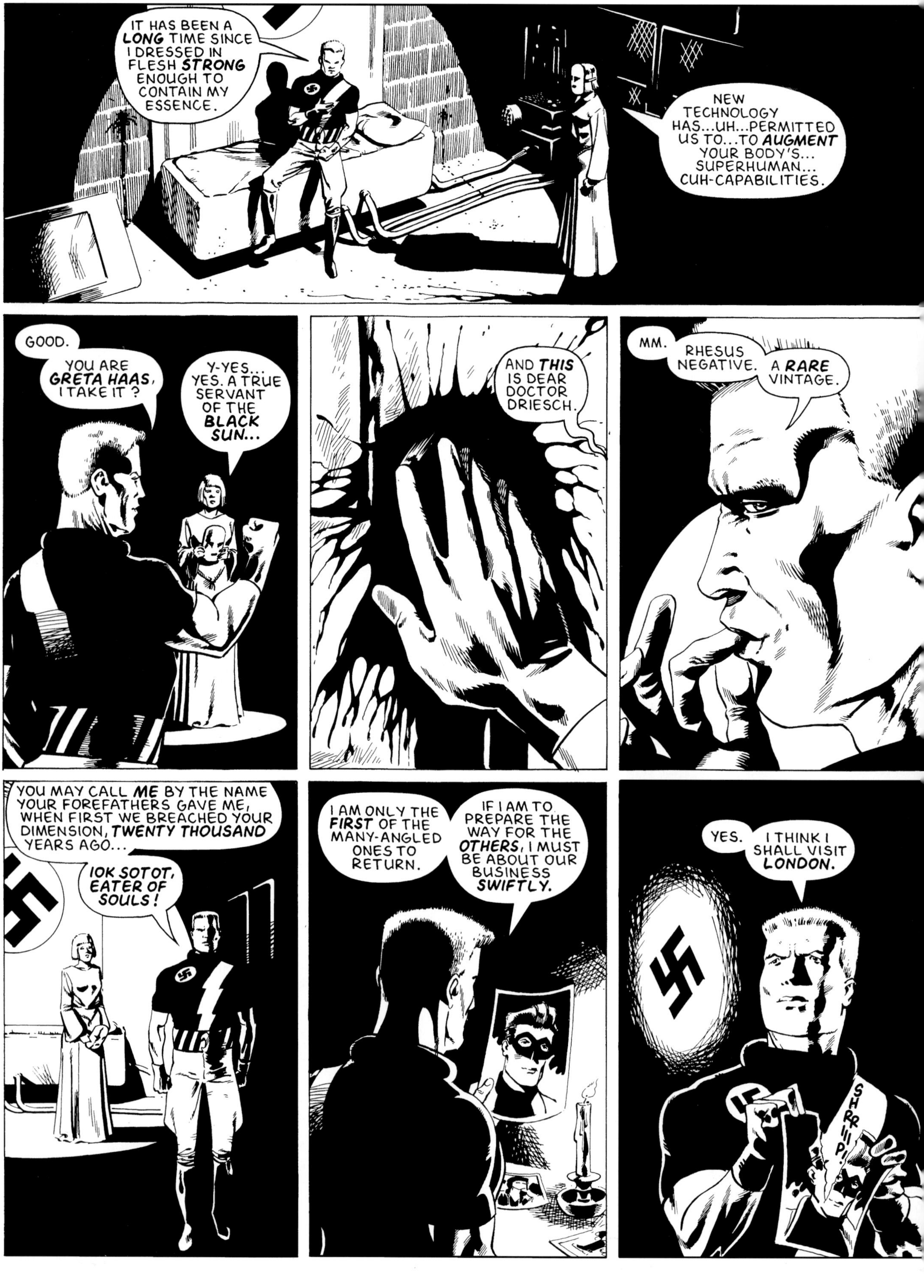
IT HAS BEEN A LONG TIME SINCE I DRESSED IN FLESH STRONG ENOUGH TO CONTAIN MY ESSENCE.
NEW TECHNOLOGY HAS...UH...PERMITTED US TO...TO AUGMENT YOUR BODY'S... SUPERHUMAN... CUH-CAPABILITIES.
GOOD.
YOU ARE GRETA HAAS, I TAKE IT ?
Y-YES... YES. A TRUE SERVANT OF THE BLACK SUN...
AND THIS IS DEAR DOCTOR DRIESCH.
MM.
RHESUS NEGATIVE.
A RARE VINTAGE.
YOU MAY CALL ME BY THE NAME YOUR FOREFATHERS GAVE ME, WHEN FIRST WE BREACHED YOUR DIMENSION, TWENTY THOUSAND YEARS AGO...
IOK SOTOT, EATER OF SOULS !
I AM ONLY THE FIRST OF THE MANY-ANGLED ONES TO RETURN.
IF I AM TO PREPARE THE WAY FOR THE OTHERS, I MUST BE ABOUT OUR BUSINESS SWIFTLY.
YES.
I THINK I SHALL VISIT LONDON.
SHRRIIP!

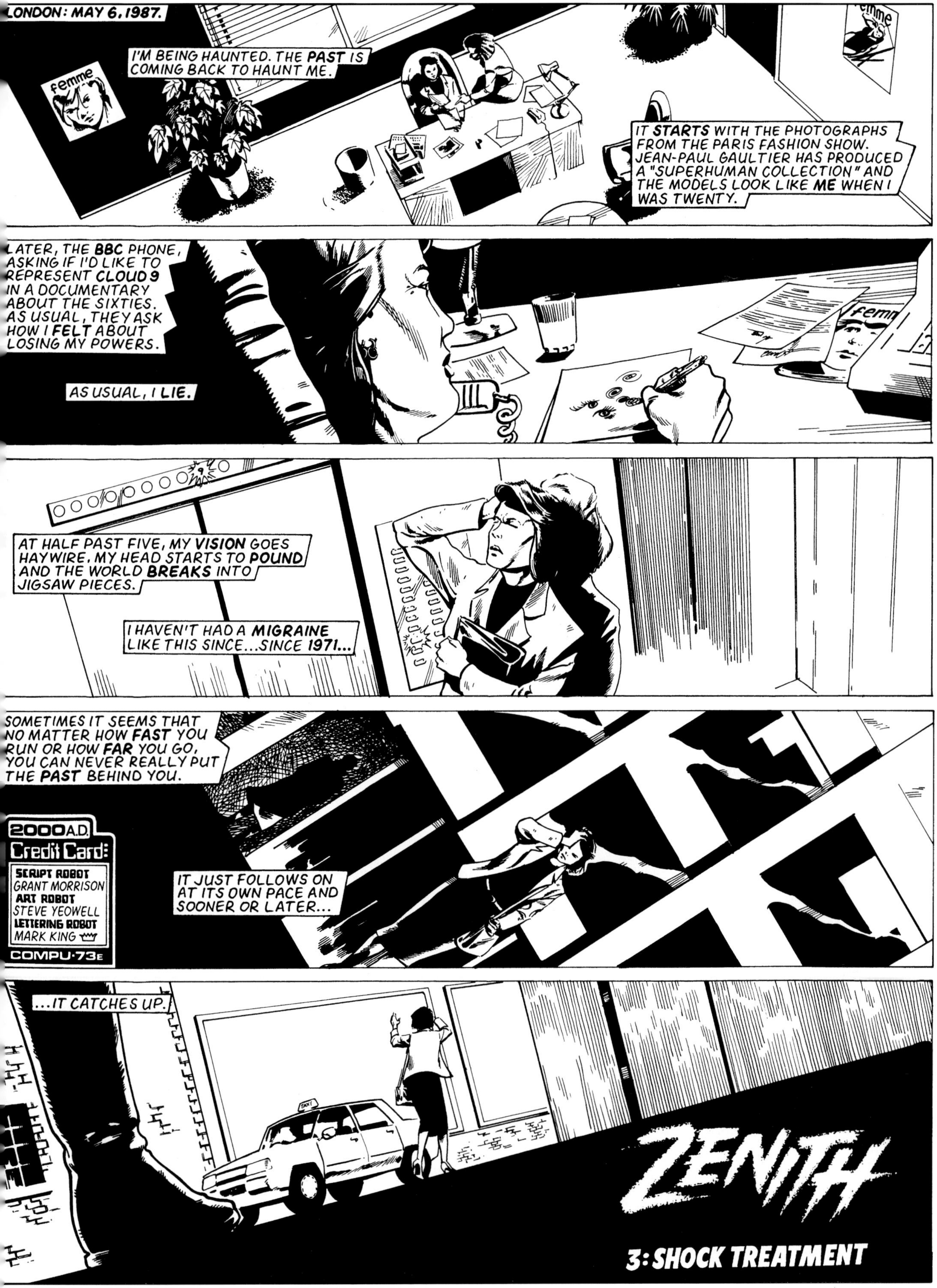
LONDON: MAY 6, 1987.
I'M BEING HAUNTED. THE PAST IS COMING BACK TO HAUNT ME.
femme
IT STARTS WITH THE PHOTOGRAPHS FROM THE PARIS FASHION SHOW. JEAN-PAUL GAULTIER HAS PRODUCED A "SUPERHUMAN COLLECTION" AND THE MODELS LOOK LIKE ME WHEN I WAS TWENTY.
LATER, THE BBC PHONE, ASKING IF I'D LIKE TO REPRESENT CLOUD 9 IN A DOCUMENTARY ABOUT THE SIXTIES. AS USUAL, THEY ASK HOW I FELT ABOUT LOSING MY POWERS.
AS USUAL, I LIE.
AT HALF PAST FIVE, MY VISION GOES HAYWIRE. MY HEAD STARTS TO POUND AND THE WORLD BREAKS INTO JIGSAW PIECES.
I HAVEN'T HAD A MIGRAINE LIKE THIS SINCE... SINCE 1971...
SOMETIMES IT SEEMS THAT NO MATTER HOW FAST YOU RUN OR HOW FAR YOU GO, YOU CAN NEVER REALLY PUT THE PAST BEHIND YOU.
2000 A.D. Credit Card: SCRIPT ROBOT GRANT MORRISON ART ROBOT STEVE YEOWELL LETTERING ROBOT MARK KING COMPU-73E
IT JUST FOLLOWS ON AT ITS OWN PACE AND SOONER OR LATER...
...IT CATCHES UP.
TAXI
ZENITH
3: SHOCK TREATMENT

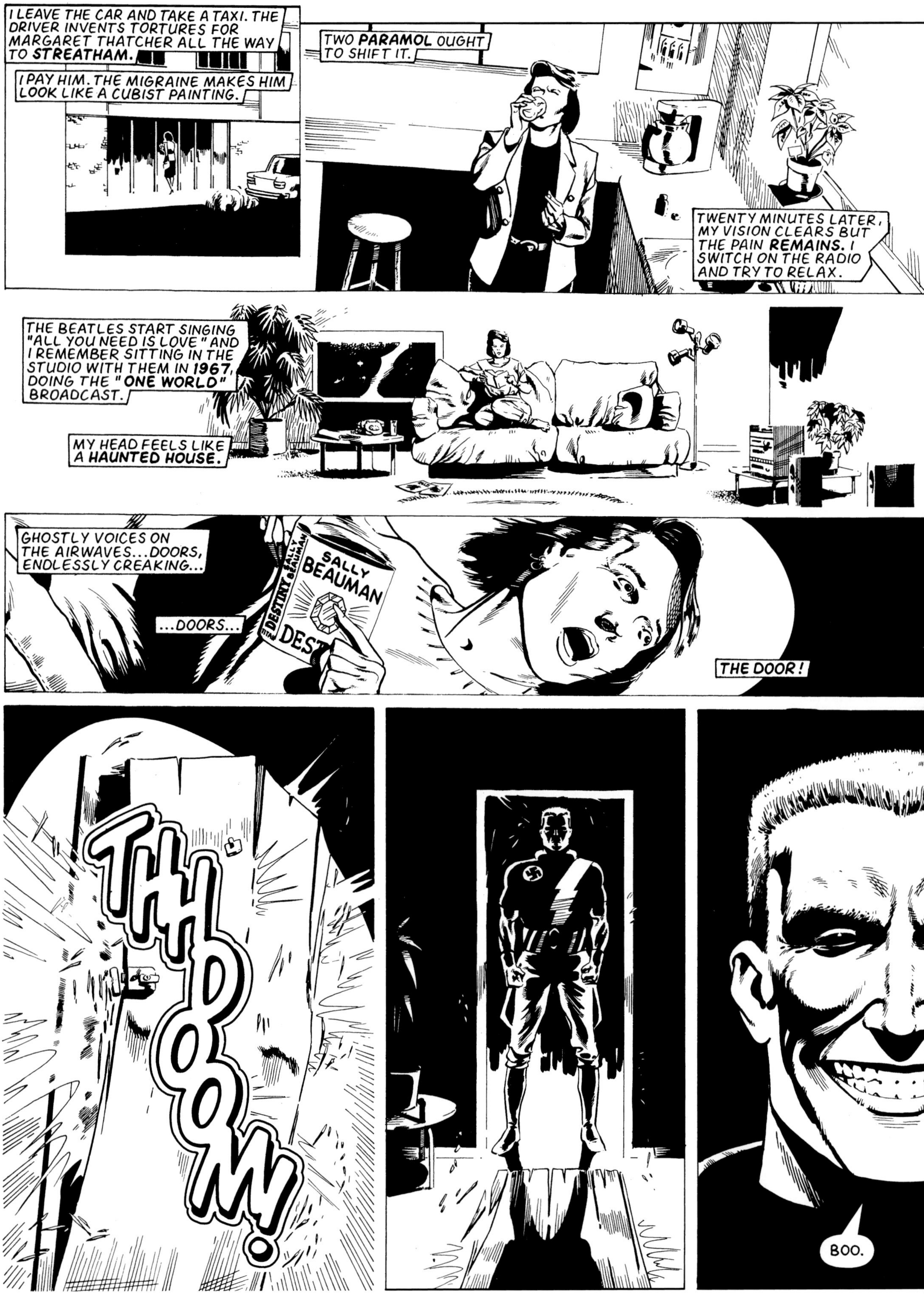

I LEAVE THE CAR AND TAKE A TAXI. THE DRIVER INVENTS TORTURES FOR MARGARET THATCHER ALL THE WAY TO STREATHAM.
I PAY HIM. THE MIGRAINE MAKES HIM LOOK LIKE A CUBIST PAINTING.
TWO PARAMOL OUGHT TO SHIFT IT.
TWENTY MINUTES LATER, MY VISION CLEARS BUT THE PAIN REMAINS. I SWITCH ON THE RADIO AND TRY TO RELAX.
THE BEATLES START SINGING "ALL YOU NEED IS LOVE" AND I REMEMBER SITTING IN THE STUDIO WITH THEM IN 1967, DOING THE "ONE WORLD" BROADCAST.
MY HEAD FEELS LIKE A HAUNTED HOUSE.
GHOSTLY VOICES ON THE AIRWAVES... DOORS, ENDLESSLY CREAKING...
SALLY BEAUMAN
DESTINY
...DOORS...
THE DOOR!
THHDOOM!
BOO.

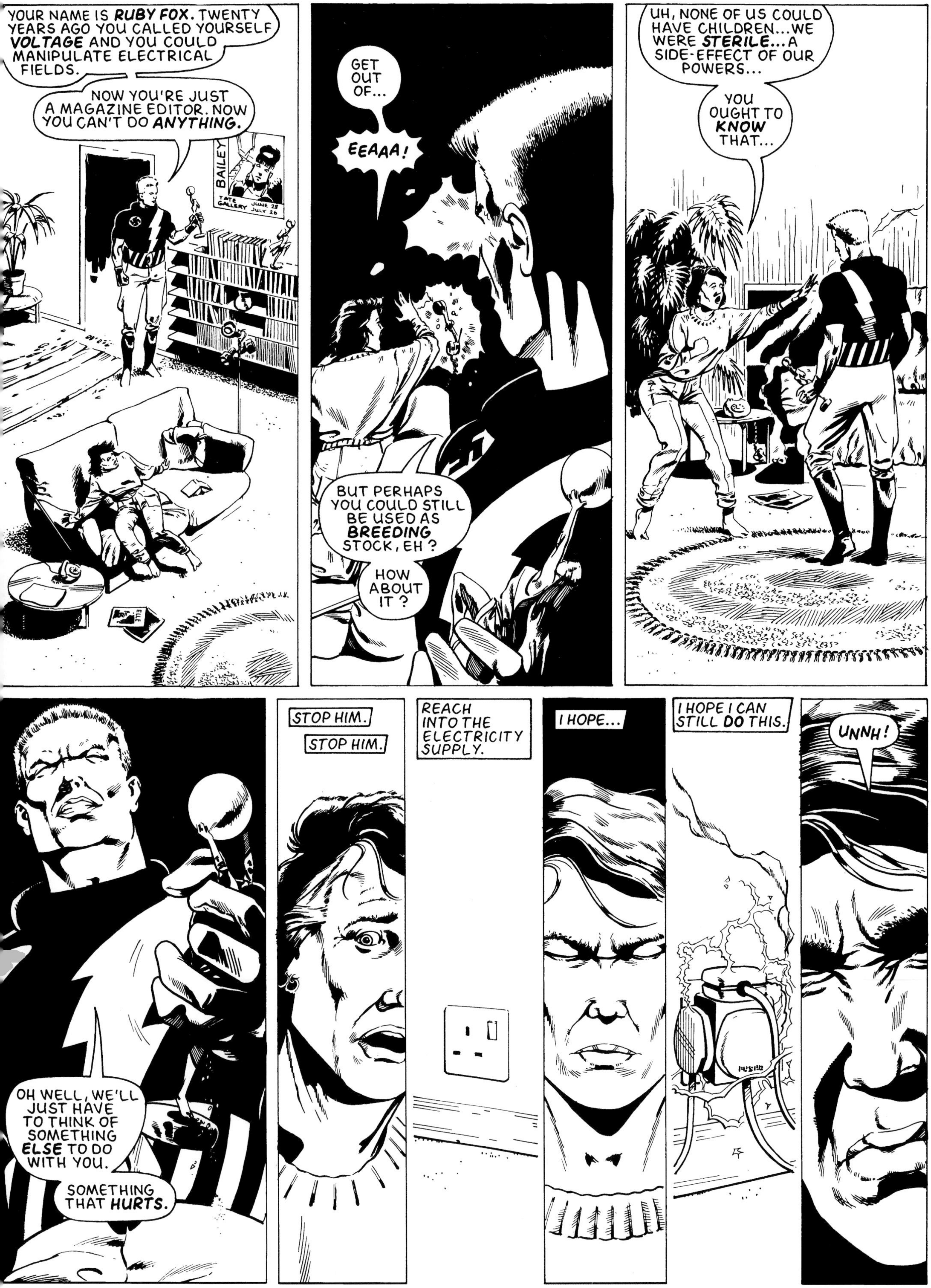
YOUR NAME IS RUBY FOX. TWENTY YEARS AGO YOU CALLED YOURSELF VOLTAGE AND YOU COULD MANIPULATE ELECTRICAL FIELDS.
NOW YOU'RE JUST A MAGAZINE EDITOR. NOW YOU CAN'T DO ANYTHING.
BAILEY
TATE GALLERY JUNE 25 JULY 26
GET OUT OF...
EEAAA!
BUT PERHAPS YOU COULD STILL BE USED AS BREEDING STOCK, EH?
HOW ABOUT IT?
UH, NONE OF US COULD HAVE CHILDREN...WE WERE STERILE...A SIDE-EFFECT OF OUR POWERS...
YOU OUGHT TO KNOW THAT...
OH WELL, WE'LL JUST HAVE TO THINK OF SOMETHING ELSE TO DO WITH YOU.
SOMETHING THAT HURTS.
STOP HIM.
STOP HIM.
REACH INTO THE ELECTRICITY SUPPLY.
I HOPE...
I HOPE I CAN STILL DO THIS.
UNNH!

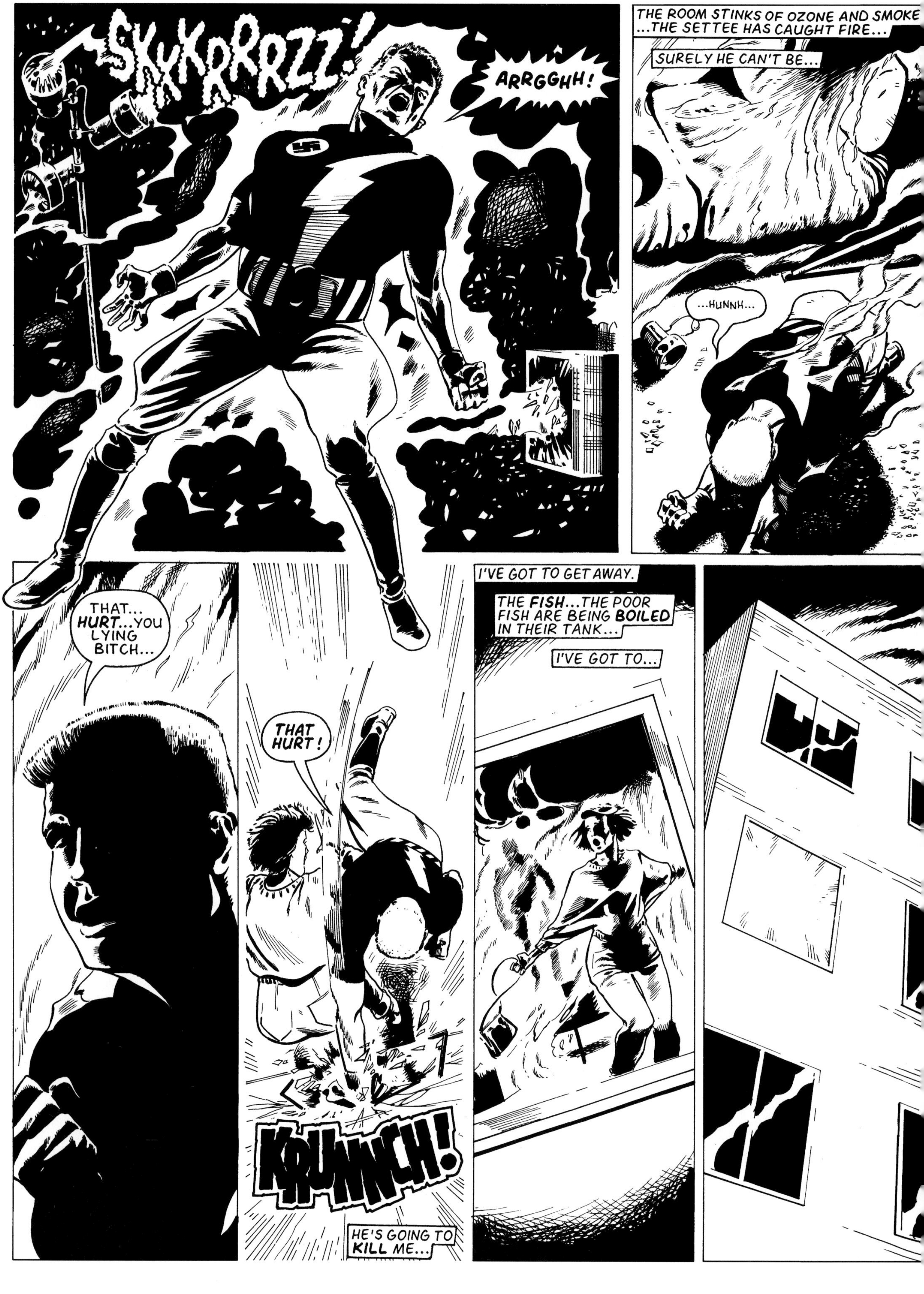
SKXKRRRZZZ!
ARRGGHH!
THE ROOM STINKS OF OZONE AND SMOKE ...THE SETTEE HAS CAUGHT FIRE...
SURELY HE CAN'T BE...
...HUNNH...
THAT... HURT...YOU LYING BITCH...
THAT HURT!
KRUNNCH!
HE'S GOING TO KILL ME...
I'VE GOT TO GET AWAY.
THE FISH...THE POOR FISH ARE BEING BOILED IN THEIR TANK...
I'VE GOT TO...

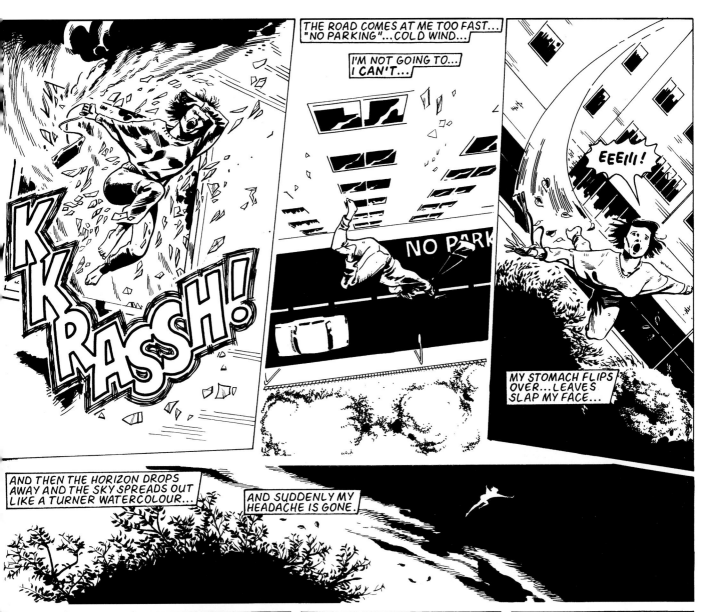

KK RASSH!

THE ROAD COMES AT ME TOO FAST... "NO PARKING"...COLD WIND...

I'M NOT GOING TO... I CAN'T...

NO PARK

EEEIII!

MY STOMACH FLIPS OVER...LEAVES SLAP MY FACE...

AND THEN THE HORIZON DROPS AWAY AND THE SKY SPREADS OUT LIKE A TURNER WATERCOLOUR...

AND SUDDENLY MY HEADACHE IS GONE.

FAR BEHIND ME NOW, MY PAST IS TURNING TO SMOKE AND CINDERS.

BUT I'M FREE NOW. I'M SAFE. EVERYTHING'S OKAY.

UNLESS...

UNLESS HE'S SURVIVED!

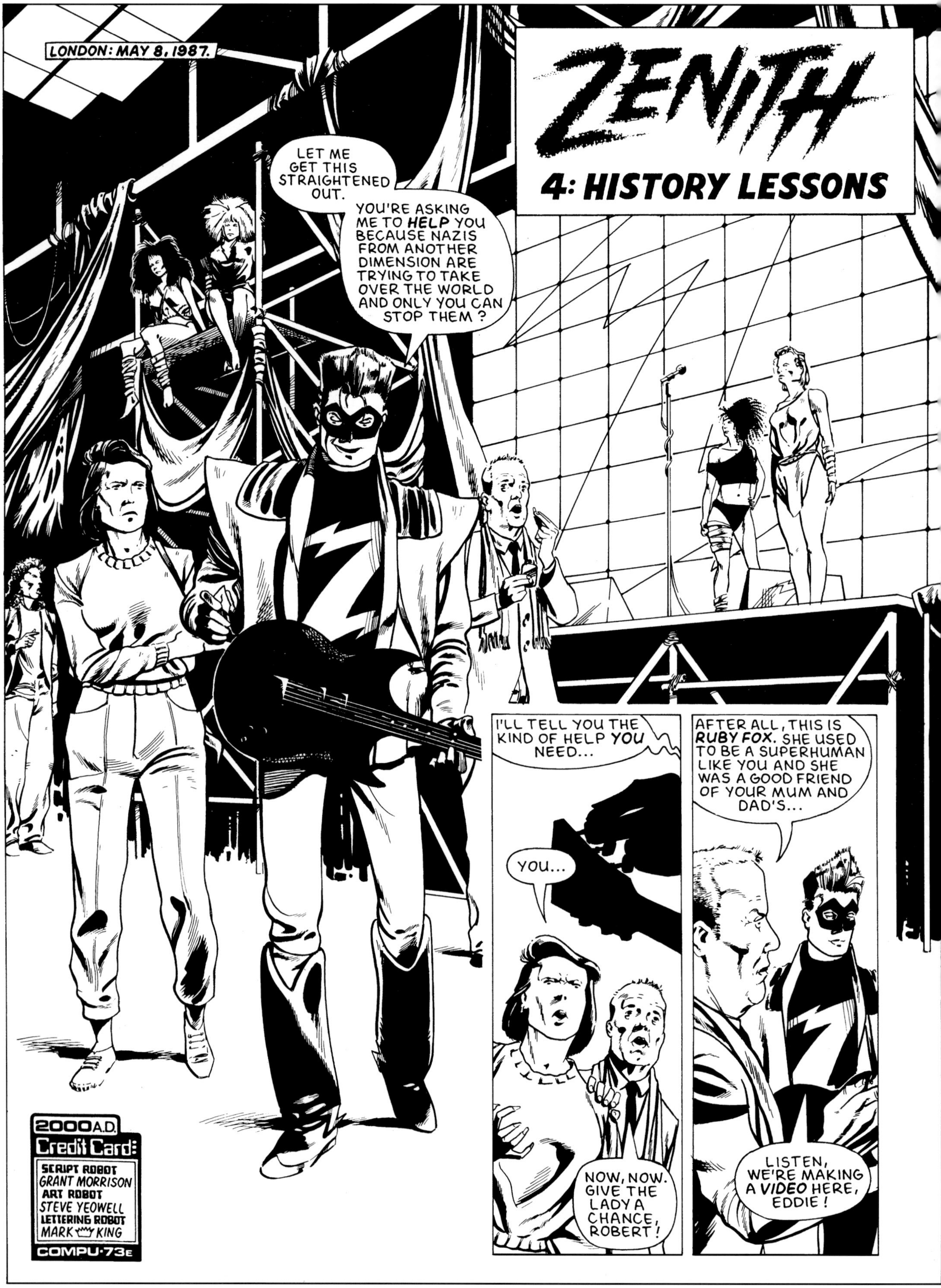
LONDON: MAY 8, 1987.
ZENITH
4: HISTORY LESSONS
LET ME GET THIS STRAIGHTENED OUT.
YOU'RE ASKING ME TO HELP YOU BECAUSE NAZIS FROM ANOTHER DIMENSION ARE TRYING TO TAKE OVER THE WORLD AND ONLY YOU CAN STOP THEM ?
I'LL TELL YOU THE KIND OF HELP YOU NEED...
YOU...
NOW, NOW. GIVE THE LADY A CHANCE, ROBERT!
AFTER ALL, THIS IS RUBY FOX. SHE USED TO BE A SUPERHUMAN LIKE YOU AND SHE WAS A GOOD FRIEND OF YOUR MUM AND DAD'S...
LISTEN, WE'RE MAKING A VIDEO HERE, EDDIE!
2000 A.D.
Credit Card:
SCRIPT ROBOT GRANT MORRISON
ART ROBOT STEVE YEOWELL
LETTERING ROBOT MARK KING
COMPU-73E

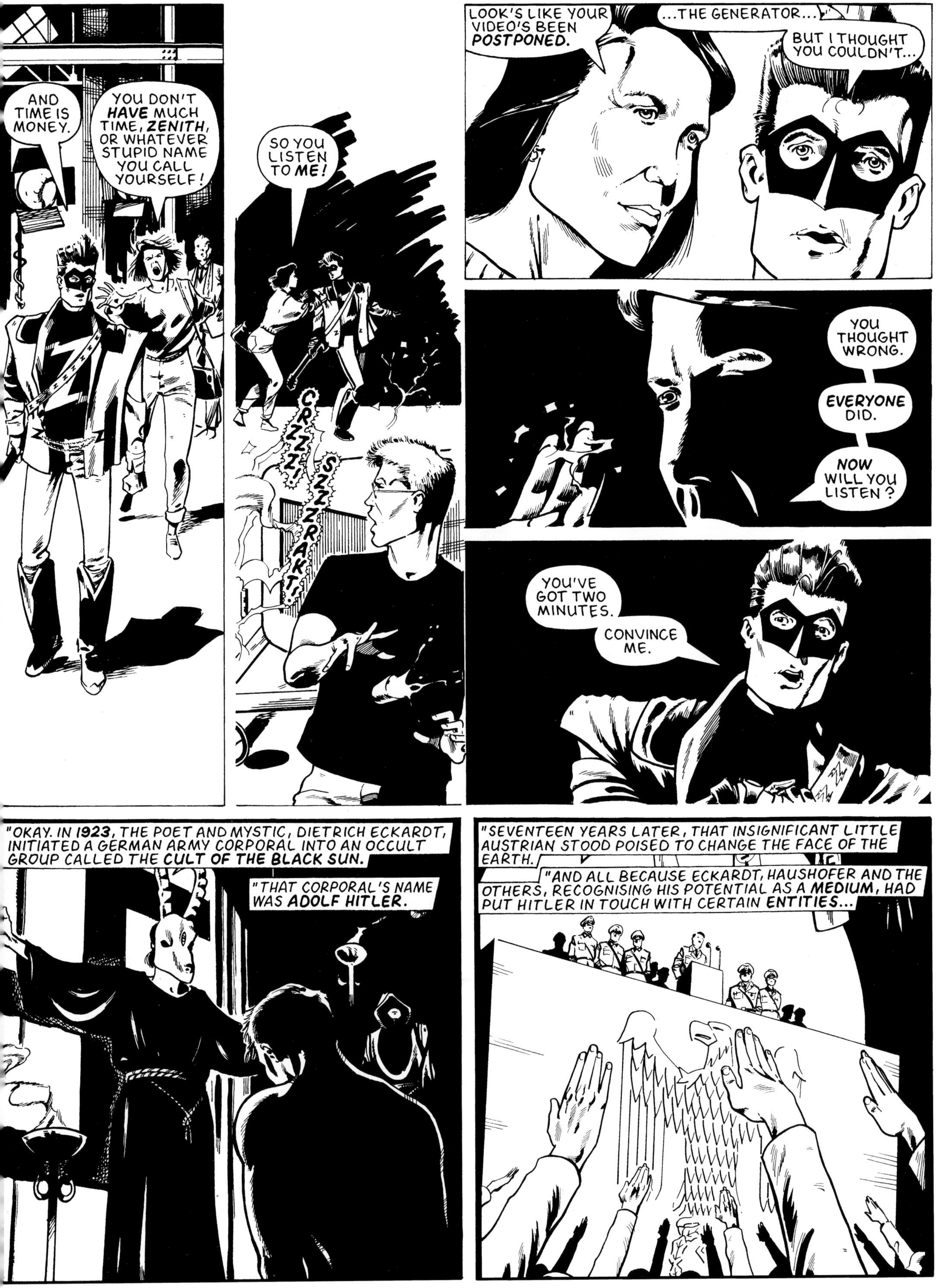

AND TIME IS MONEY.
YOU DON'T HAVE MUCH TIME, ZENITH, OR WHATEVER STUPID NAME YOU CALL YOURSELF!
SO YOU LISTEN TO ME!
CRZZZZT!
SZZZRAKT!
LOOK'S LIKE YOUR VIDEO'S BEEN POSTPONED.
...THE GENERATOR...
BUT I THOUGHT YOU COULDN'T...
YOU THOUGHT WRONG.
EVERYONE DID.
NOW WILL YOU LISTEN?
YOU'VE GOT TWO MINUTES.
CONVINCE ME.
"OKAY. IN 1923, THE POET AND MYSTIC, DIETRICH ECKARDT, INITIATED A GERMAN ARMY CORPORAL INTO AN OCCULT GROUP CALLED THE CULT OF THE BLACK SUN.
"THAT CORPORAL'S NAME WAS ADOLF HITLER.
"SEVENTEEN YEARS LATER, THAT INSIGNIFICANT LITTLE AUSTRIAN STOOD POISED TO CHANGE THE FACE OF THE EARTH.
"AND ALL BECAUSE ECKARDT, HAUSHOFER AND THE OTHERS, RECOGNISING HIS POTENTIAL AS A MEDIUM, HAD PUT HITLER IN TOUCH WITH CERTAIN ENTITIES...

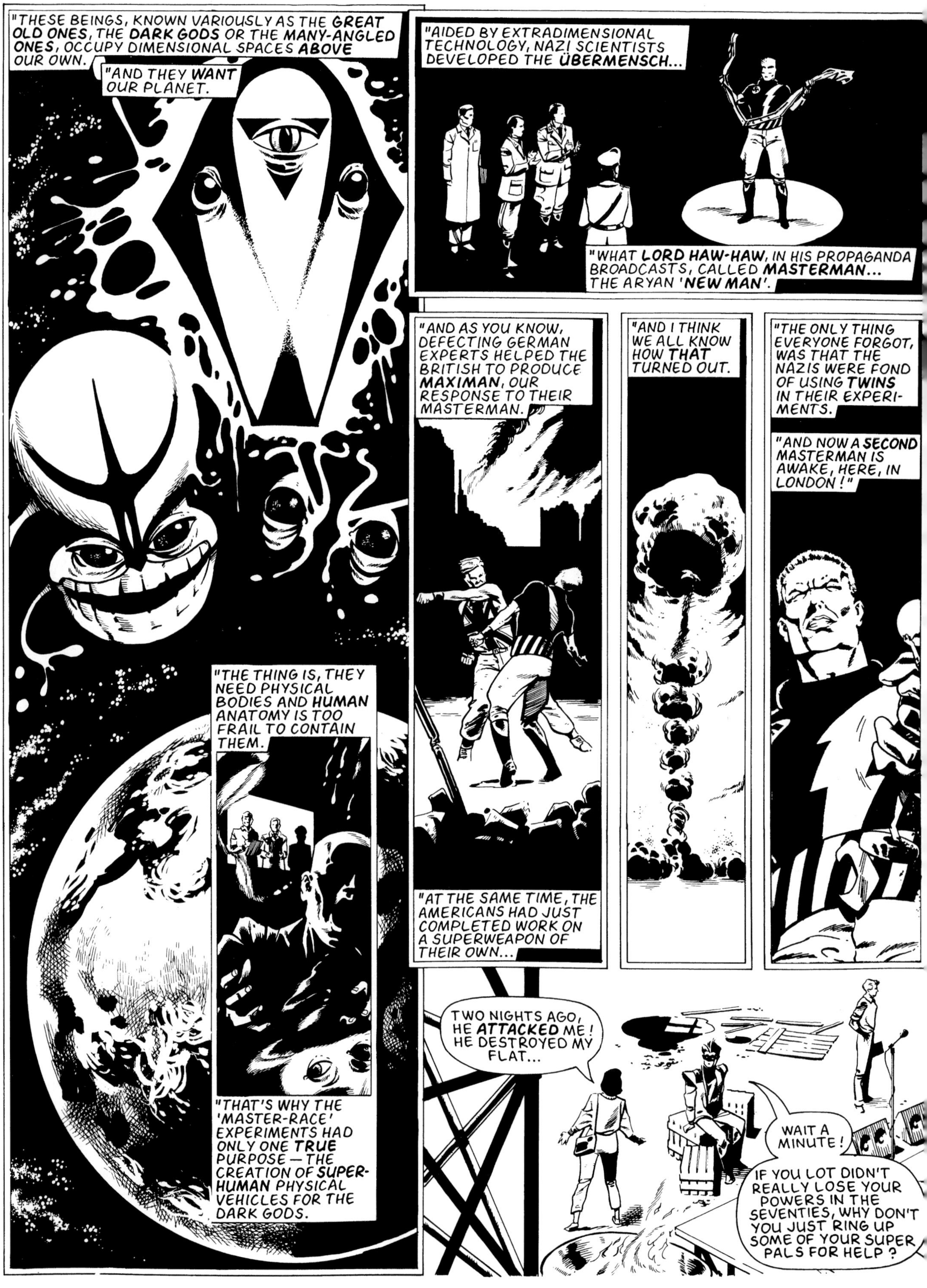
"THESE BEINGS, KNOWN VARIOUSLY AS THE GREAT OLD ONES, THE DARK GODS OR THE MANY-ANGLED ONES, OCCUPY DIMENSIONAL SPACES ABOVE OUR OWN.
"AND THEY WANT OUR PLANET.
"THE THING IS, THEY NEED PHYSICAL BODIES AND HUMAN ANATOMY IS TOO FRAIL TO CONTAIN THEM.
"THAT'S WHY THE 'MASTER-RACE' EXPERIMENTS HAD ONLY ONE TRUE PURPOSE — THE CREATION OF SUPER-HUMAN PHYSICAL VEHICLES FOR THE DARK GODS.
"AIDED BY EXTRADIMENSIONAL TECHNOLOGY, NAZI SCIENTISTS DEVELOPED THE ÜBERMENSCH...
"WHAT LORD HAW-HAW, IN HIS PROPAGANDA BROADCASTS, CALLED MASTERMAN... THE ARYAN 'NEW MAN'.
"AND AS YOU KNOW, DEFECTING GERMAN EXPERTS HELPED THE BRITISH TO PRODUCE MAXIMAN, OUR RESPONSE TO THEIR MASTERMAN.
"AT THE SAME TIME, THE AMERICANS HAD JUST COMPLETED WORK ON A SUPERWEAPON OF THEIR OWN...
"AND I THINK WE ALL KNOW HOW THAT TURNED OUT.
"THE ONLY THING EVERYONE FORGOT, WAS THAT THE NAZIS WERE FOND OF USING TWINS IN THEIR EXPERIMENTS.
"AND NOW A SECOND MASTERMAN IS AWAKE, HERE, IN LONDON!"
TWO NIGHTS AGO, HE ATTACKED ME! HE DESTROYED MY FLAT...
WAIT A MINUTE!
IF YOU LOT DIDN'T REALLY LOSE YOUR POWERS IN THE SEVENTIES, WHY DON'T YOU JUST RING UP SOME OF YOUR SUPER PALS FOR HELP?

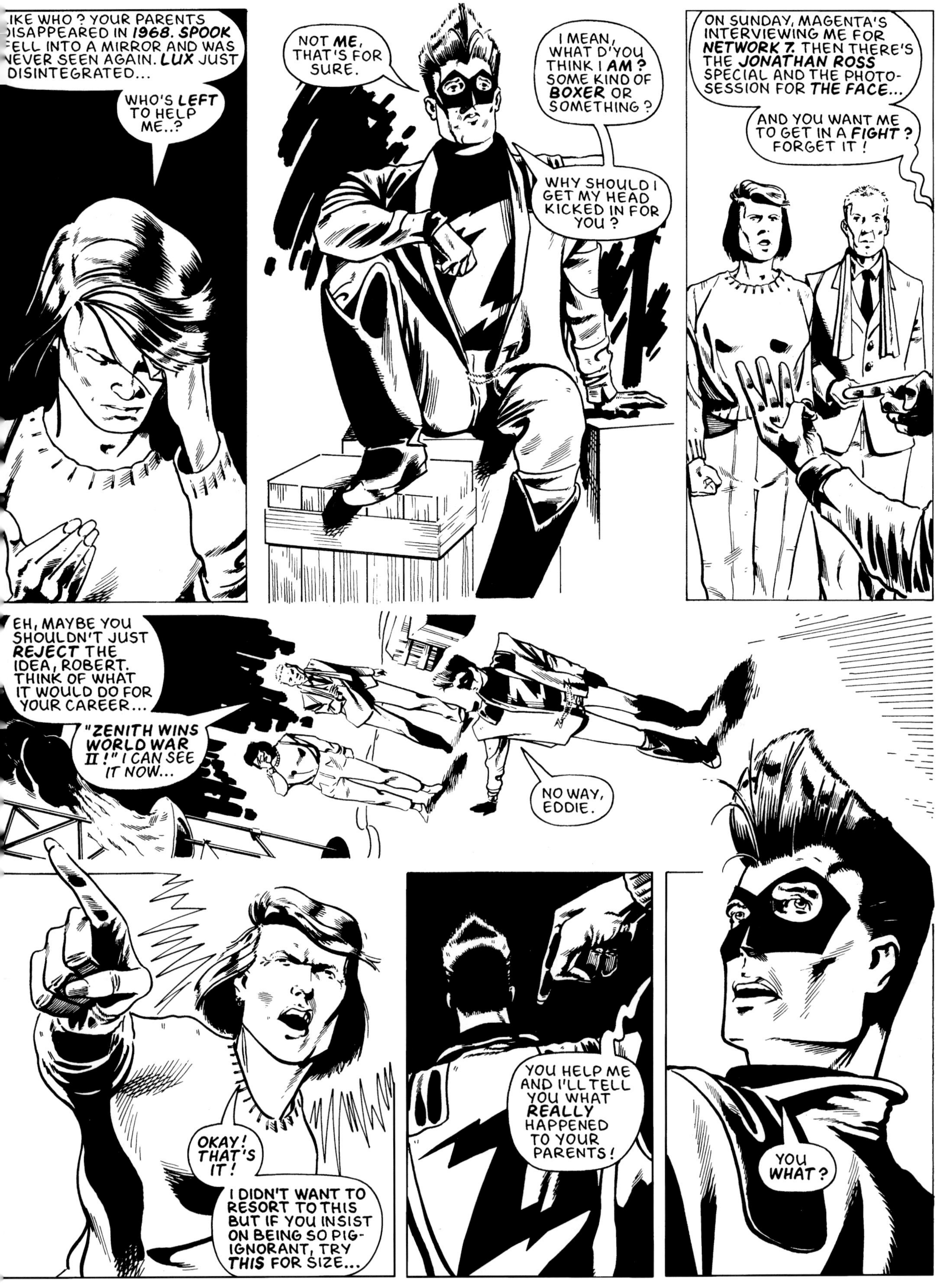
LIKE WHO? YOUR PARENTS DISAPPEARED IN 1968. SPOOK FELL INTO A MIRROR AND WAS NEVER SEEN AGAIN. LUX JUST DISINTEGRATED...
WHO'S LEFT TO HELP ME..?
NOT ME, THAT'S FOR SURE.
I MEAN, WHAT D'YOU THINK I AM? SOME KIND OF BOXER OR SOMETHING?
WHY SHOULD I GET MY HEAD KICKED IN FOR YOU?
ON SUNDAY, MAGENTA'S INTERVIEWING ME FOR NETWORK 7. THEN THERE'S THE JONATHAN ROSS SPECIAL AND THE PHOTO-SESSION FOR THE FACE...
AND YOU WANT ME TO GET IN A FIGHT? FORGET IT!
EH, MAYBE YOU SHOULDN'T JUST REJECT THE IDEA, ROBERT. THINK OF WHAT IT WOULD DO FOR YOUR CAREER...
"ZENITH WINS WORLD WAR II!" I CAN SEE IT NOW...
NO WAY, EDDIE.
OKAY! THAT'S IT!
I DIDN'T WANT TO RESORT TO THIS BUT IF YOU INSIST ON BEING SO PIG-IGNORANT, TRY THIS FOR SIZE...
YOU HELP ME AND I'LL TELL YOU WHAT REALLY HAPPENED TO YOUR PARENTS!
YOU WHAT?

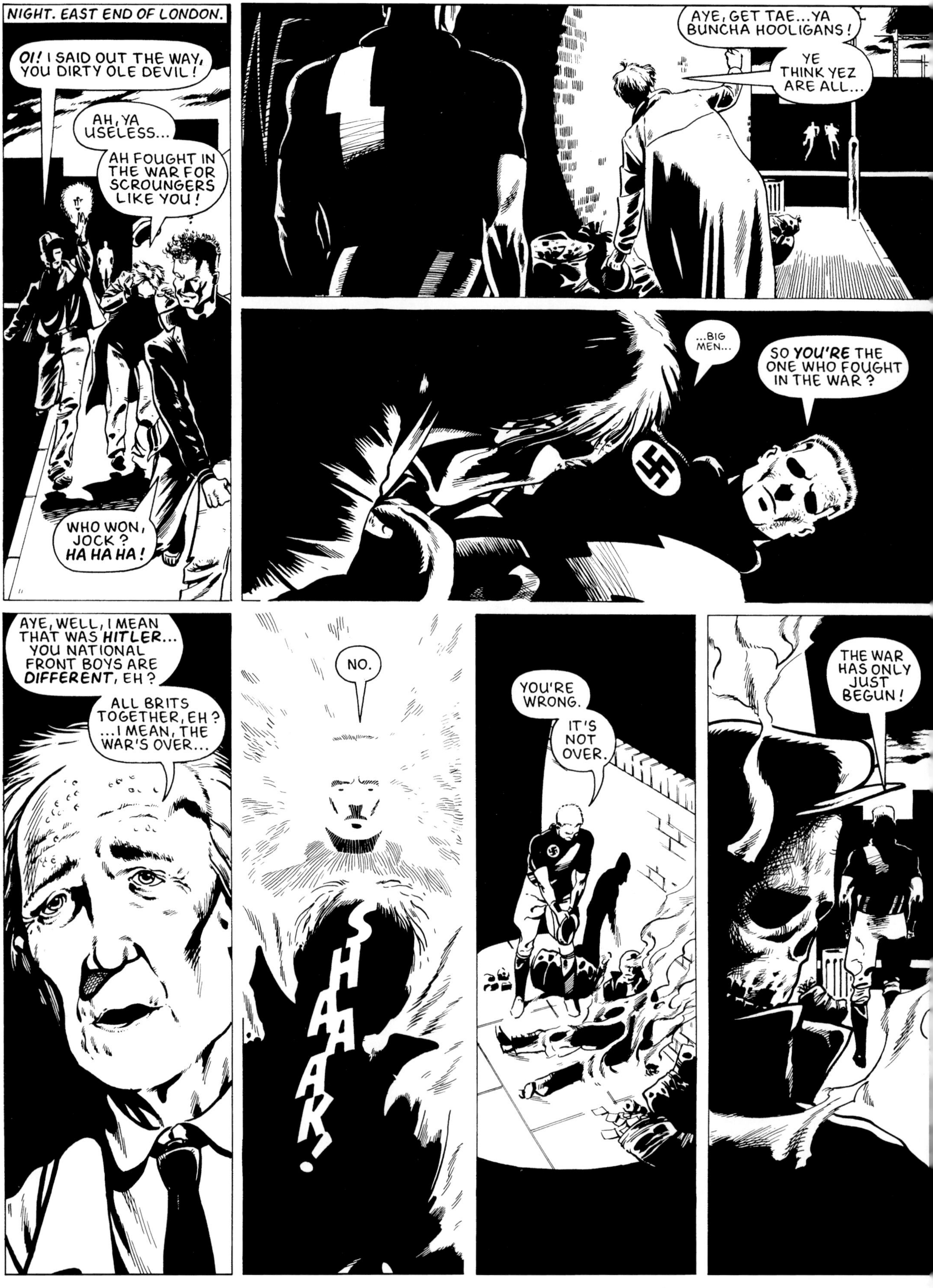

NIGHT. EAST END OF LONDON.
OI! I SAID OUT THE WAY, YOU DIRTY OLE DEVIL!
AH, YA USELESS...
AH FOUGHT IN THE WAR FOR SCROUNGERS LIKE YOU!
WHO WON, JOCK? HA HA HA!
AYE, GET TAE... YA BUNCHA HOOLIGANS!
YE THINK YEZ ARE ALL...
...BIG MEN...
SO YOU'RE THE ONE WHO FOUGHT IN THE WAR?
AYE, WELL, I MEAN THAT WAS HITLER... YOU NATIONAL FRONT BOYS ARE DIFFERENT, EH?
ALL BRITS TOGETHER, EH? ...I MEAN, THE WAR'S OVER...
NO.
SHAAAK!
YOU'RE WRONG.
IT'S NOT OVER.
THE WAR HAS ONLY JUST BEGUN!

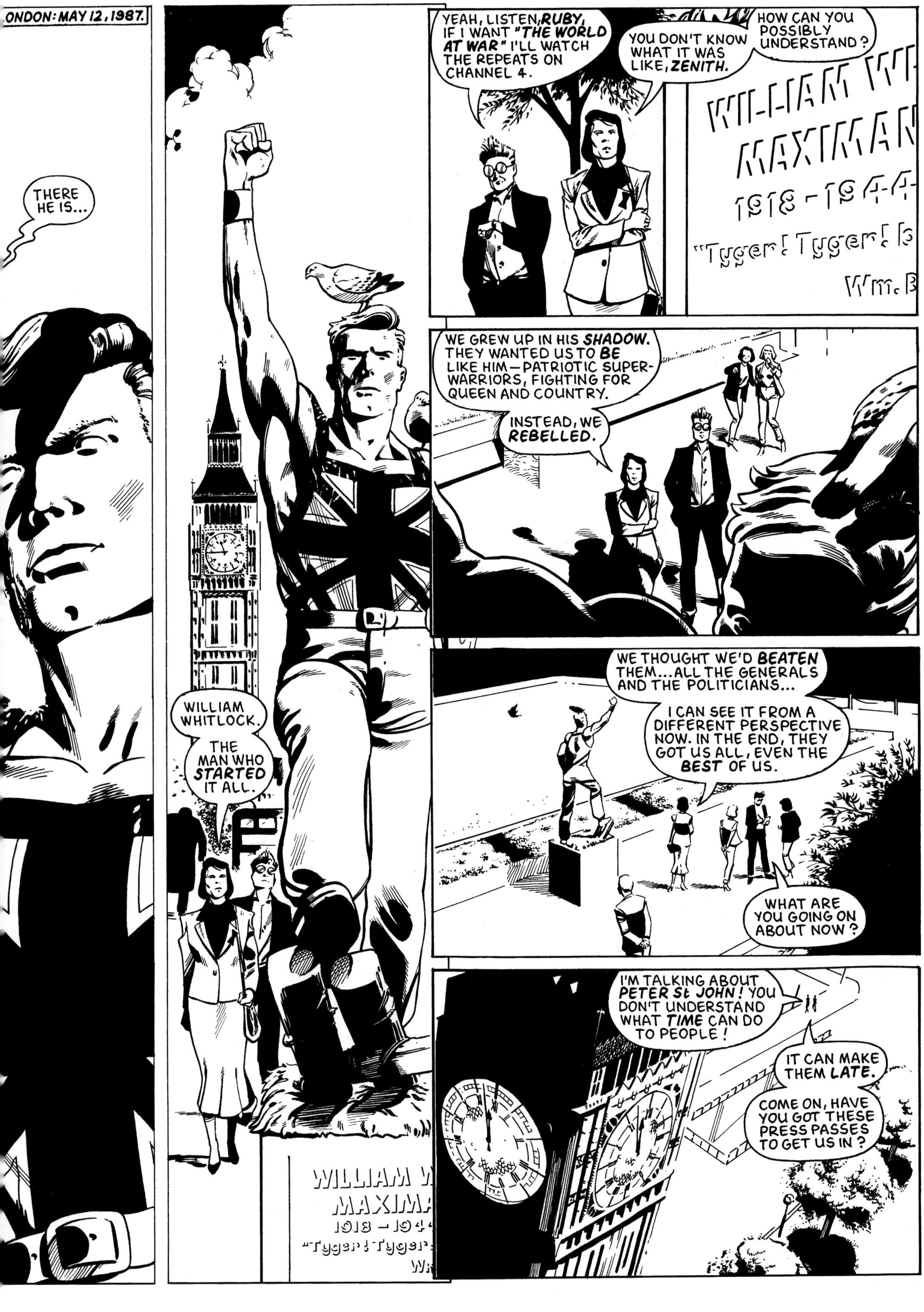
ONDON: MAY 12, 1987.
THERE HE IS...
WILLIAM WHITLOCK.
THE MAN WHO STARTED IT ALL.
WILLIAM W
MAXIMA
1918 – 194
"Tyger! Tyger!
Wi
YEAH, LISTEN, RUBY, IF I WANT "THE WORLD AT WAR" I'LL WATCH THE REPEATS ON CHANNEL 4.
YOU DON'T KNOW WHAT IT WAS LIKE, ZENITH.
HOW CAN YOU POSSIBLY UNDERSTAND?
WILLIAM W
MAXIMAN
1918 - 1944
"Tyger! Tyger! B
Wm. B
WE GREW UP IN HIS SHADOW. THEY WANTED US TO BE LIKE HIM—PATRIOTIC SUPER-WARRIORS, FIGHTING FOR QUEEN AND COUNTRY.
INSTEAD, WE REBELLED.
WE THOUGHT WE'D BEATEN THEM... ALL THE GENERALS AND THE POLITICIANS...
I CAN SEE IT FROM A DIFFERENT PERSPECTIVE NOW. IN THE END, THEY GOT US ALL, EVEN THE BEST OF US.
WHAT ARE YOU GOING ON ABOUT NOW?
I'M TALKING ABOUT PETER St JOHN! YOU DON'T UNDERSTAND WHAT TIME CAN DO TO PEOPLE!
IT CAN MAKE THEM LATE.
COME ON, HAVE YOU GOT THESE PRESS PASSES TO GET US IN?

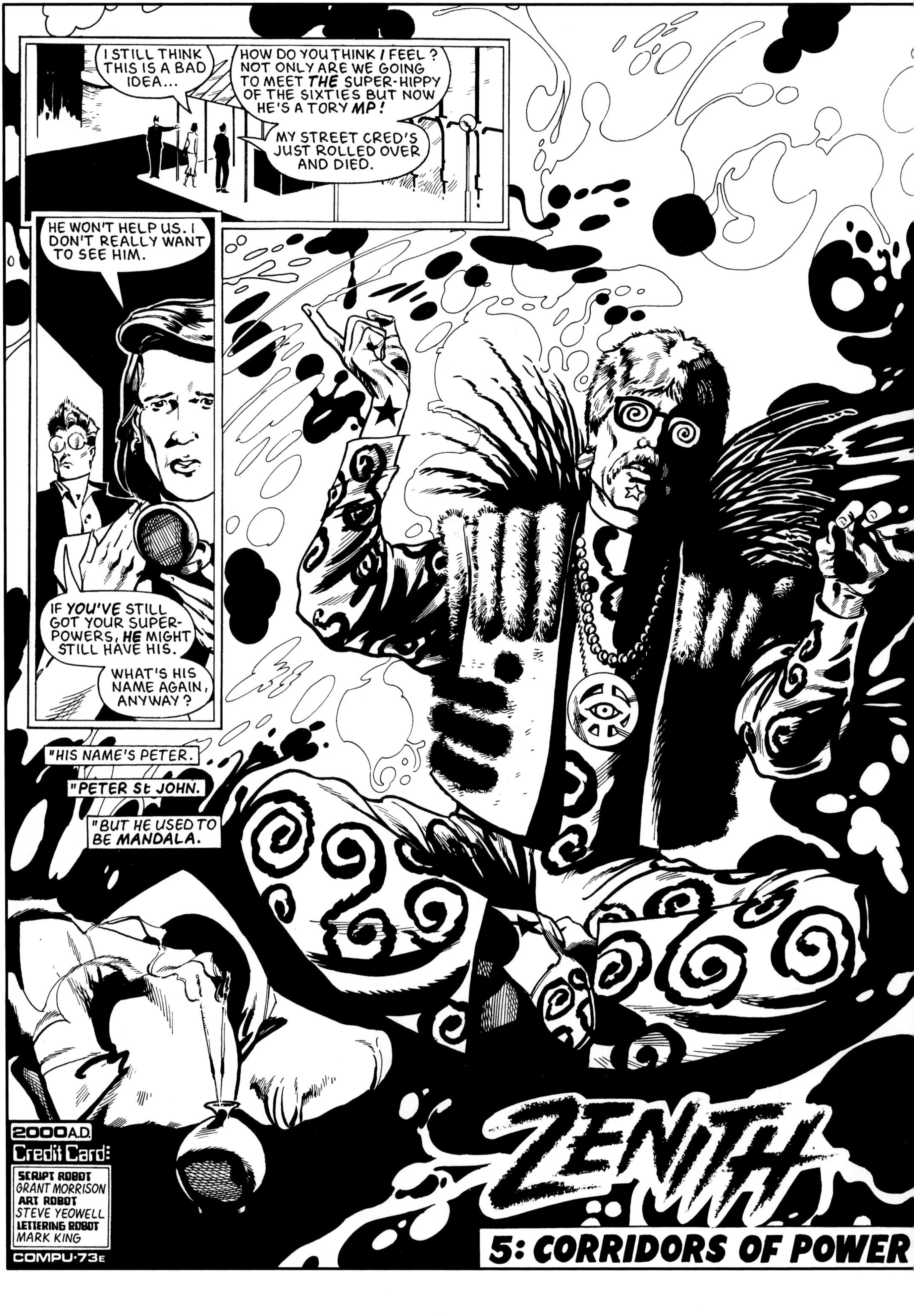

I STILL THINK THIS IS A BAD IDEA...
HOW DO YOU THINK I FEEL? NOT ONLY ARE WE GOING TO MEET THE SUPER-HIPPY OF THE SIXTIES BUT NOW HE'S A TORY MP!
MY STREET CRED'S JUST ROLLED OVER AND DIED.
HE WON'T HELP US. I DON'T REALLY WANT TO SEE HIM.
IF YOU'VE STILL GOT YOUR SUPER-POWERS, HE MIGHT STILL HAVE HIS.
WHAT'S HIS NAME AGAIN, ANYWAY?
"HIS NAME'S PETER.
"PETER St JOHN.
"BUT HE USED TO BE MANDALA.
2000 A.D. Credit Card:
SCRIPT ROBOT GRANT MORRISON
ART ROBOT STEVE YEOWELL
LETTERING ROBOT MARK KING
COMPU·73E
ZENITH
5: CORRIDORS OF POWER

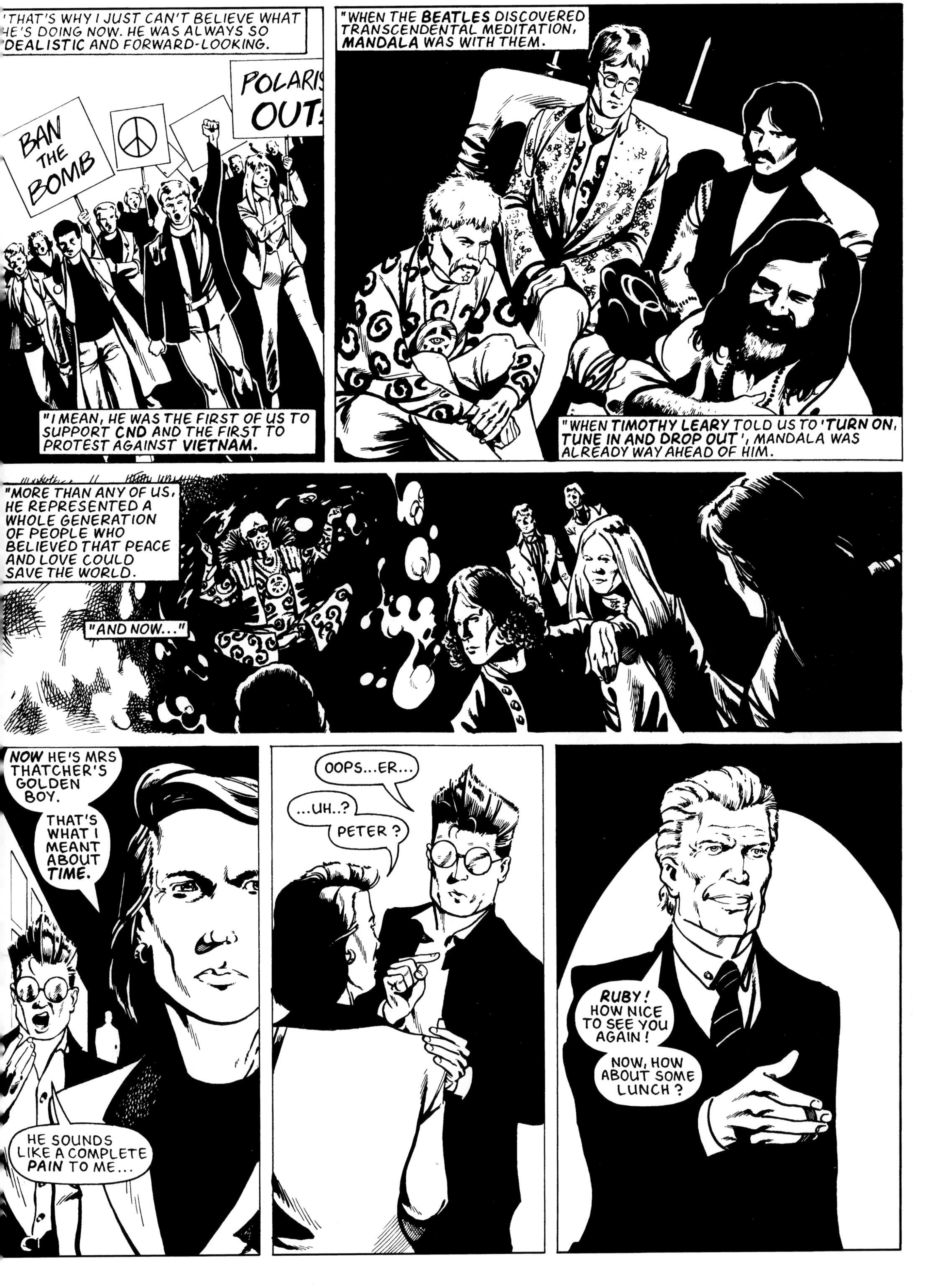
"THAT'S WHY I JUST CAN'T BELIEVE WHAT HE'S DOING NOW. HE WAS ALWAYS SO IDEALISTIC AND FORWARD-LOOKING.
POLARIS OUT!
BAN THE BOMB
"I MEAN, HE WAS THE FIRST OF US TO SUPPORT CND AND THE FIRST TO PROTEST AGAINST VIETNAM.
"WHEN THE BEATLES DISCOVERED TRANSCENDENTAL MEDITATION, MANDALA WAS WITH THEM.
"WHEN TIMOTHY LEARY TOLD US TO 'TURN ON, TUNE IN AND DROP OUT', MANDALA WAS ALREADY WAY AHEAD OF HIM.
"MORE THAN ANY OF US, HE REPRESENTED A WHOLE GENERATION OF PEOPLE WHO BELIEVED THAT PEACE AND LOVE COULD SAVE THE WORLD.
"AND NOW..."
NOW HE'S MRS THATCHER'S GOLDEN BOY.
THAT'S WHAT I MEANT ABOUT TIME.
HE SOUNDS LIKE A COMPLETE PAIN TO ME...
OOPS...ER...
...UH..?
PETER ?
RUBY! HOW NICE TO SEE YOU AGAIN!
NOW, HOW ABOUT SOME LUNCH ?

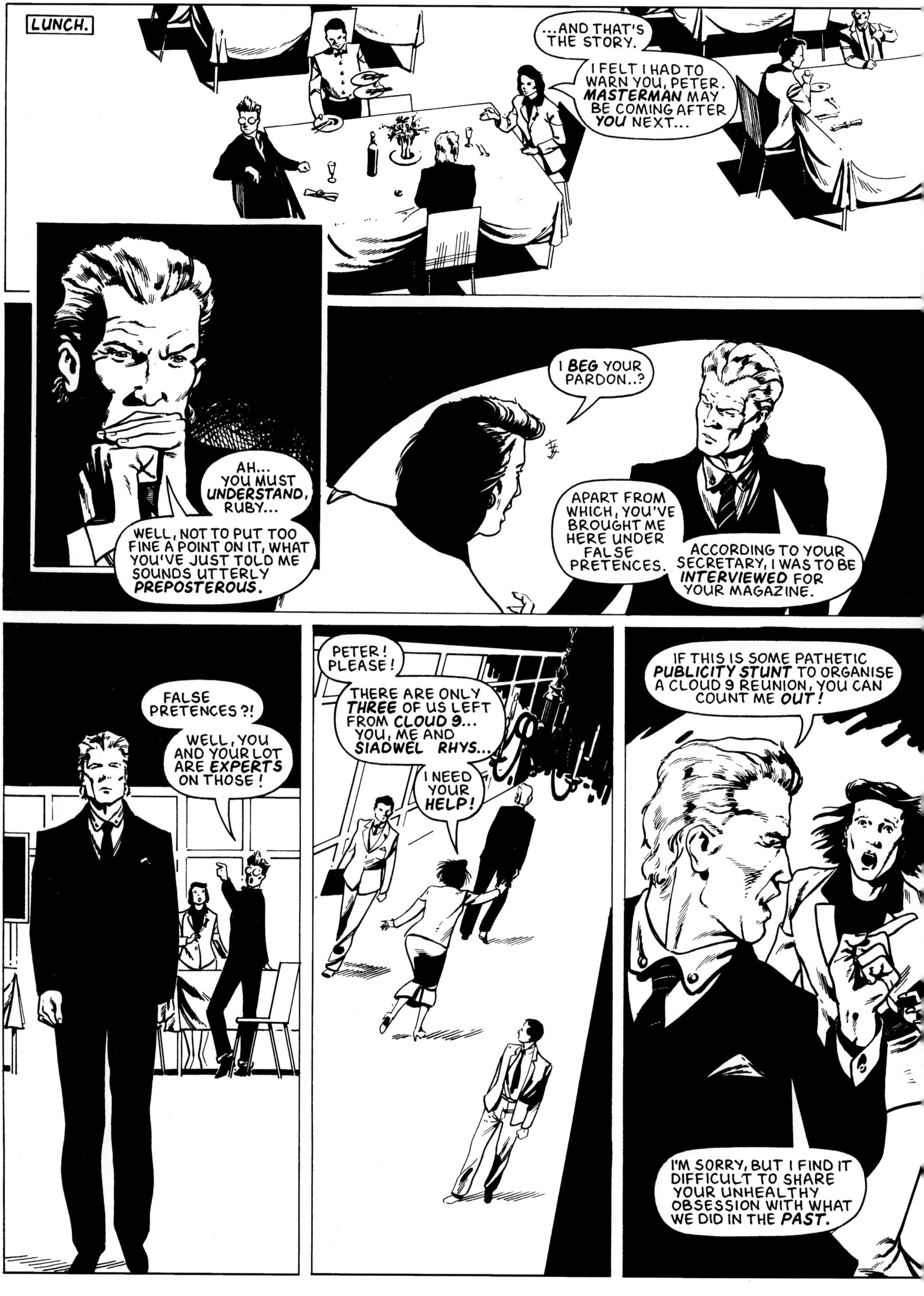
LUNCH.
...AND THAT'S THE STORY.
I FELT I HAD TO WARN YOU, PETER. MASTERMAN MAY BE COMING AFTER YOU NEXT...
AH... YOU MUST UNDERSTAND, RUBY...
WELL, NOT TO PUT TOO FINE A POINT ON IT, WHAT YOU'VE JUST TOLD ME SOUNDS UTTERLY PREPOSTEROUS.
I BEG YOUR PARDON..?
APART FROM WHICH, YOU'VE BROUGHT ME HERE UNDER FALSE PRETENCES.
ACCORDING TO YOUR SECRETARY, I WAS TO BE INTERVIEWED FOR YOUR MAGAZINE.
FALSE PRETENCES?!
WELL, YOU AND YOUR LOT ARE EXPERTS ON THOSE!
PETER! PLEASE!
THERE ARE ONLY THREE OF US LEFT FROM CLOUD 9... YOU, ME AND SIADWEL RHYS...
I NEED YOUR HELP!
IF THIS IS SOME PATHETIC PUBLICITY STUNT TO ORGANISE A CLOUD 9 REUNION, YOU CAN COUNT ME OUT!
I'M SORRY, BUT I FIND IT DIFFICULT TO SHARE YOUR UNHEALTHY OBSESSION WITH WHAT WE DID IN THE PAST.

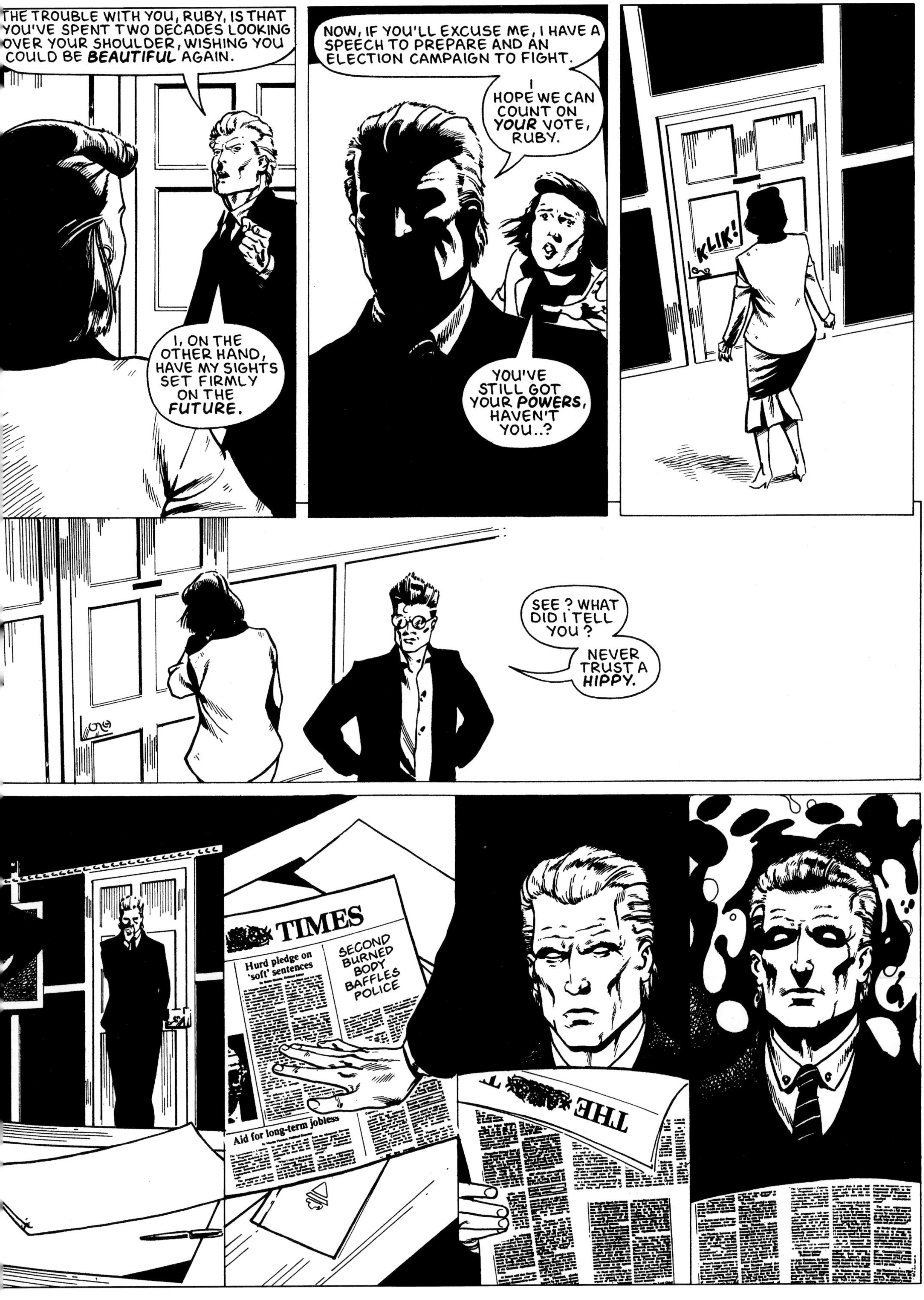

THE TROUBLE WITH YOU, RUBY, IS THAT YOU'VE SPENT TWO DECADES LOOKING OVER YOUR SHOULDER, WISHING YOU COULD BE BEAUTIFUL AGAIN.
I, ON THE OTHER HAND, HAVE MY SIGHTS SET FIRMLY ON THE FUTURE.
NOW, IF YOU'LL EXCUSE ME, I HAVE A SPEECH TO PREPARE AND AN ELECTION CAMPAIGN TO FIGHT.
I HOPE WE CAN COUNT ON YOUR VOTE, RUBY.
YOU'VE STILL GOT YOUR POWERS, HAVEN'T YOU..?
KLIK!
SEE ? WHAT DID I TELL YOU ?
NEVER TRUST A HIPPY.
TIMES
Hurd pledge on 'soft' sentences
SECOND BURNED BODY BAFFLES POLICE
Aid for long-term jobless
THE

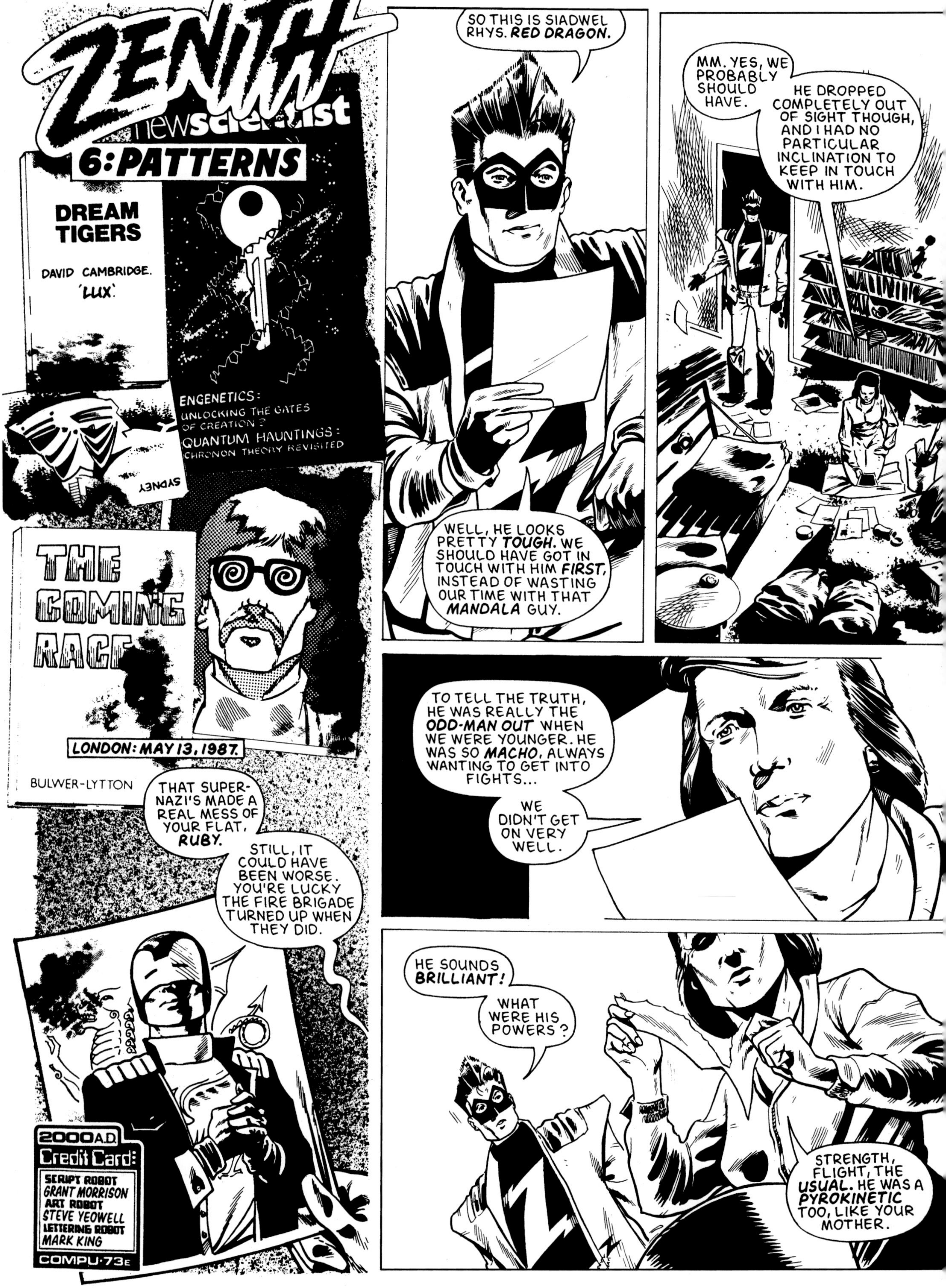
ZENITH
new scientist
6: PATTERNS
DREAM TIGERS
DAVID CAMBRIDGE.
'LUX'.
ENGENETICS: UNLOCKING THE GATES OF CREATION?
QUANTUM HAUNTINGS: CHRONON THEORY REVISITED
SYDNEY
THE COMING RACE
LONDON: MAY 13, 1987.
BULWER-LYTTON
THAT SUPER-NAZI'S MADE A REAL MESS OF YOUR FLAT, RUBY.
STILL, IT COULD HAVE BEEN WORSE. YOU'RE LUCKY THE FIRE BRIGADE TURNED UP WHEN THEY DID.
2000 A.D. Credit Card:
SCRIPT ROBOT GRANT MORRISON
ART ROBOT STEVE YEOWELL
LETTERING ROBOT MARK KING
COMPU·73E
SO THIS IS SIADWEL RHYS. RED DRAGON.
WELL, HE LOOKS PRETTY TOUGH. WE SHOULD HAVE GOT IN TOUCH WITH HIM FIRST, INSTEAD OF WASTING OUR TIME WITH THAT MANDALA GUY.
MM. YES, WE PROBABLY SHOULD HAVE.
HE DROPPED COMPLETELY OUT OF SIGHT THOUGH, AND I HAD NO PARTICULAR INCLINATION TO KEEP IN TOUCH WITH HIM.
TO TELL THE TRUTH, HE WAS REALLY THE ODD-MAN OUT WHEN WE WERE YOUNGER. HE WAS SO MACHO, ALWAYS WANTING TO GET INTO FIGHTS...
WE DIDN'T GET ON VERY WELL.
HE SOUNDS BRILLIANT!
WHAT WERE HIS POWERS?
STRENGTH, FLIGHT, THE USUAL. HE WAS A PYROKINETIC TOO, LIKE YOUR MOTHER.

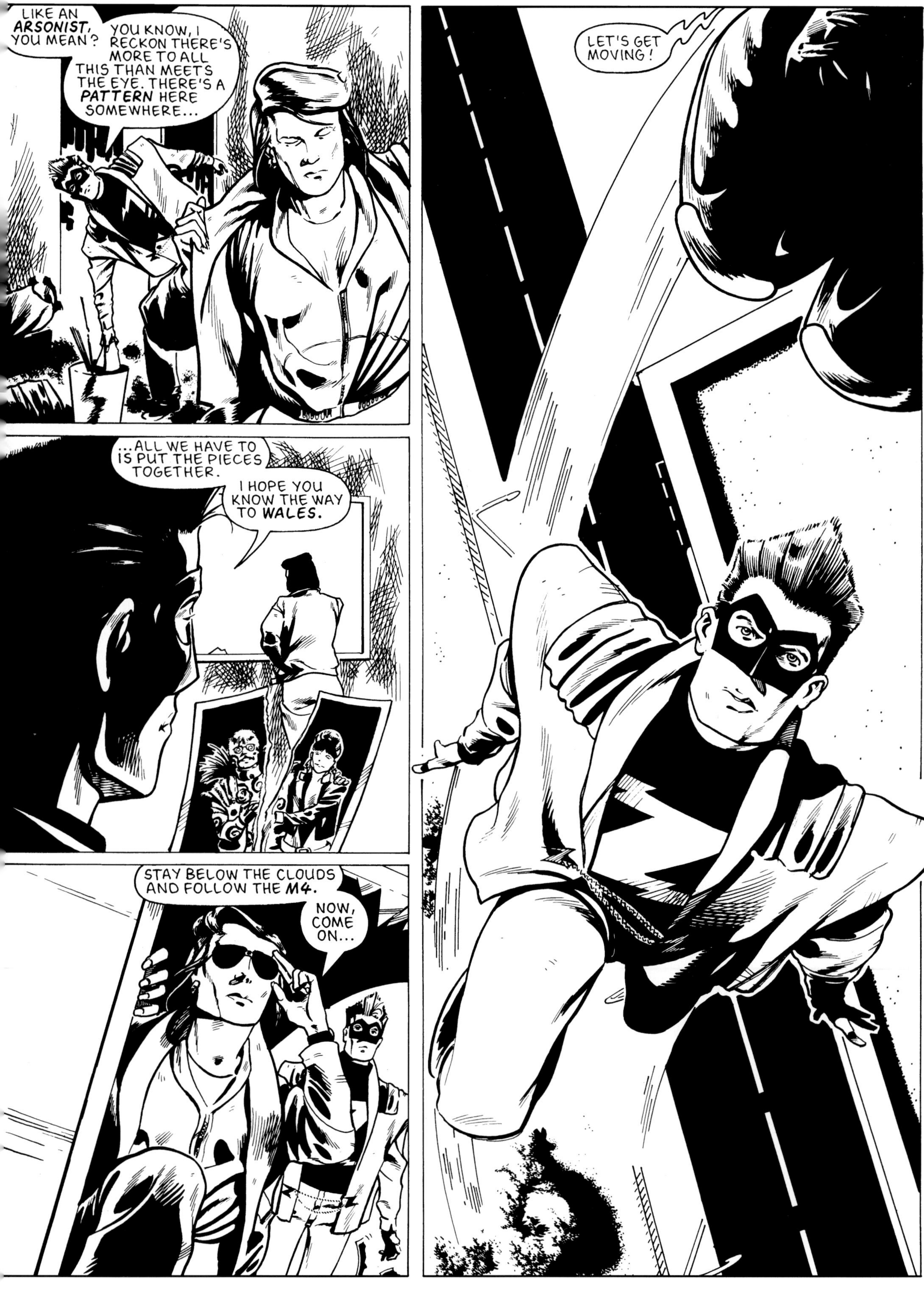

LIKE AN ARSONIST, YOU MEAN?
YOU KNOW, I RECKON THERE'S MORE TO ALL THIS THAN MEETS THE EYE. THERE'S A PATTERN HERE SOMEWHERE...
...ALL WE HAVE TO IS PUT THE PIECES TOGETHER.
I HOPE YOU KNOW THE WAY TO WALES.
STAY BELOW THE CLOUDS AND FOLLOW THE M4.
NOW, COME ON...
LET'S GET MOVING!

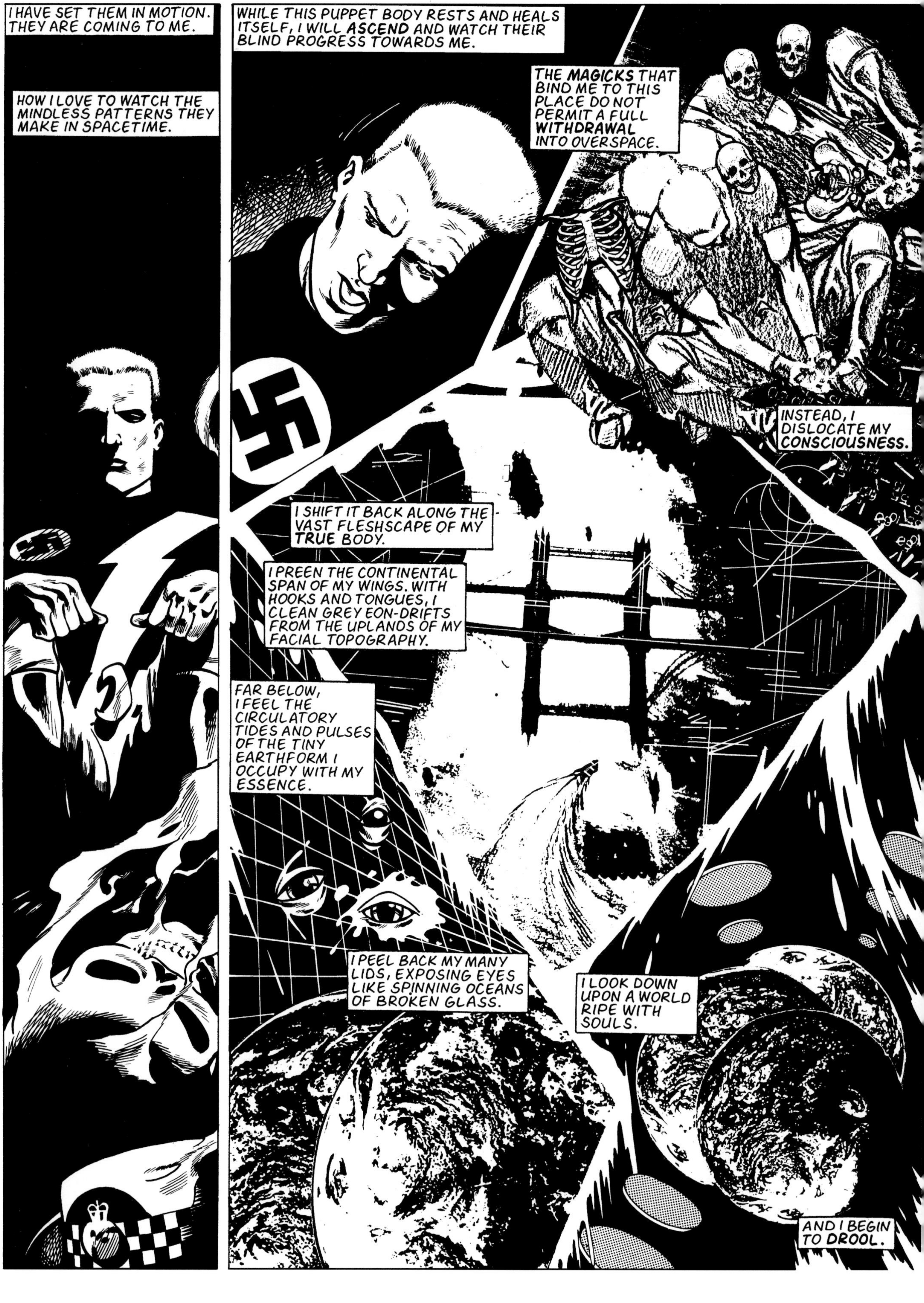
I HAVE SET THEM IN MOTION. THEY ARE COMING TO ME.
HOW I LOVE TO WATCH THE MINDLESS PATTERNS THEY MAKE IN SPACETIME.
WHILE THIS PUPPET BODY RESTS AND HEALS ITSELF, I WILL ASCEND AND WATCH THEIR BLIND PROGRESS TOWARDS ME.
THE MAGICKS THAT BIND ME TO THIS PLACE DO NOT PERMIT A FULL WITHDRAWAL INTO OVERSPACE.
INSTEAD, I DISLOCATE MY CONSCIOUSNESS.
I SHIFT IT BACK ALONG THE VAST FLESHSCAPE OF MY TRUE BODY.
I PREEN THE CONTINENTAL SPAN OF MY WINGS. WITH HOOKS AND TONGUES, I CLEAN GREY EON-DRIFTS FROM THE UPLANDS OF MY FACIAL TOPOGRAPHY.
FAR BELOW, I FEEL THE CIRCULATORY TIDES AND PULSES OF THE TINY EARTHFORM I OCCUPY WITH MY ESSENCE.
I PEEL BACK MY MANY LIDS, EXPOSING EYES LIKE SPINNING OCEANS OF BROKEN GLASS.
I LOOK DOWN UPON A WORLD RIPE WITH SOULS.
AND I BEGIN TO DROOL.

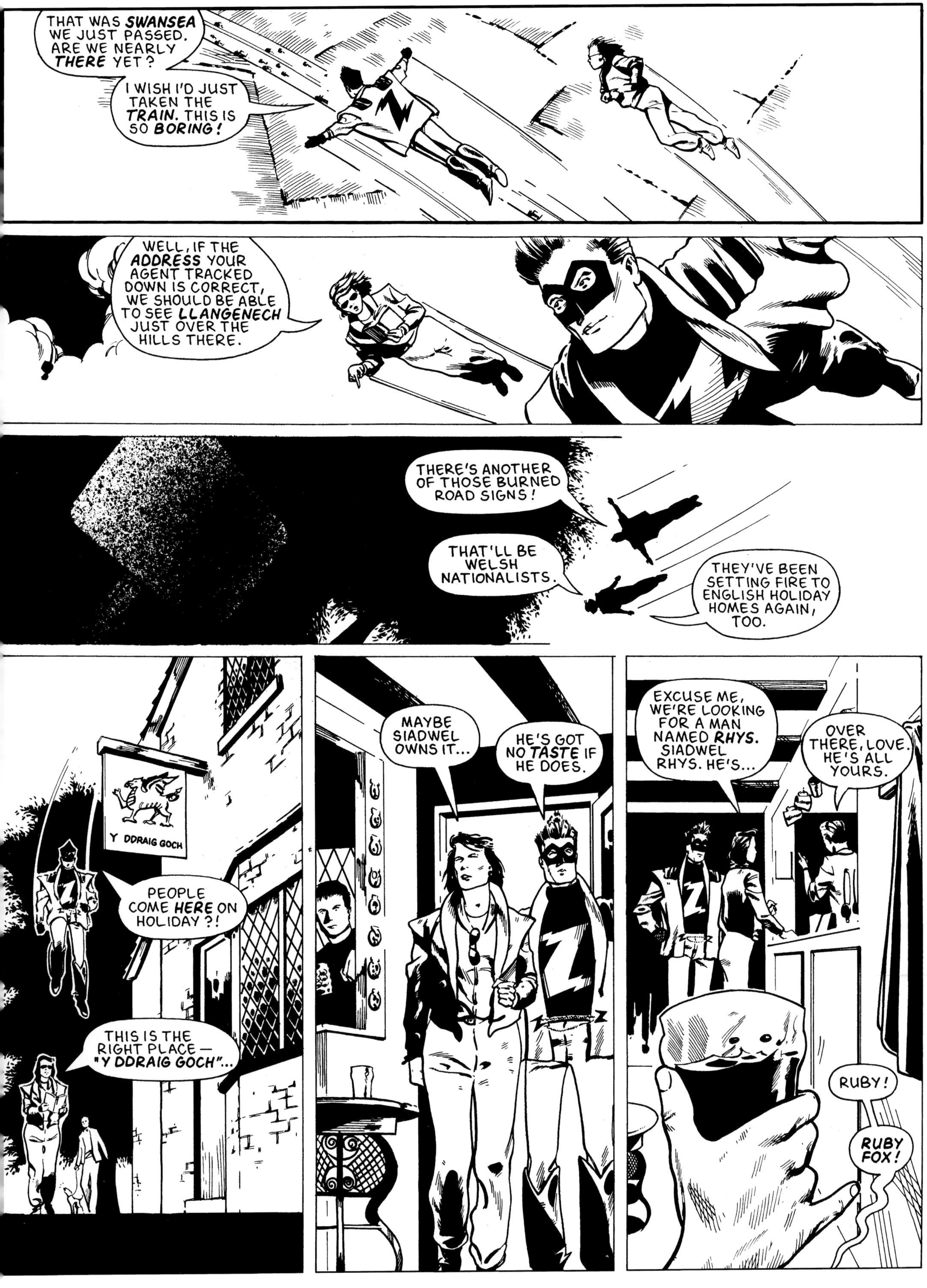

THAT WAS SWANSEA WE JUST PASSED. ARE WE NEARLY THERE YET?
I WISH I'D JUST TAKEN THE TRAIN. THIS IS SO BORING!
WELL, IF THE ADDRESS YOUR AGENT TRACKED DOWN IS CORRECT, WE SHOULD BE ABLE TO SEE LLANGENECH JUST OVER THE HILLS THERE.
THERE'S ANOTHER OF THOSE BURNED ROAD SIGNS!
THAT'LL BE WELSH NATIONALISTS.
THEY'VE BEEN SETTING FIRE TO ENGLISH HOLIDAY HOMES AGAIN, TOO.
Y DDRAIG GOCH
PEOPLE COME HERE ON HOLIDAY?!
THIS IS THE RIGHT PLACE — "Y DDRAIG GOCH"...
MAYBE SIADWEL OWNS IT...
HE'S GOT NO TASTE IF HE DOES.
EXCUSE ME, WE'RE LOOKING FOR A MAN NAMED RHYS. SIADWEL RHYS. HE'S...
OVER THERE, LOVE. HE'S ALL YOURS.
RUBY!
RUBY FOX!

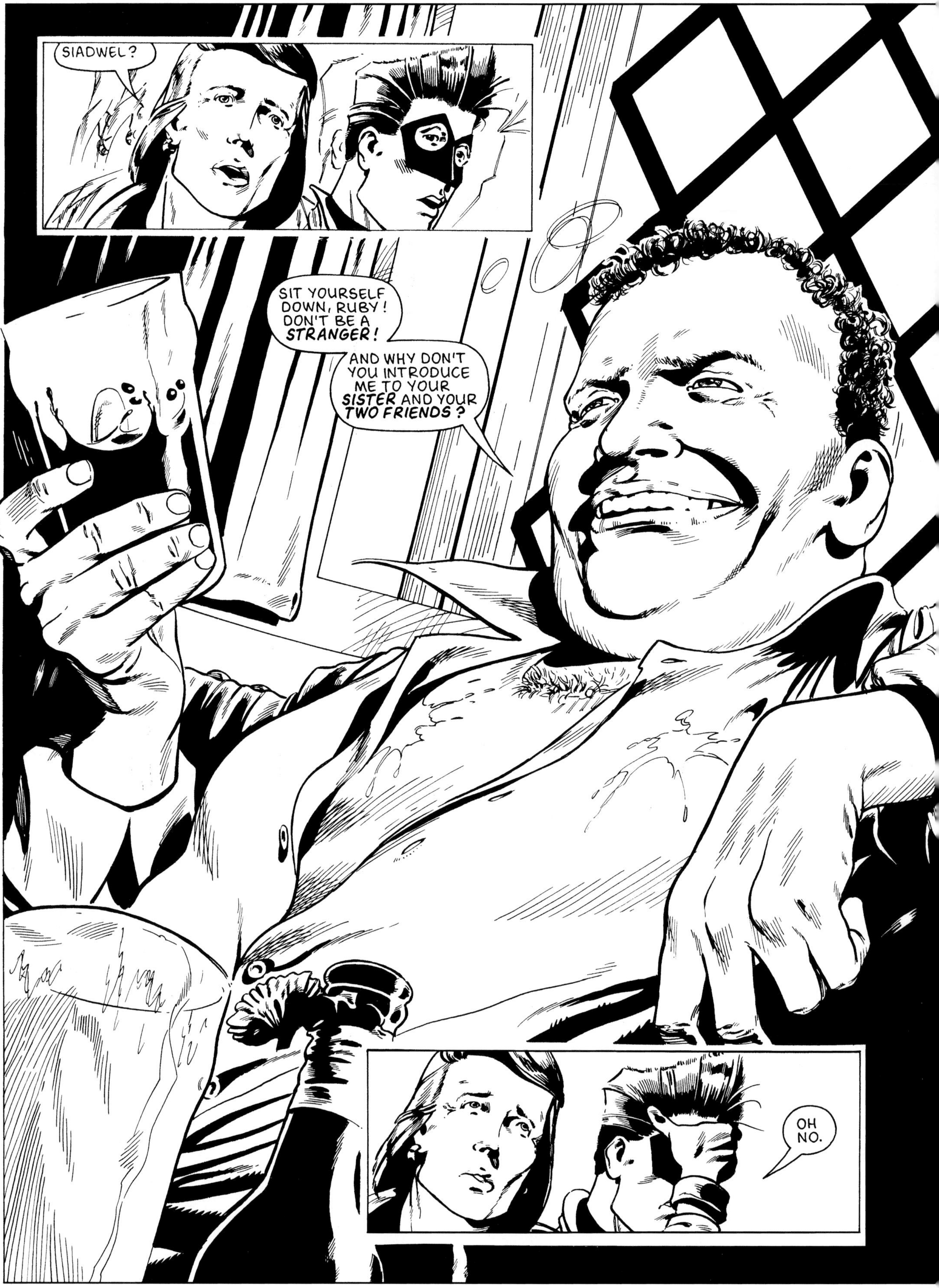
SIADWEL?
SIT YOURSELF DOWN, RUBY! DON'T BE A STRANGER!
AND WHY DON'T YOU INTRODUCE ME TO YOUR SISTER AND YOUR TWO FRIENDS?
OH NO.

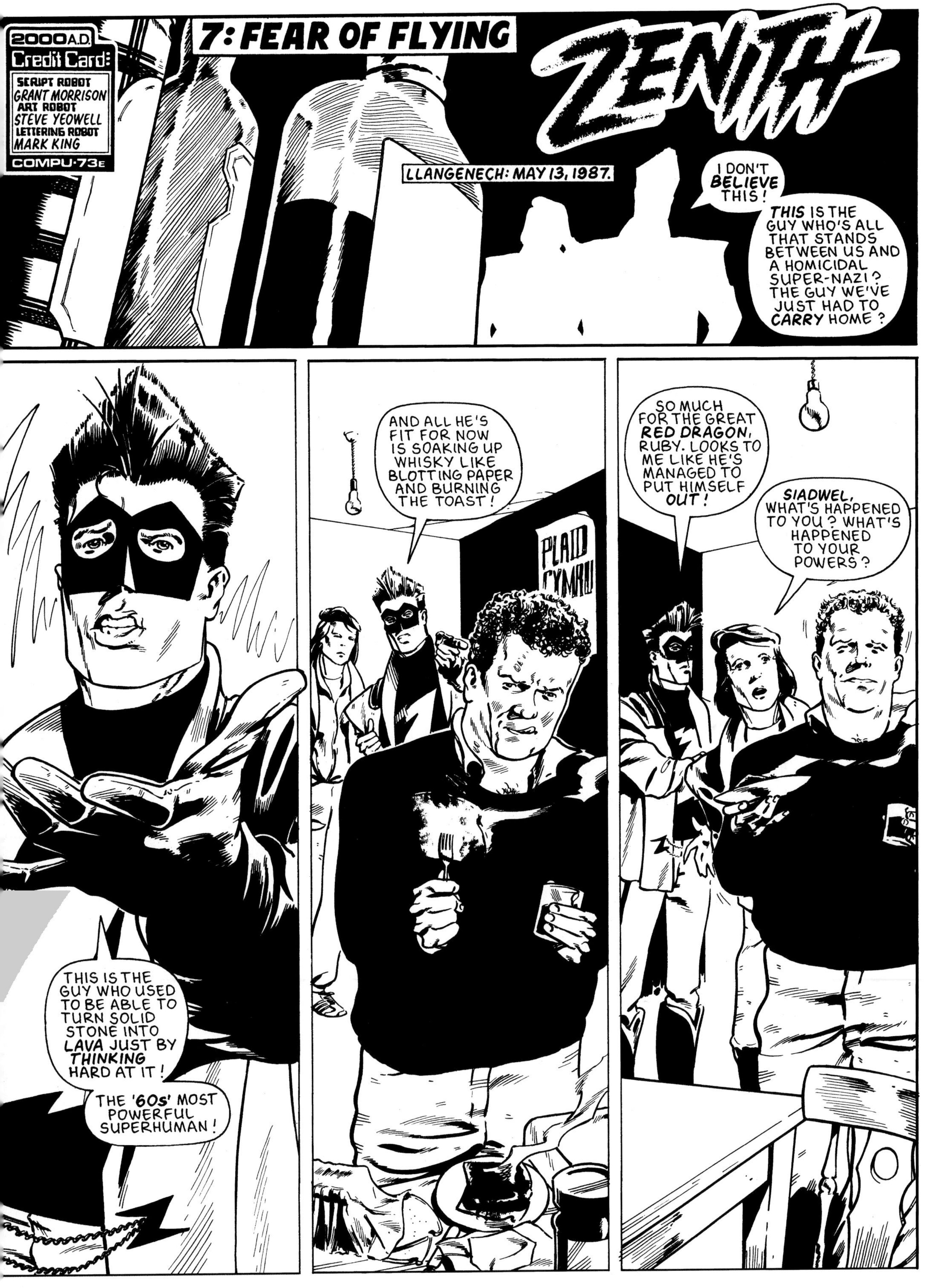
2000 A.D. Credit Card:
SCRIPT ROBOT GRANT MORRISON
ART ROBOT STEVE YEOWELL
LETTERING ROBOT MARK KING
COMPU·73E
7: FEAR OF FLYING
ZENITH
LLANGENECH: MAY 13, 1987.
I DON'T BELIEVE THIS!
THIS IS THE GUY WHO'S ALL THAT STANDS BETWEEN US AND A HOMICIDAL SUPER-NAZI? THE GUY WE'VE JUST HAD TO CARRY HOME?
THIS IS THE GUY WHO USED TO BE ABLE TO TURN SOLID STONE INTO LAVA JUST BY THINKING HARD AT IT!
THE '60s' MOST POWERFUL SUPERHUMAN!
AND ALL HE'S FIT FOR NOW IS SOAKING UP WHISKY LIKE BLOTTING PAPER AND BURNING THE TOAST!
PLAID CYMRU
SO MUCH FOR THE GREAT RED DRAGON, RUBY. LOOKS TO ME LIKE HE'S MANAGED TO PUT HIMSELF OUT!
SIADWEL, WHAT'S HAPPENED TO YOU? WHAT'S HAPPENED TO YOUR POWERS?

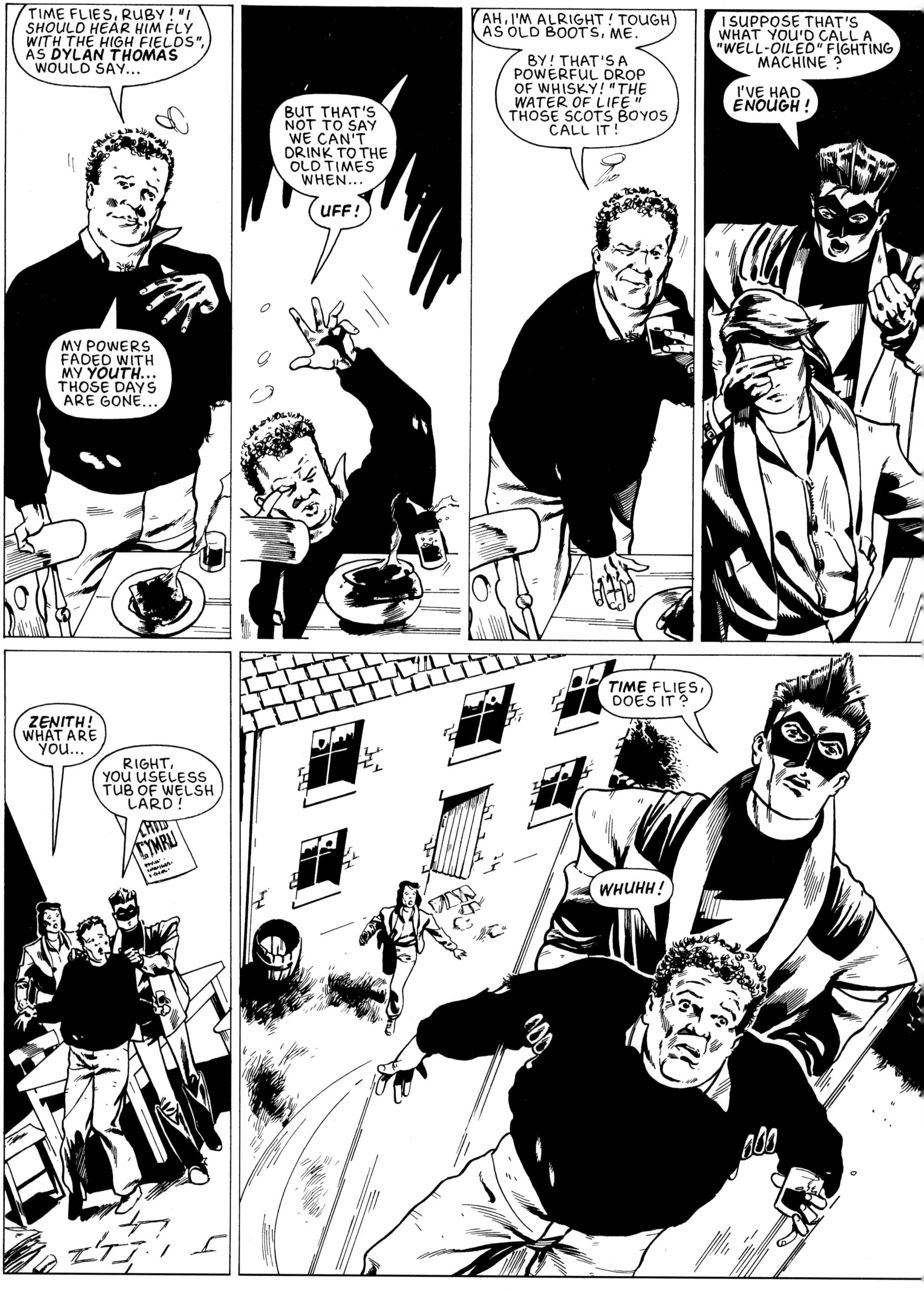

TIME FLIES, RUBY! "I SHOULD HEAR HIM FLY WITH THE HIGH FIELDS", AS DYLAN THOMAS WOULD SAY...
MY POWERS FADED WITH MY YOUTH... THOSE DAYS ARE GONE...
BUT THAT'S NOT TO SAY WE CAN'T DRINK TO THE OLD TIMES WHEN...
UFF!
AH, I'M ALRIGHT! TOUGH AS OLD BOOTS, ME.
BY! THAT'S A POWERFUL DROP OF WHISKY! "THE WATER OF LIFE" THOSE SCOTS BOYOS CALL IT!
I SUPPOSE THAT'S WHAT YOU'D CALL A "WELL-OILED" FIGHTING MACHINE?
I'VE HAD ENOUGH!
ZENITH! WHAT ARE YOU...
RIGHT, YOU USELESS TUB OF WELSH LARD!
TIME FLIES, DOES IT?
WHUHH!

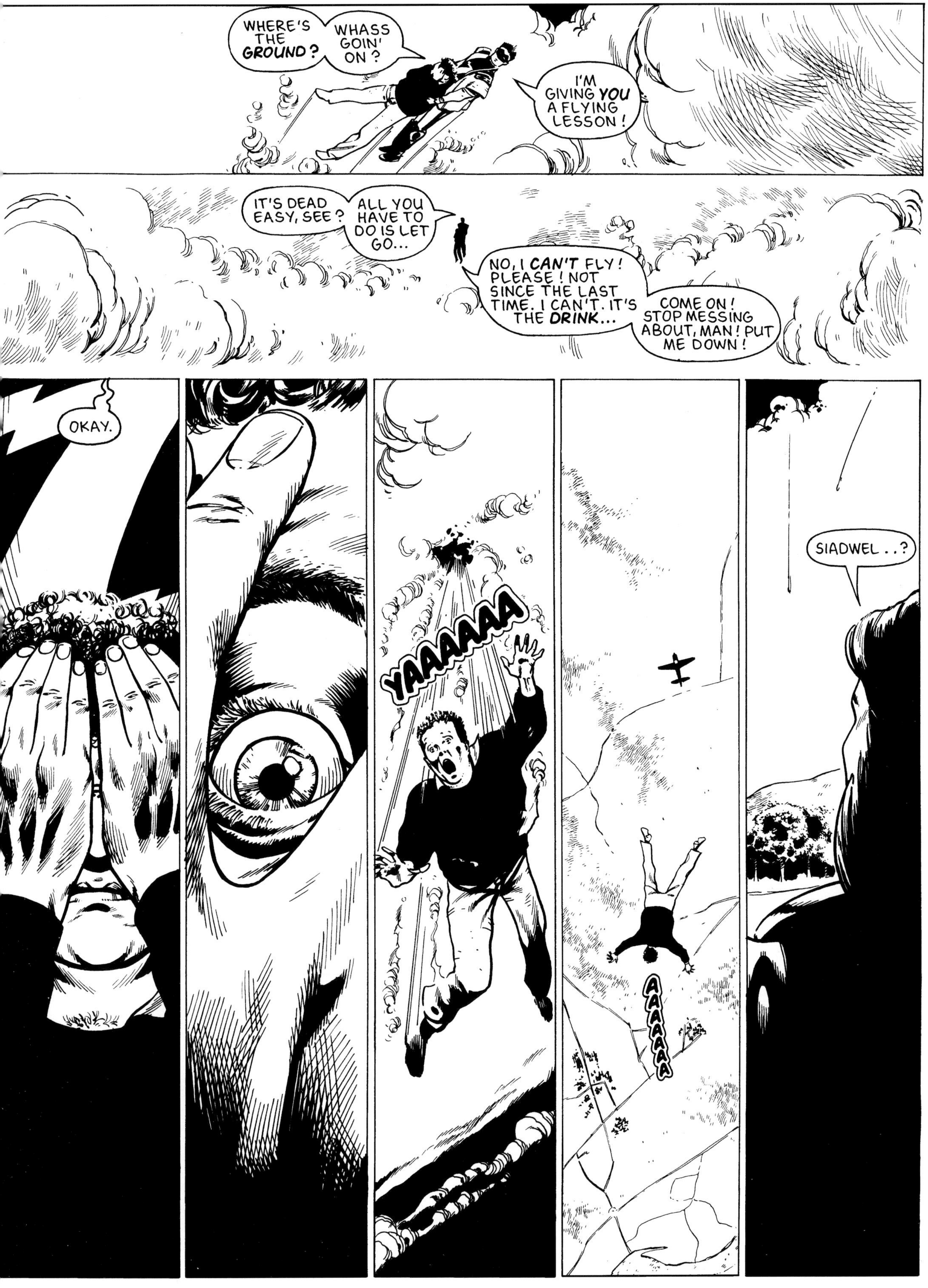
WHERE'S THE GROUND?
WHASS GOIN' ON?
I'M GIVING YOU A FLYING LESSON!
IT'S DEAD EASY, SEE?
ALL YOU HAVE TO DO IS LET GO...
NO, I CAN'T FLY! PLEASE! NOT SINCE THE LAST TIME. I CAN'T. IT'S THE DRINK...
COME ON! STOP MESSING ABOUT, MAN! PUT ME DOWN!
OKAY.
YAAAAAA
AAAAAA
SIADWEL..?

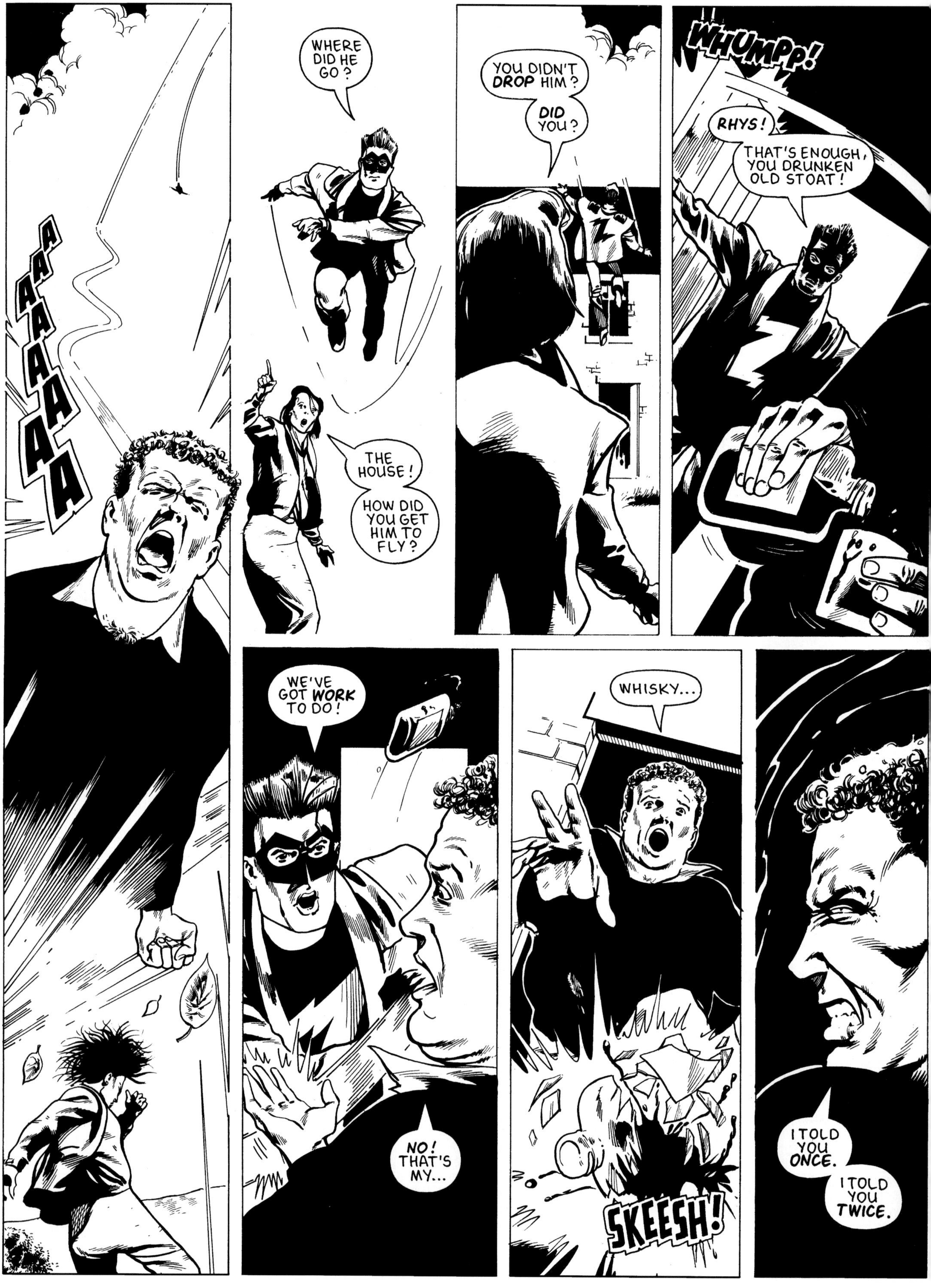
AAAAAAAAAA
WHERE DID HE GO?
THE HOUSE!
HOW DID YOU GET HIM TO FLY?
YOU DIDN'T DROP HIM?
DID YOU?
WHUMPP!
RHYS!
THAT'S ENOUGH, YOU DRUNKEN OLD STOAT!
WE'VE GOT WORK TO DO!
NO! THAT'S MY...
WHISKY...
SKEESH!
I TOLD YOU ONCE.
I TOLD YOU TWICE.

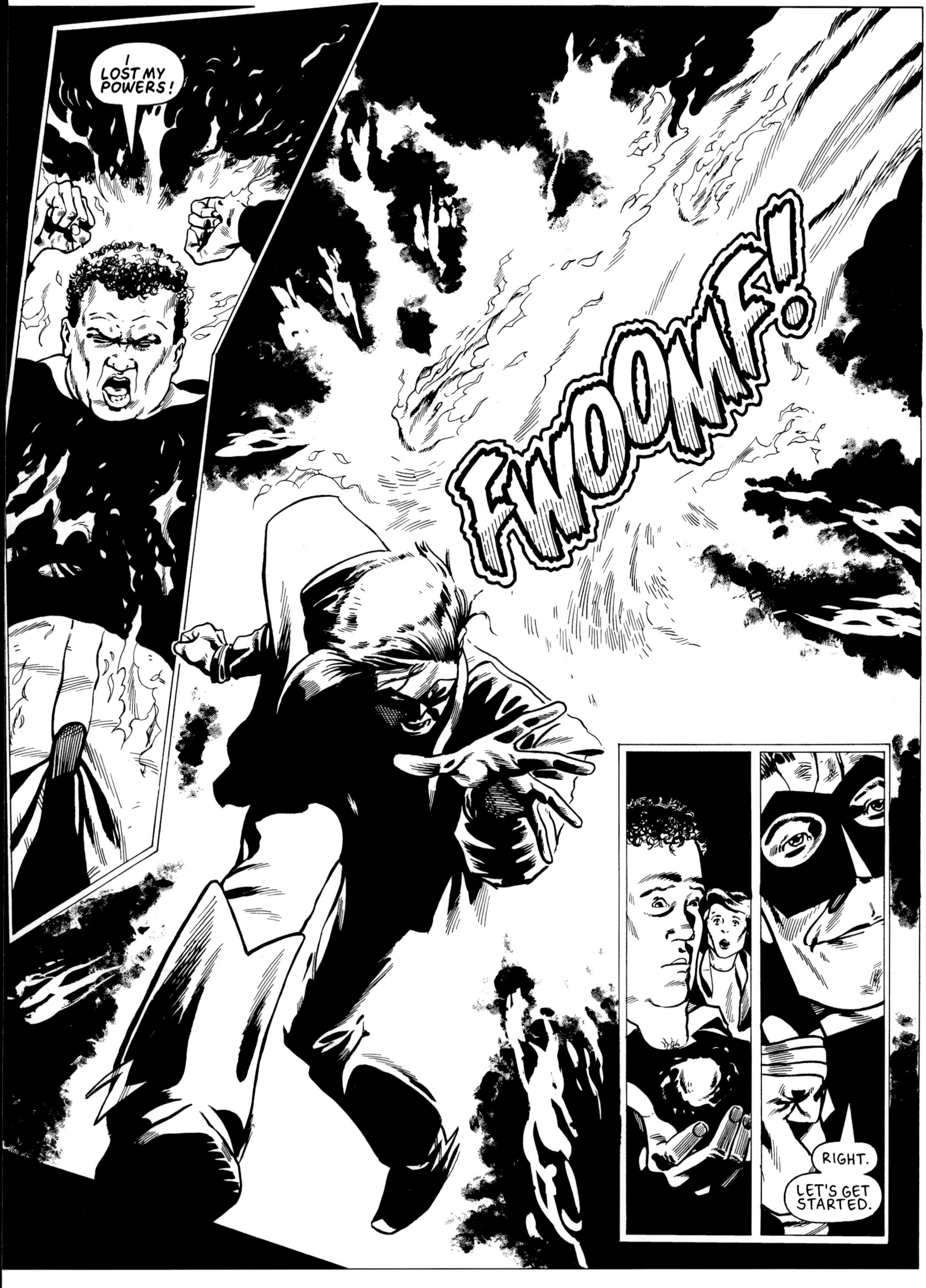

I LOST MY POWERS!
FWOOMF!
RIGHT.
LET'S GET STARTED.

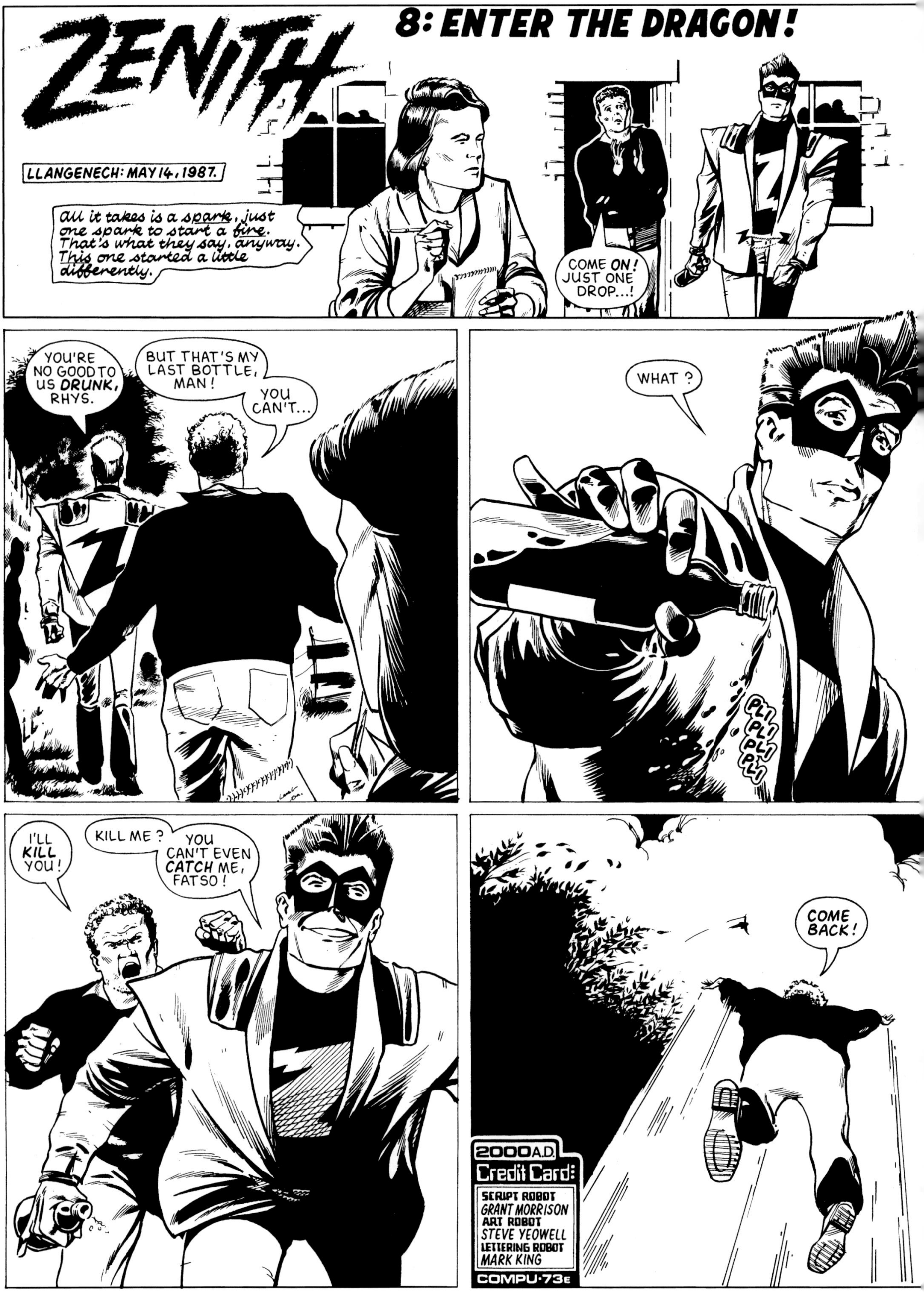
ZENITH
8: ENTER THE DRAGON!
LLANGENECH: MAY 14, 1987.
All it takes is a spark, just one spark to start a fire. That's what they say, anyway. This one started a little differently.
COME ON! JUST ONE DROP...!
YOU'RE NO GOOD TO US DRUNK, RHYS.
BUT THAT'S MY LAST BOTTLE, MAN!
YOU CAN'T...
WHAT ?
PLI PLI PLI PLI
I'LL KILL YOU!
KILL ME ?
YOU CAN'T EVEN CATCH ME, FATSO!
COME BACK!
2000 A.D. Credit Card:
SCRIPT ROBOT GRANT MORRISON
ART ROBOT STEVE YEOWELL
LETTERING ROBOT MARK KING
COMPU·73E

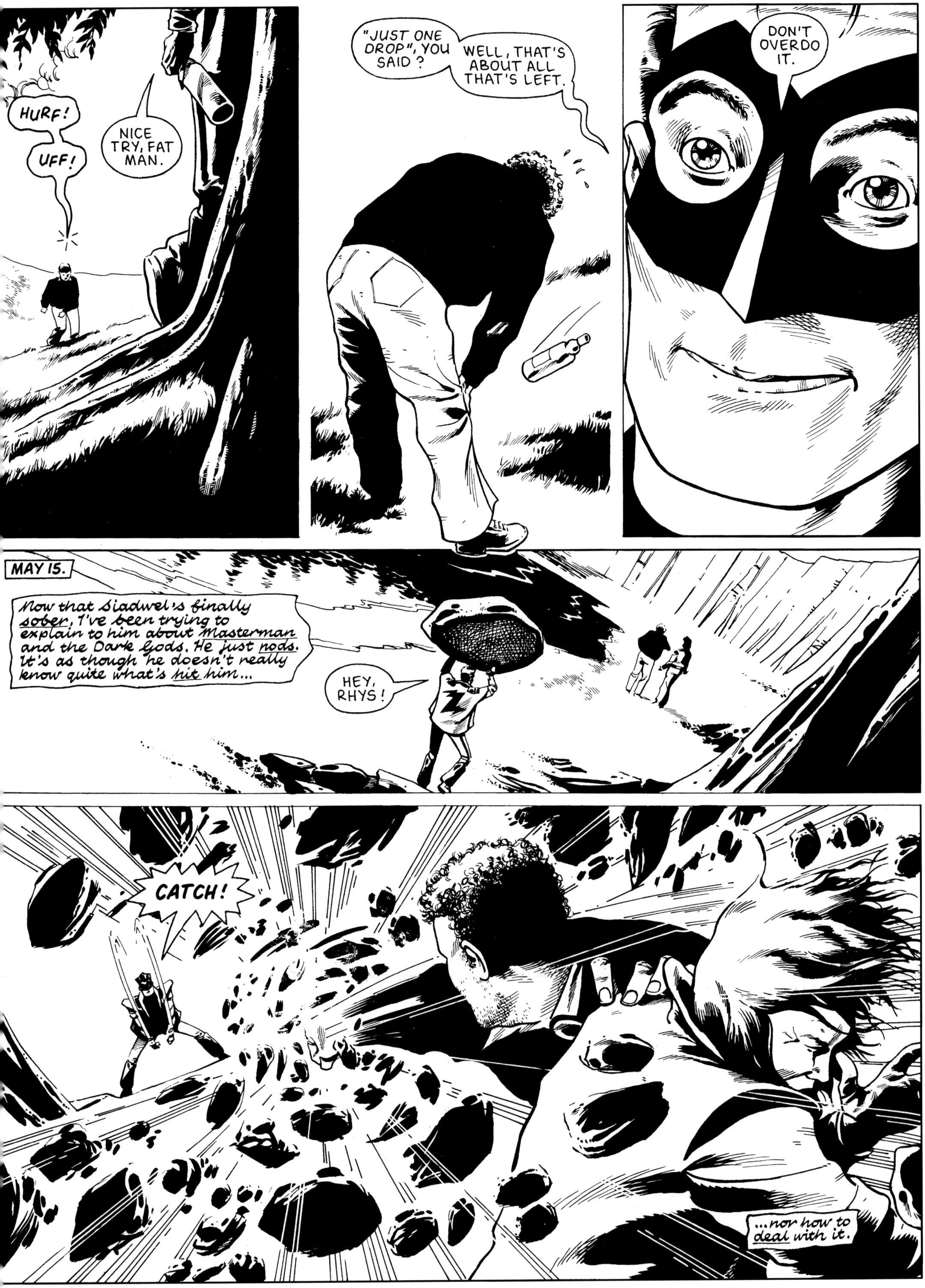
HURF!
UFF!
NICE TRY, FAT MAN.
"JUST ONE DROP", YOU SAID?
WELL, THAT'S ABOUT ALL THAT'S LEFT.
DON'T OVERDO IT.
MAY 15.
Now that Siadwel's finally sober, I've been trying to explain to him about Masterman and the Dark Gods. He just nods. It's as though he doesn't really know quite what's hit him...
HEY, RHYS!
CATCH!
...nor how to deal with it.

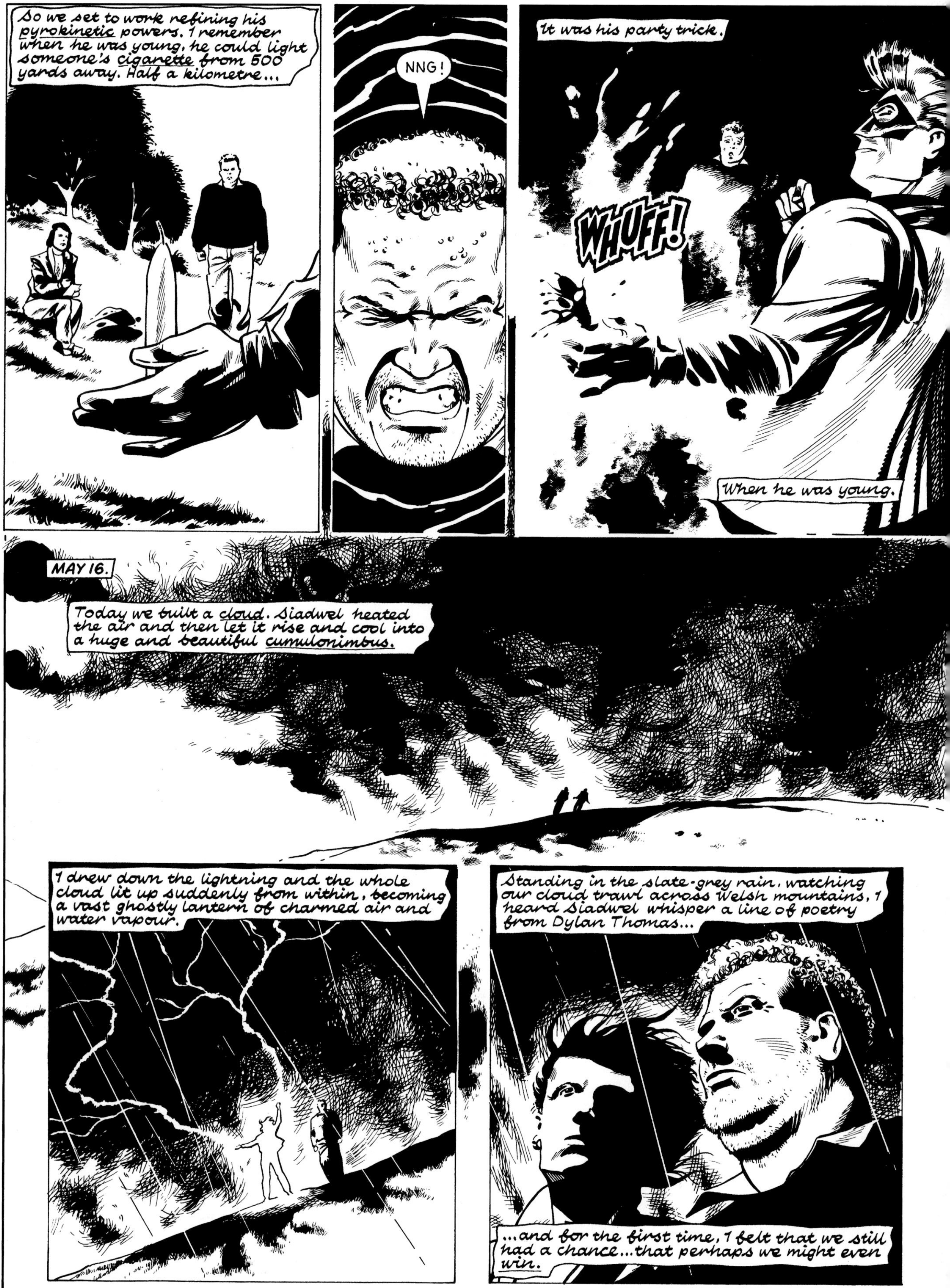
So we set to work refining his pyrokinetic powers. I remember when he was young, he could light someone's cigarette from 500 yards away. Half a kilometre...
NNG!
It was his party trick.
WHUFF!
When he was young.
MAY 16.
Today we built a cloud. Siadwel heated the air and then let it rise and cool into a huge and beautiful cumulonimbus.
I drew down the lightning and the whole cloud lit up suddenly from within, becoming a vast ghostly lantern of charmed air and water vapour.
Standing in the slate-grey rain, watching our cloud trawl across Welsh mountains, I heard Siadwel whisper a line of poetry from Dylan Thomas...
...and for the first time, I felt that we still had a chance...that perhaps we might even win.

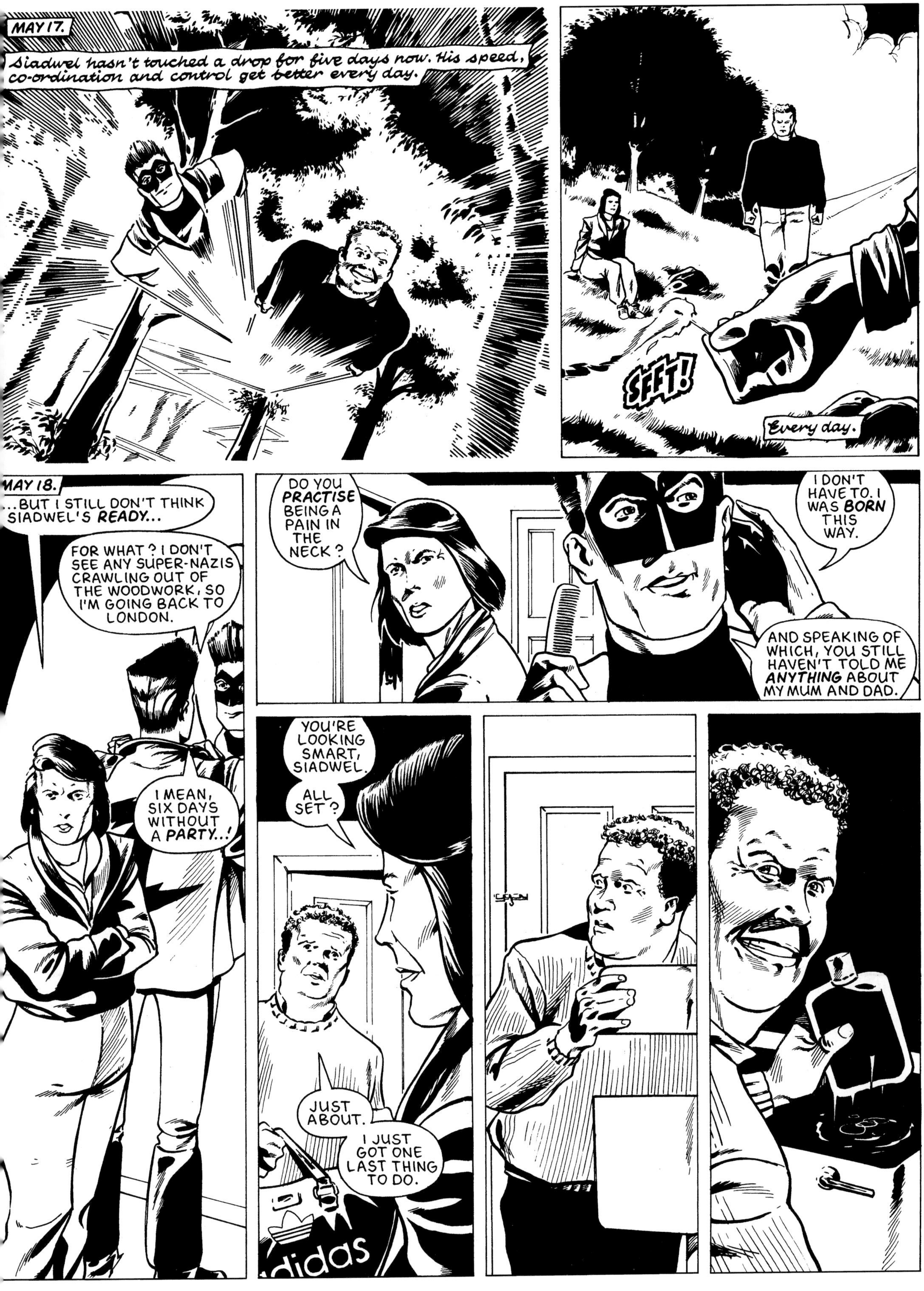
MAY 17.
Siadwel hasn't touched a drop for five days now. His speed, co-ordination and control get better every day.
SFFT!
Every day.
MAY 18.
...BUT I STILL DON'T THINK SIADWEL'S READY...
FOR WHAT? I DON'T SEE ANY SUPER-NAZIS CRAWLING OUT OF THE WOODWORK, SO I'M GOING BACK TO LONDON.
I MEAN, SIX DAYS WITHOUT A PARTY...!
DO YOU PRACTISE BEING A PAIN IN THE NECK?
I DON'T HAVE TO. I WAS BORN THIS WAY.
AND SPEAKING OF WHICH, YOU STILL HAVEN'T TOLD ME ANYTHING ABOUT MY MUM AND DAD.
YOU'RE LOOKING SMART, SIADWEL.
ALL SET?
JUST ABOUT.
I JUST GOT ONE LAST THING TO DO.

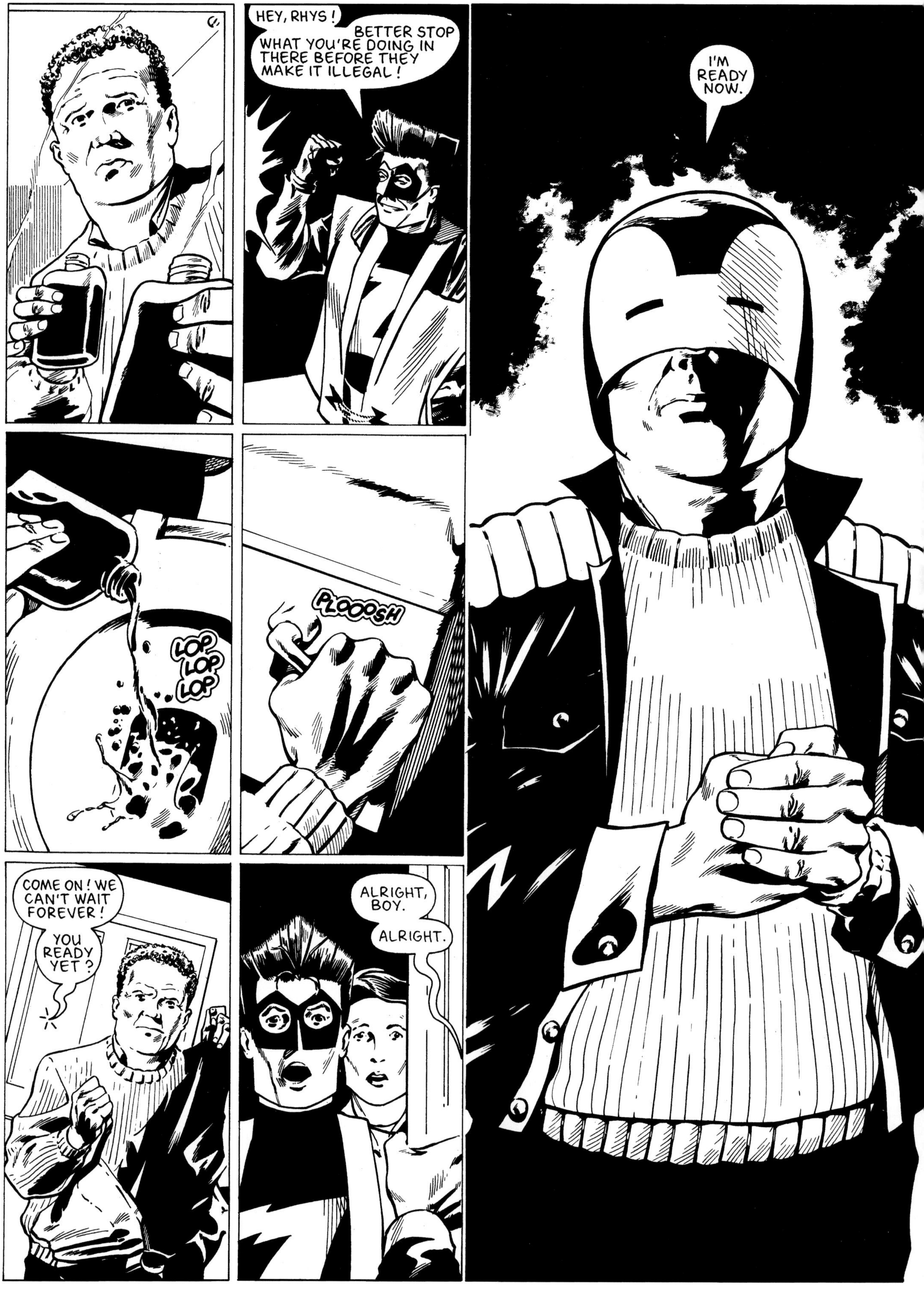

HEY, RHYS! BETTER STOP WHAT YOU'RE DOING IN THERE BEFORE THEY MAKE IT ILLEGAL!
I'M READY NOW.
LOP LOP LOP
PLOOOSH
COME ON! WE CAN'T WAIT FOREVER!
YOU READY YET?
ALRIGHT, BOY.
ALRIGHT.

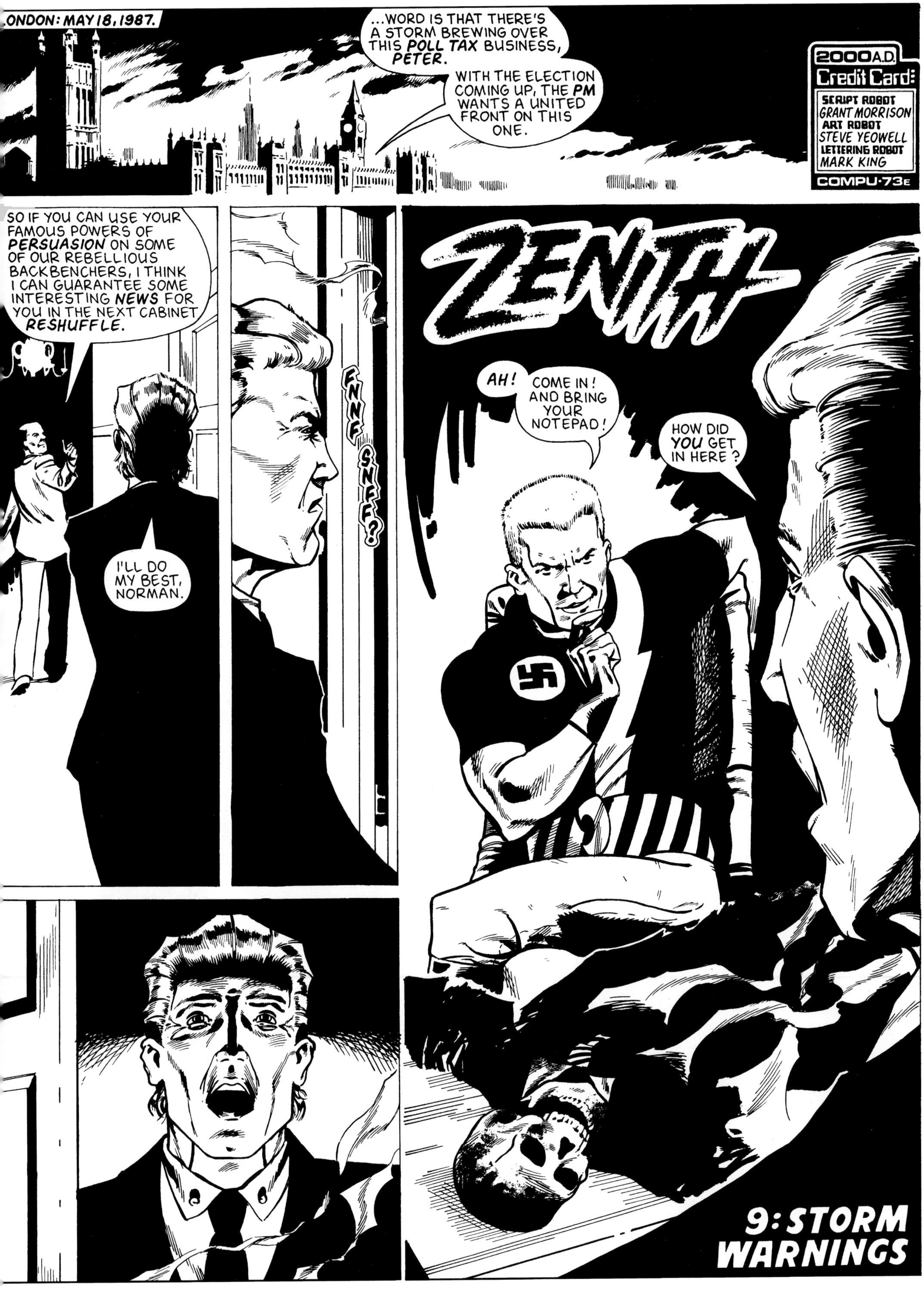
ONDON: MAY 18, 1987.
...WORD IS THAT THERE'S A STORM BREWING OVER THIS POLL TAX BUSINESS, PETER.
WITH THE ELECTION COMING UP, THE PM WANTS A UNITED FRONT ON THIS ONE.
2000 A.D. Credit Card: SCRIPT ROBOT GRANT MORRISON ART ROBOT STEVE YEOWELL LETTERING ROBOT MARK KING COMPU-73E
SO IF YOU CAN USE YOUR FAMOUS POWERS OF PERSUASION ON SOME OF OUR REBELLIOUS BACKBENCHERS, I THINK I CAN GUARANTEE SOME INTERESTING NEWS FOR YOU IN THE NEXT CABINET RESHUFFLE.
I'LL DO MY BEST, NORMAN.
FNNF SNFF?
ZENITH
AH!
COME IN! AND BRING YOUR NOTEPAD!
HOW DID YOU GET IN HERE?
9: STORM WARNINGS

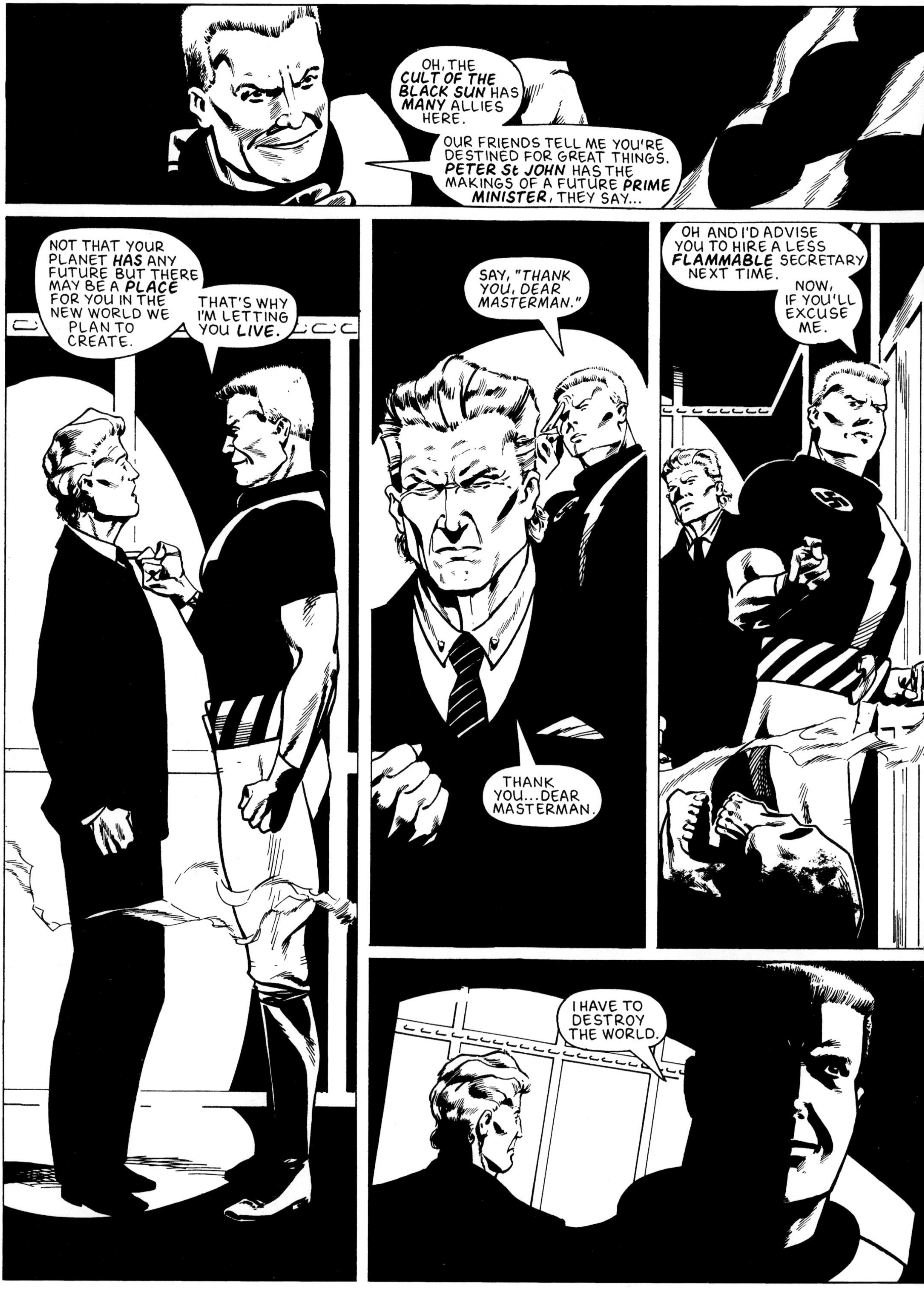

OH, THE CULT OF THE BLACK SUN HAS MANY ALLIES HERE.
OUR FRIENDS TELL ME YOU'RE DESTINED FOR GREAT THINGS. PETER St JOHN HAS THE MAKINGS OF A FUTURE PRIME MINISTER, THEY SAY...
NOT THAT YOUR PLANET HAS ANY FUTURE BUT THERE MAY BE A PLACE FOR YOU IN THE NEW WORLD WE PLAN TO CREATE.
THAT'S WHY I'M LETTING YOU LIVE.
SAY, "THANK YOU, DEAR MASTERMAN."
THANK YOU... DEAR MASTERMAN.
OH AND I'D ADVISE YOU TO HIRE A LESS FLAMMABLE SECRETARY NEXT TIME.
NOW, IF YOU'LL EXCUSE ME.
I HAVE TO DESTROY THE WORLD.

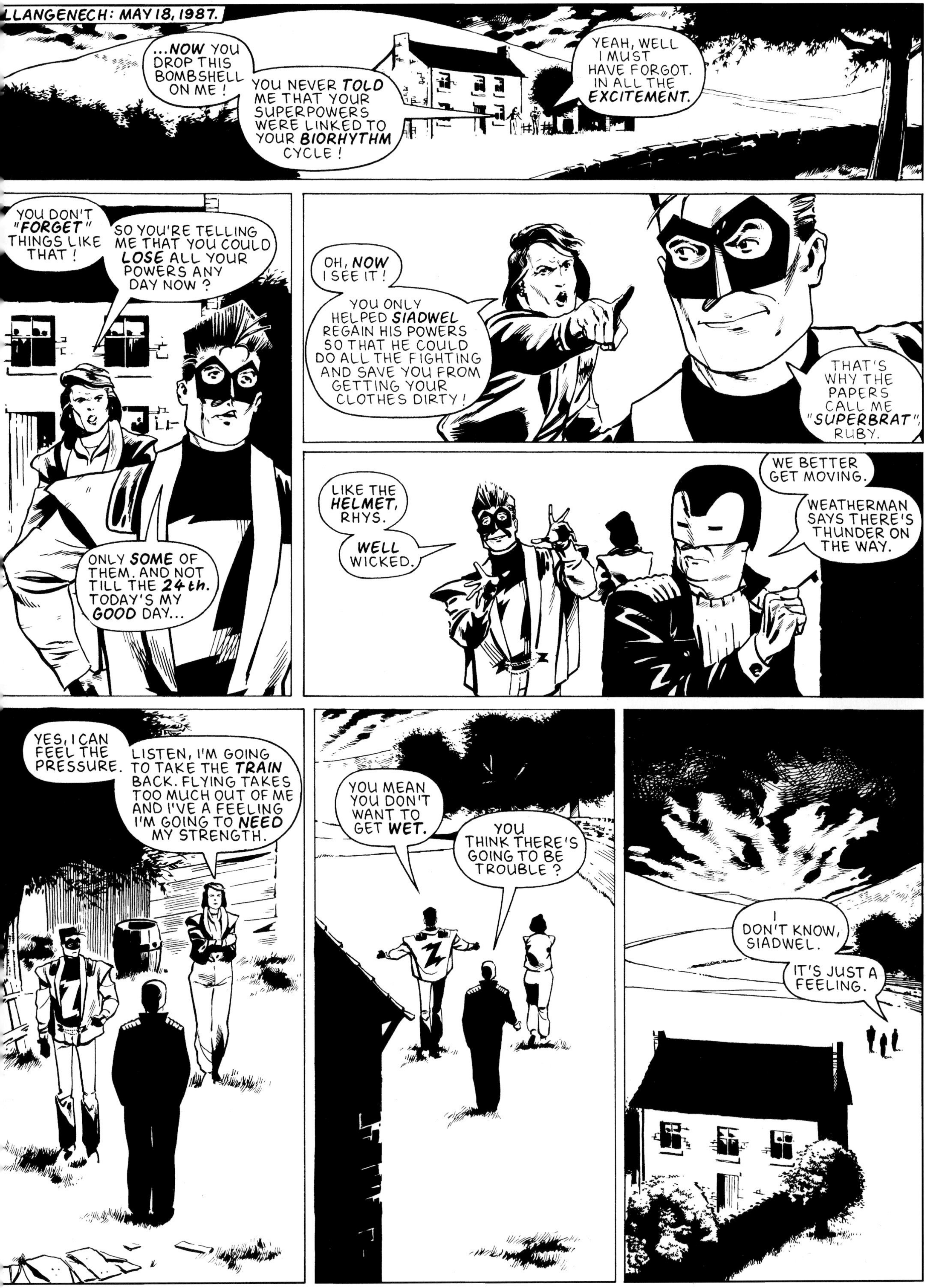

LLANGENECH: MAY 18, 1987.
...NOW YOU DROP THIS BOMBSHELL ON ME!
YOU NEVER TOLD ME THAT YOUR SUPERPOWERS WERE LINKED TO YOUR BIORHYTHM CYCLE!
YEAH, WELL I MUST HAVE FORGOT. IN ALL THE EXCITEMENT.
YOU DON'T "FORGET" THINGS LIKE THAT!
SO YOU'RE TELLING ME THAT YOU COULD LOSE ALL YOUR POWERS ANY DAY NOW?
ONLY SOME OF THEM. AND NOT TILL THE 24th. TODAY'S MY GOOD DAY...
OH, NOW I SEE IT!
YOU ONLY HELPED SIADWEL REGAIN HIS POWERS SO THAT HE COULD DO ALL THE FIGHTING AND SAVE YOU FROM GETTING YOUR CLOTHES DIRTY!
THAT'S WHY THE PAPERS CALL ME "SUPERBRAT", RUBY.
LIKE THE HELMET, RHYS.
WELL WICKED.
WE BETTER GET MOVING.
WEATHERMAN SAYS THERE'S THUNDER ON THE WAY.
YES, I CAN FEEL THE PRESSURE.
LISTEN, I'M GOING TO TAKE THE TRAIN BACK. FLYING TAKES TOO MUCH OUT OF ME AND I'VE A FEELING I'M GOING TO NEED MY STRENGTH.
YOU MEAN YOU DON'T WANT TO GET WET.
YOU THINK THERE'S GOING TO BE TROUBLE?
I DON'T KNOW, SIADWEL.
IT'S JUST A FEELING.

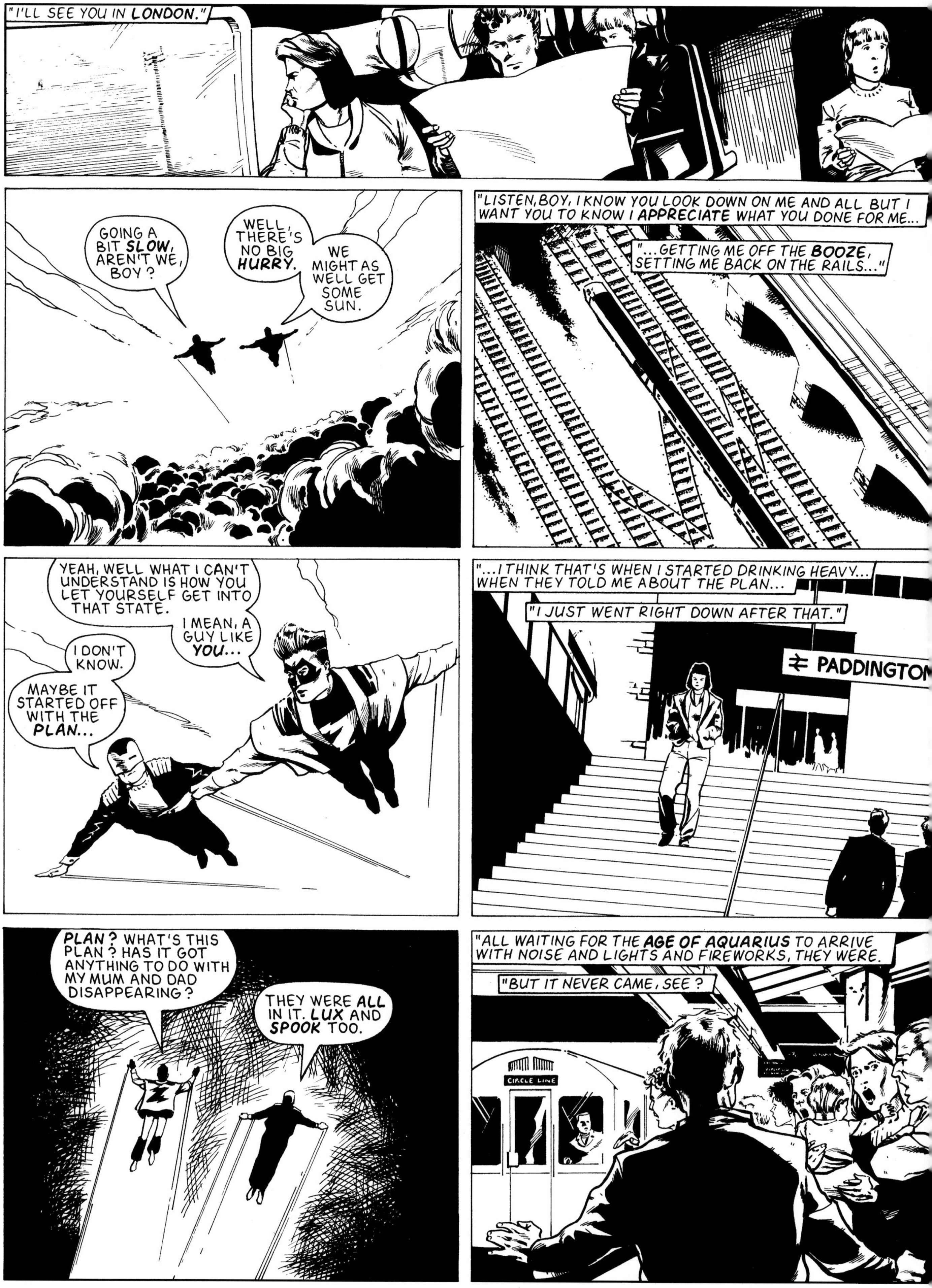
"I'LL SEE YOU IN LONDON."
GOING A BIT SLOW, AREN'T WE, BOY?
WELL, THERE'S NO BIG HURRY.
WE MIGHT AS WELL GET SOME SUN.
"LISTEN, BOY, I KNOW YOU LOOK DOWN ON ME AND ALL BUT I WANT YOU TO KNOW I APPRECIATE WHAT YOU DONE FOR ME...
"...GETTING ME OFF THE BOOZE, SETTING ME BACK ON THE RAILS..."
YEAH, WELL WHAT I CAN'T UNDERSTAND IS HOW YOU LET YOURSELF GET INTO THAT STATE.
I MEAN, A GUY LIKE YOU...
I DON'T KNOW.
MAYBE IT STARTED OFF WITH THE PLAN...
"...I THINK THAT'S WHEN I STARTED DRINKING HEAVY... WHEN THEY TOLD ME ABOUT THE PLAN...
"I JUST WENT RIGHT DOWN AFTER THAT."
PADDINGTON
PLAN? WHAT'S THIS PLAN? HAS IT GOT ANYTHING TO DO WITH MY MUM AND DAD DISAPPEARING?
THEY WERE ALL IN IT. LUX AND SPOOK TOO.
"ALL WAITING FOR THE AGE OF AQUARIUS TO ARRIVE WITH NOISE AND LIGHTS AND FIREWORKS, THEY WERE.
"BUT IT NEVER CAME, SEE?
CIRCLE LINE

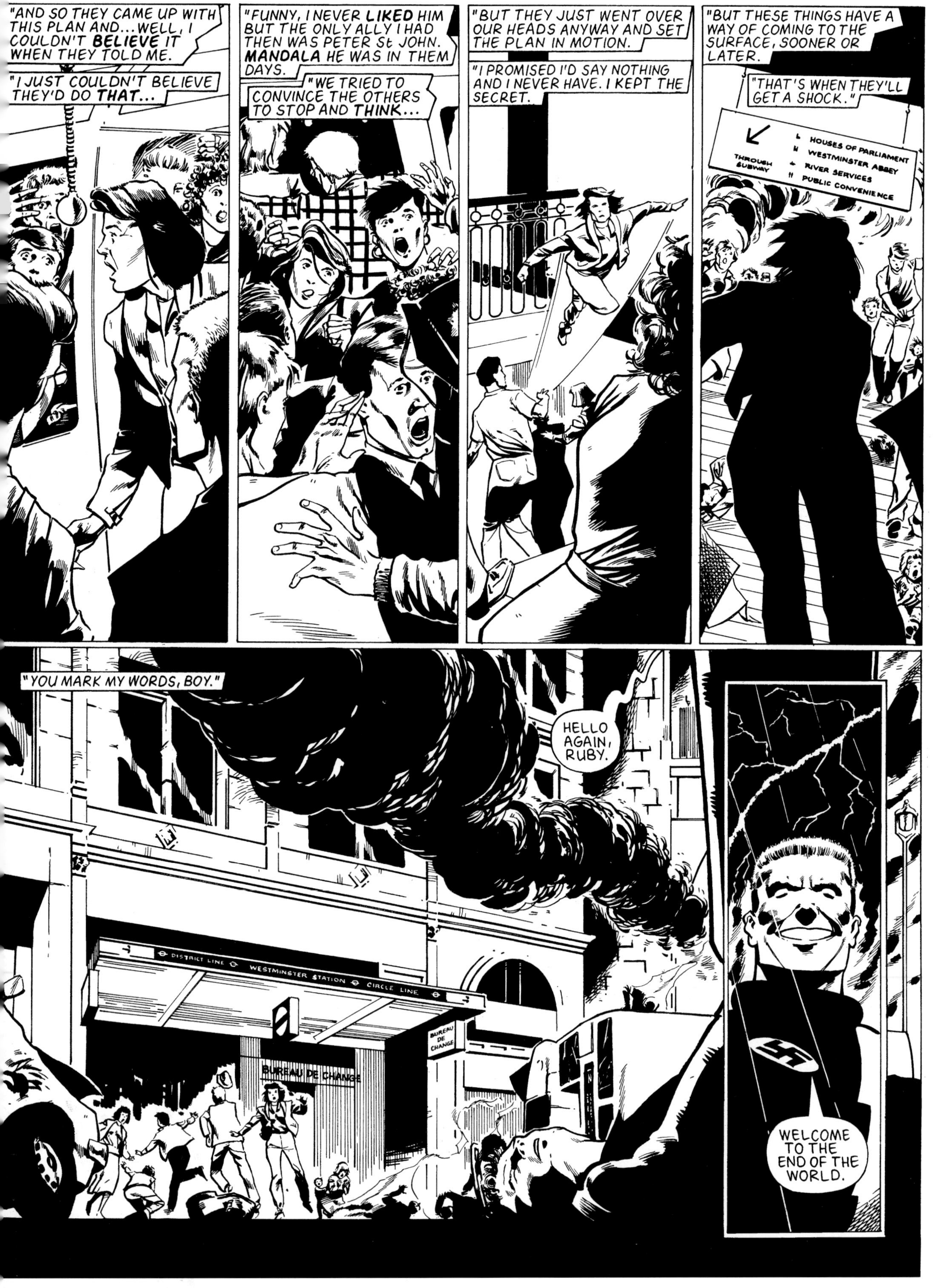
"AND SO THEY CAME UP WITH THIS PLAN AND... WELL, I COULDN'T BELIEVE IT WHEN THEY TOLD ME.
"I JUST COULDN'T BELIEVE THEY'D DO THAT...
"FUNNY, I NEVER LIKED HIM BUT THE ONLY ALLY I HAD THEN WAS PETER St JOHN. MANDALA HE WAS IN THEM DAYS.
"WE TRIED TO CONVINCE THE OTHERS TO STOP AND THINK...
"BUT THEY JUST WENT OVER OUR HEADS ANYWAY AND SET THE PLAN IN MOTION.
"I PROMISED I'D SAY NOTHING AND I NEVER HAVE. I KEPT THE SECRET.
"BUT THESE THINGS HAVE A WAY OF COMING TO THE SURFACE, SOONER OR LATER.
"THAT'S WHEN THEY'LL GET A SHOCK."
THROUGH SUBWAY
HOUSES OF PARLIAMENT
WESTMINSTER ABBEY
RIVER SERVICES
PUBLIC CONVENIENCE
"YOU MARK MY WORDS, BOY."
HELLO AGAIN, RUBY.
DISTRICT LINE
WESTMINSTER STATION
CIRCLE LINE
BUREAU DE CHANGE
BUREAU DE CHANGE
WELCOME TO THE END OF THE WORLD.

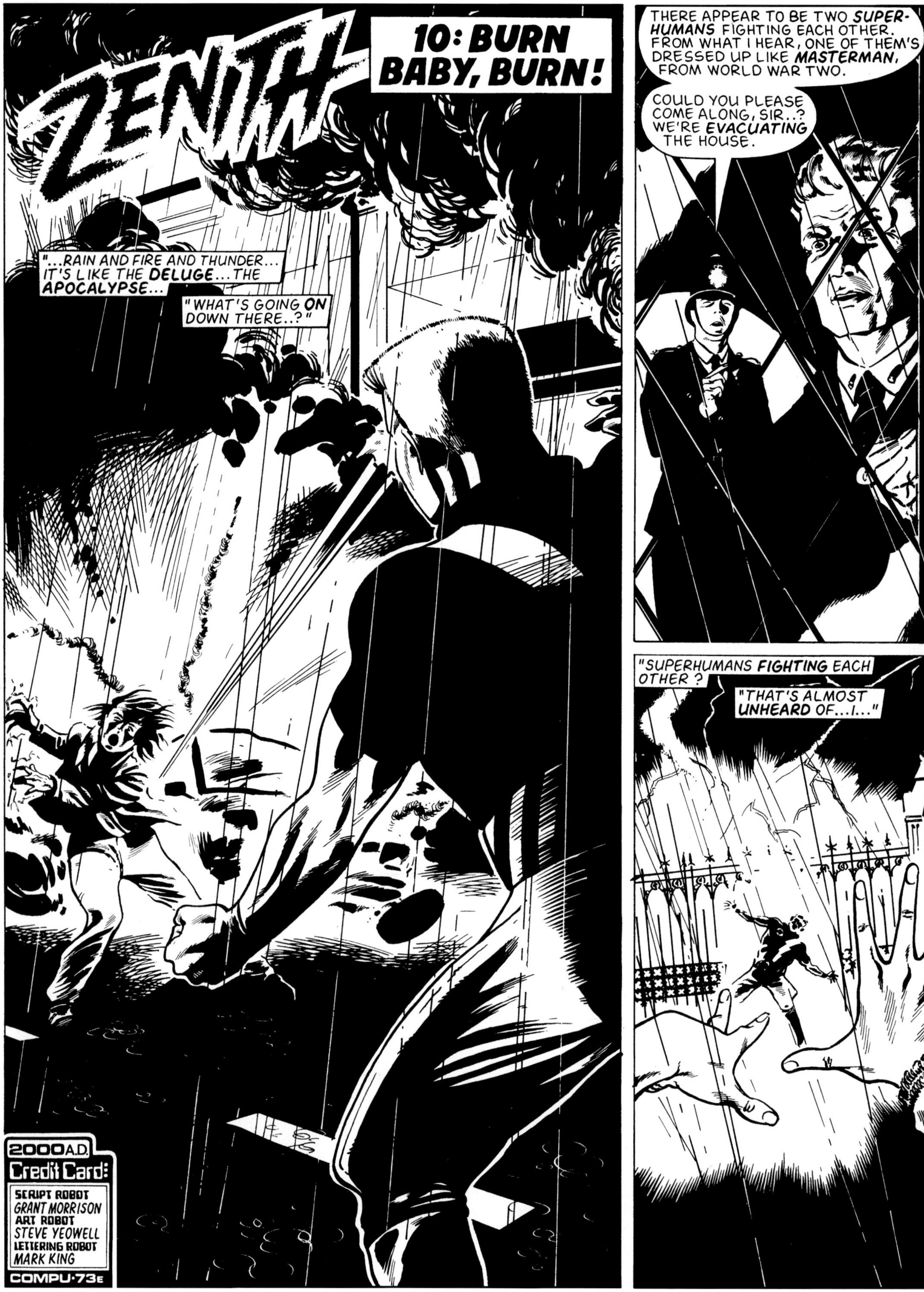
ZENITH
10: BURN BABY, BURN!
"...RAIN AND FIRE AND THUNDER... IT'S LIKE THE DELUGE... THE APOCALYPSE...
"WHAT'S GOING ON DOWN THERE..?"
2000 A.D. Credit Card:
SCRIPT ROBOT GRANT MORRISON
ART ROBOT STEVE YEOWELL
LETTERING ROBOT MARK KING
COMPU·73E
THERE APPEAR TO BE TWO SUPER-HUMANS FIGHTING EACH OTHER. FROM WHAT I HEAR, ONE OF THEM'S DRESSED UP LIKE MASTERMAN, FROM WORLD WAR TWO.
COULD YOU PLEASE COME ALONG, SIR..? WE'RE EVACUATING THE HOUSE.
"SUPERHUMANS FIGHTING EACH OTHER?
"THAT'S ALMOST UNHEARD OF...I..."

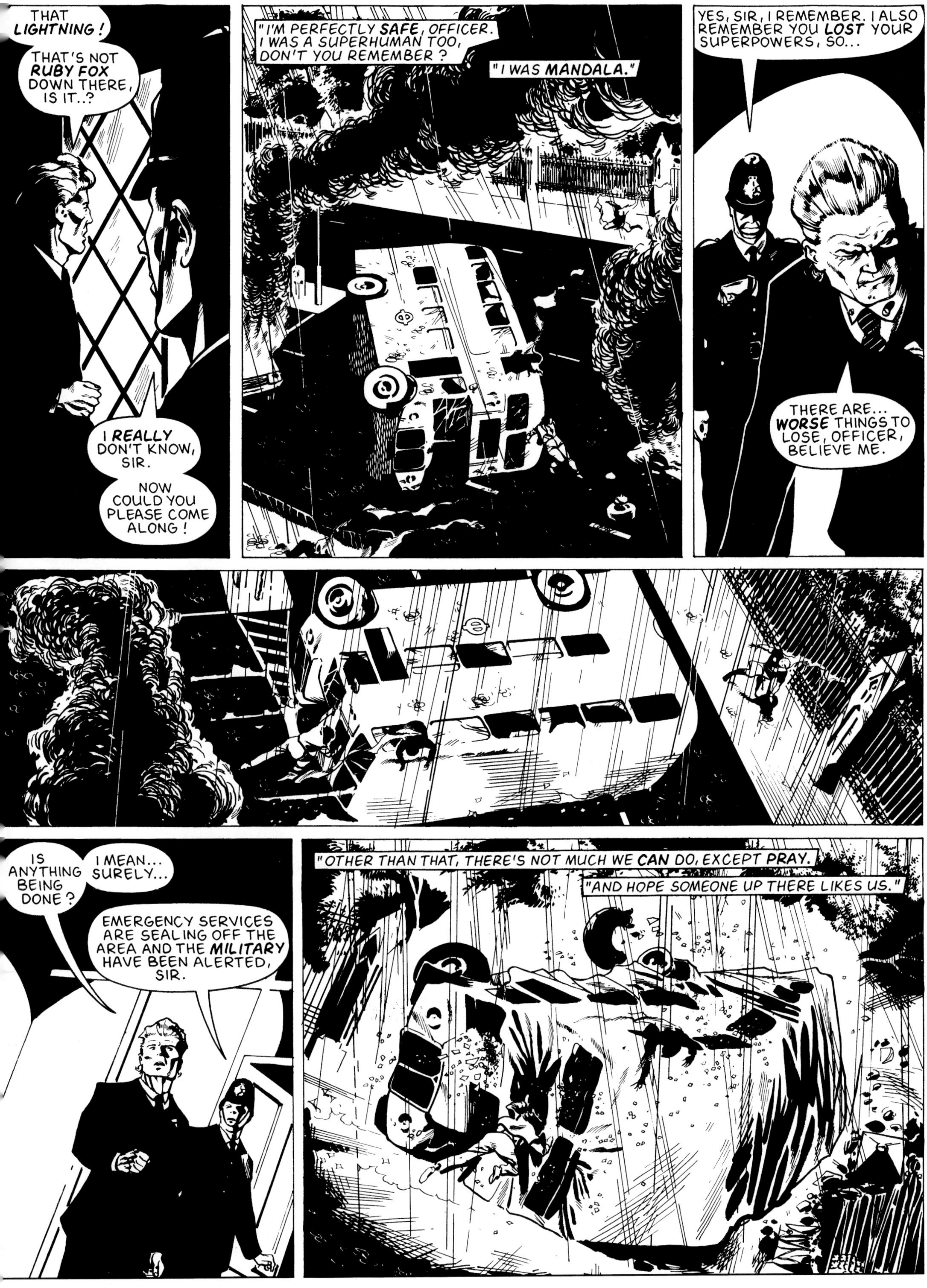
THAT LIGHTNING!
THAT'S NOT RUBY FOX DOWN THERE, IS IT..?
I REALLY DON'T KNOW, SIR.
NOW COULD YOU PLEASE COME ALONG!
"I'M PERFECTLY SAFE, OFFICER. I WAS A SUPERHUMAN TOO, DON'T YOU REMEMBER?
"I WAS MANDALA."
YES, SIR, I REMEMBER. I ALSO REMEMBER YOU LOST YOUR SUPERPOWERS, SO...
THERE ARE... WORSE THINGS TO LOSE, OFFICER, BELIEVE ME.
IS ANYTHING BEING DONE?
I MEAN... SURELY...
EMERGENCY SERVICES ARE SEALING OFF THE AREA AND THE MILITARY HAVE BEEN ALERTED, SIR.
"OTHER THAN THAT, THERE'S NOT MUCH WE CAN DO, EXCEPT PRAY.
"AND HOPE SOMEONE UP THERE LIKES US."

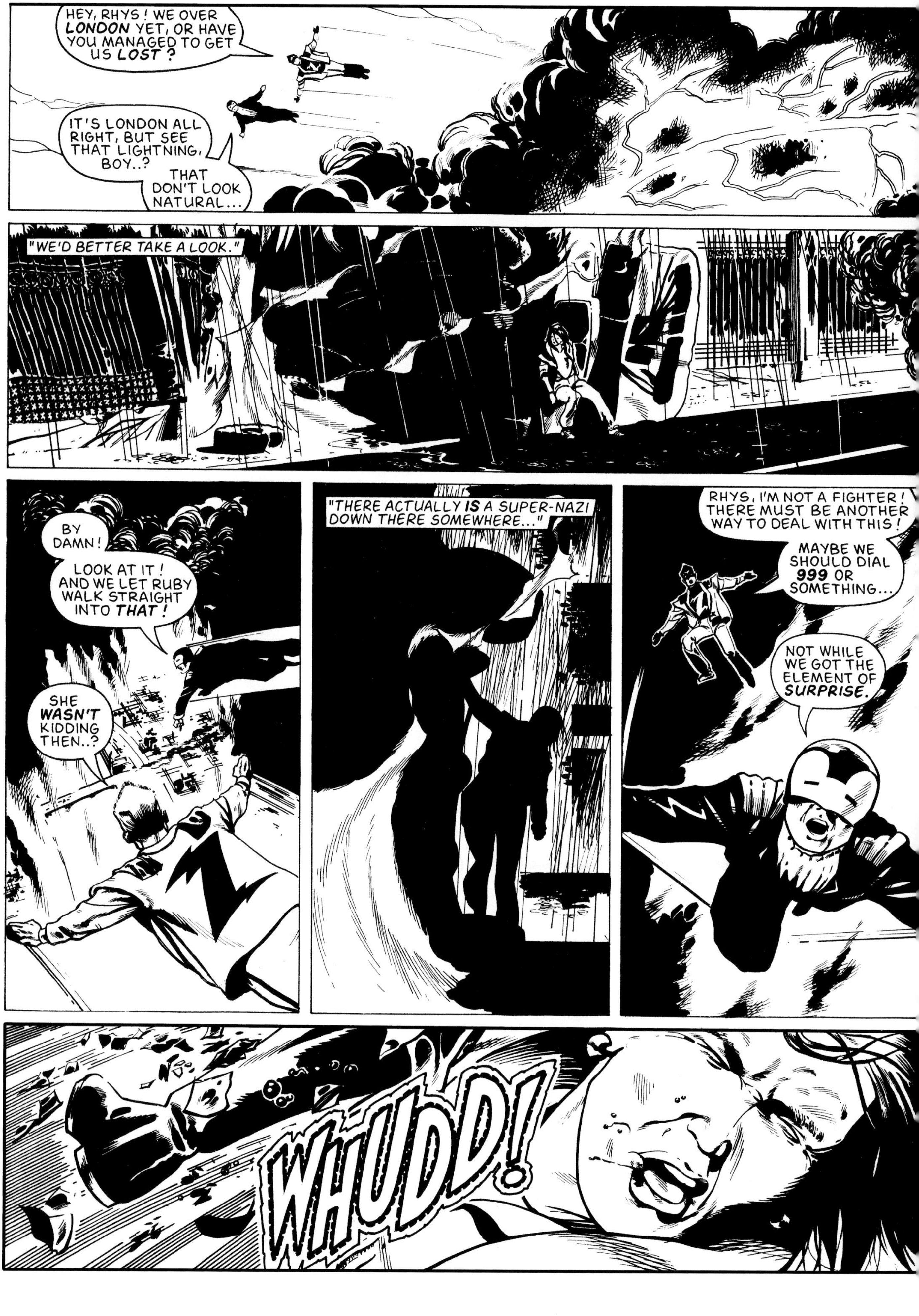
HEY, RHYS ! WE OVER LONDON YET, OR HAVE YOU MANAGED TO GET US LOST ?
IT'S LONDON ALL RIGHT, BUT SEE THAT LIGHTNING, BOY..?
THAT DON'T LOOK NATURAL...
"WE'D BETTER TAKE A LOOK."
BY DAMN !
LOOK AT IT ! AND WE LET RUBY WALK STRAIGHT INTO THAT !
SHE WASN'T KIDDING THEN..?
"THERE ACTUALLY IS A SUPER-NAZI DOWN THERE SOMEWHERE..."
RHYS, I'M NOT A FIGHTER ! THERE MUST BE ANOTHER WAY TO DEAL WITH THIS !
MAYBE WE SHOULD DIAL 999 OR SOMETHING...
NOT WHILE WE GOT THE ELEMENT OF SURPRISE.
WHUDD!

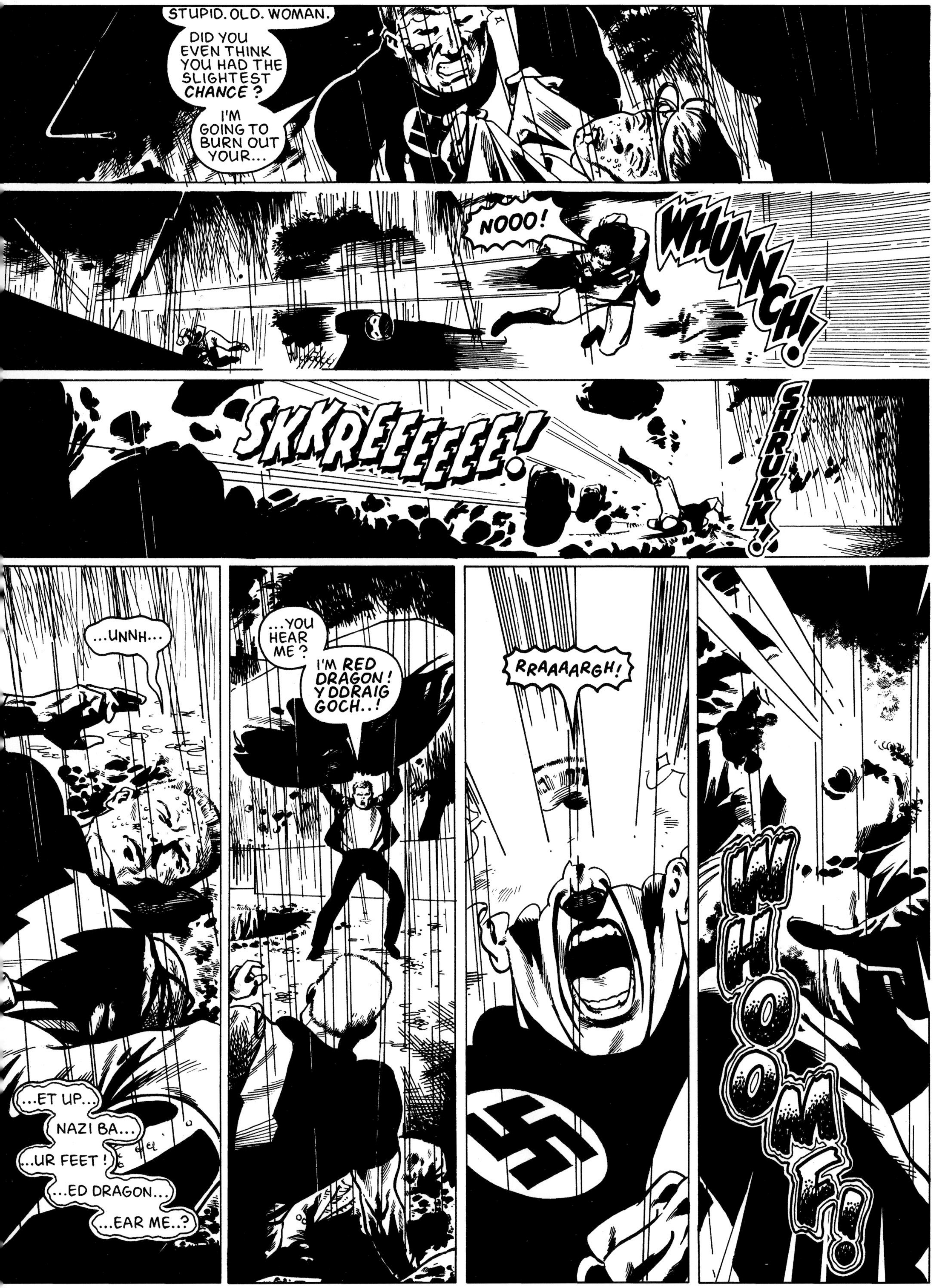

STUPID. OLD. WOMAN.
DID YOU EVEN THINK YOU HAD THE SLIGHTEST CHANCE ?
I'M GOING TO BURN OUT YOUR...
NOOO!
WHUNNCH!
SKKREEEEEEE!
SHRUKK!
...UNNH...
...ET UP...
NAZI BA...
...UR FEET !
...ED DRAGON...
...EAR ME..?
...YOU HEAR ME ?
I'M RED DRAGON! Y DDRAIG GOCH..!
RRAAAARGH!
WHOOOM!

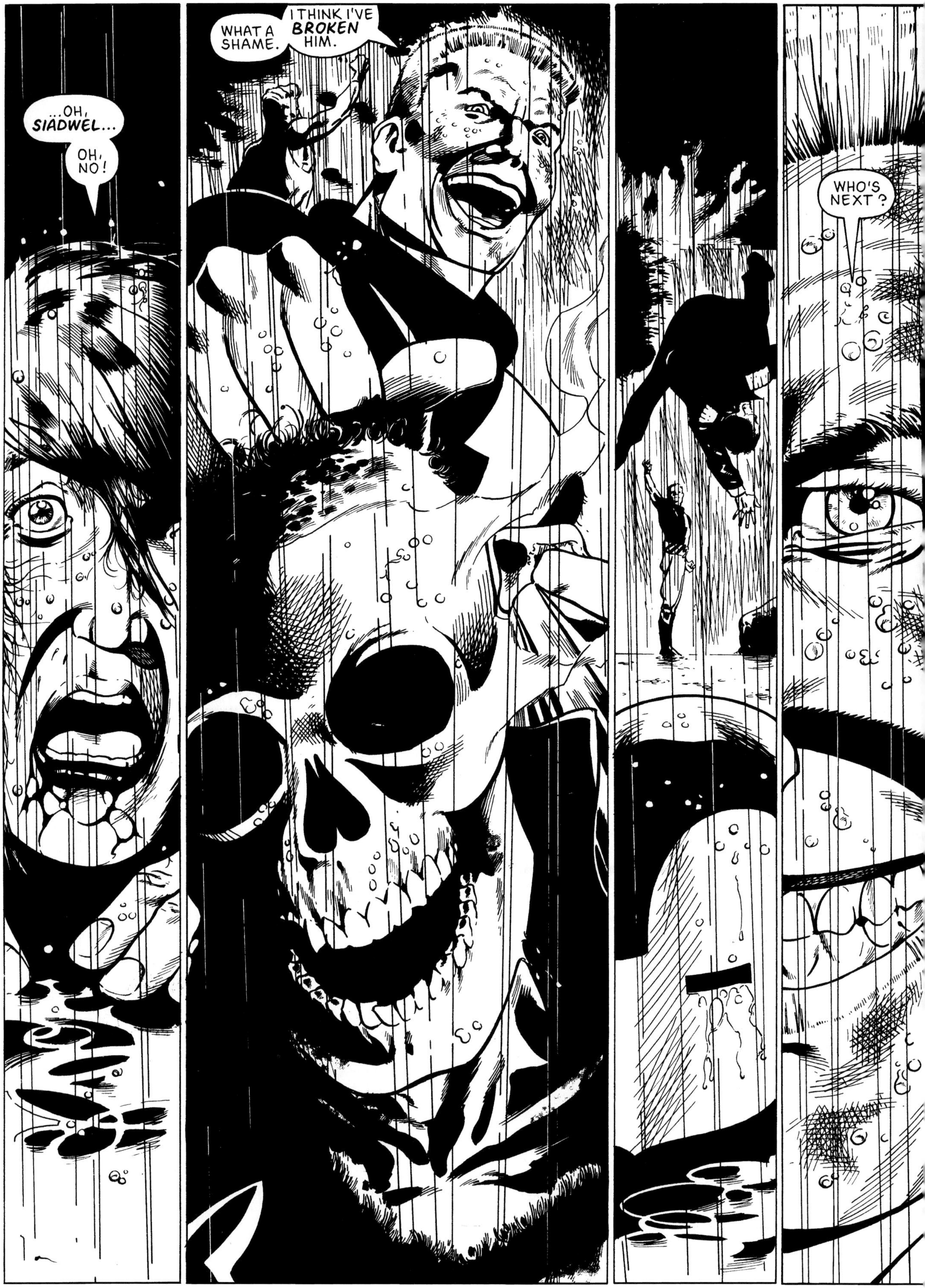
...OH, SIADWEL...
OH, NO!
WHAT A SHAME.
I THINK I'VE BROKEN HIM.
WHO'S NEXT?

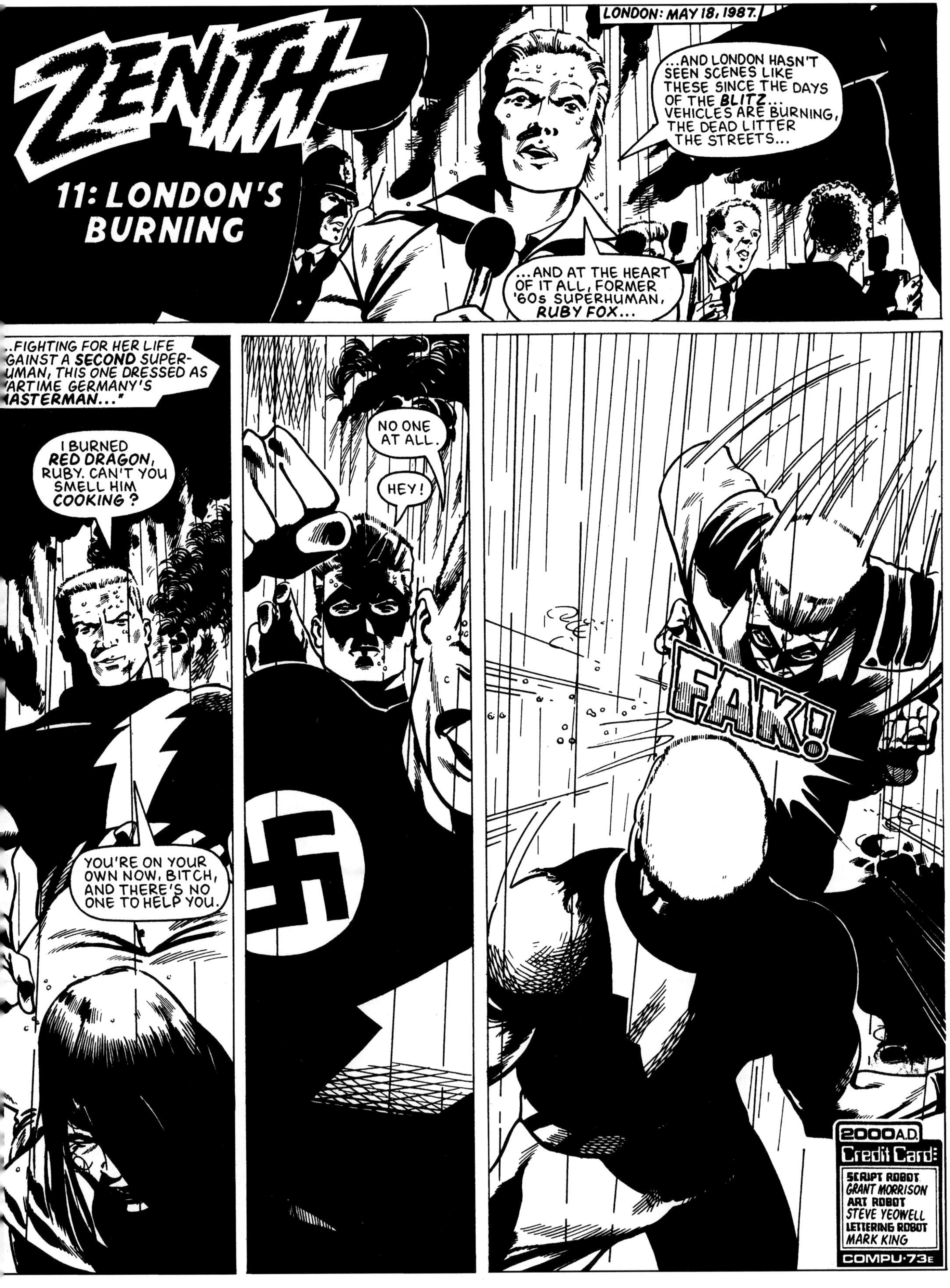

ZENITH
11: LONDON'S BURNING
LONDON: MAY 18, 1987.
...AND LONDON HASN'T SEEN SCENES LIKE THESE SINCE THE DAYS OF THE BLITZ... VEHICLES ARE BURNING, THE DEAD LITTER THE STREETS...
...AND AT THE HEART OF IT ALL, FORMER '60s SUPERHUMAN, RUBY FOX...
..FIGHTING FOR HER LIFE GAINST A SECOND SUPER-UMAN, THIS ONE DRESSED AS 'ARTIME GERMANY'S ASTERMAN..."
I BURNED RED DRAGON, RUBY. CAN'T YOU SMELL HIM COOKING?
YOU'RE ON YOUR OWN NOW, BITCH, AND THERE'S NO ONE TO HELP YOU.
NO ONE AT ALL.
HEY!
FAK!
2000 A.D. Credit Card:
SCRIPT ROBOT GRANT MORRISON
ART ROBOT STEVE YEOWELL
LETTERING ROBOT MARK KING
COMPU-73E

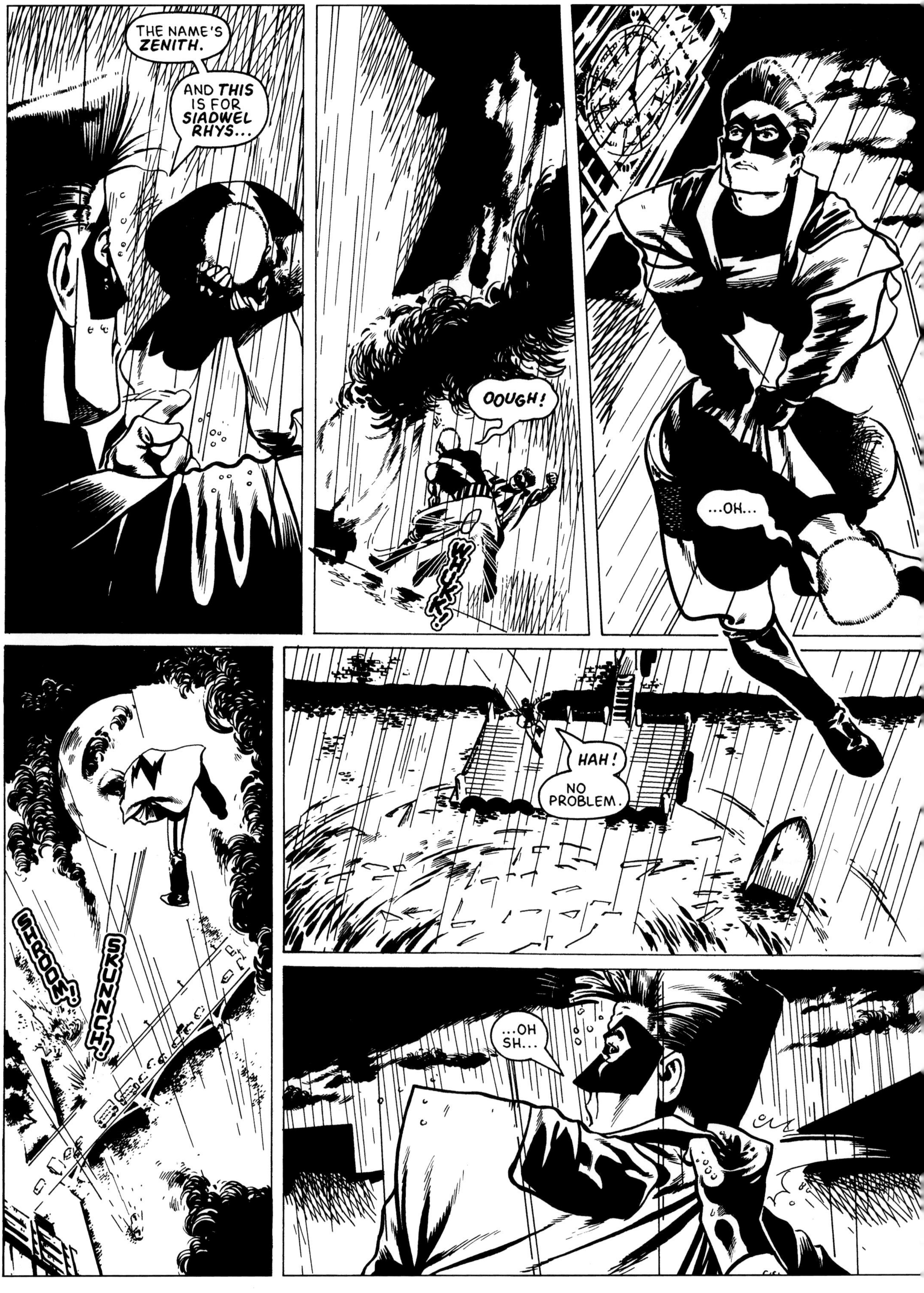
THE NAME'S ZENITH.
AND THIS IS FOR SIADWEL RHYS...
OOUGH!
WHUK!
...OH...
SHROOM!
SKRUNCH!
HAH!
NO PROBLEM.
...OH SH...

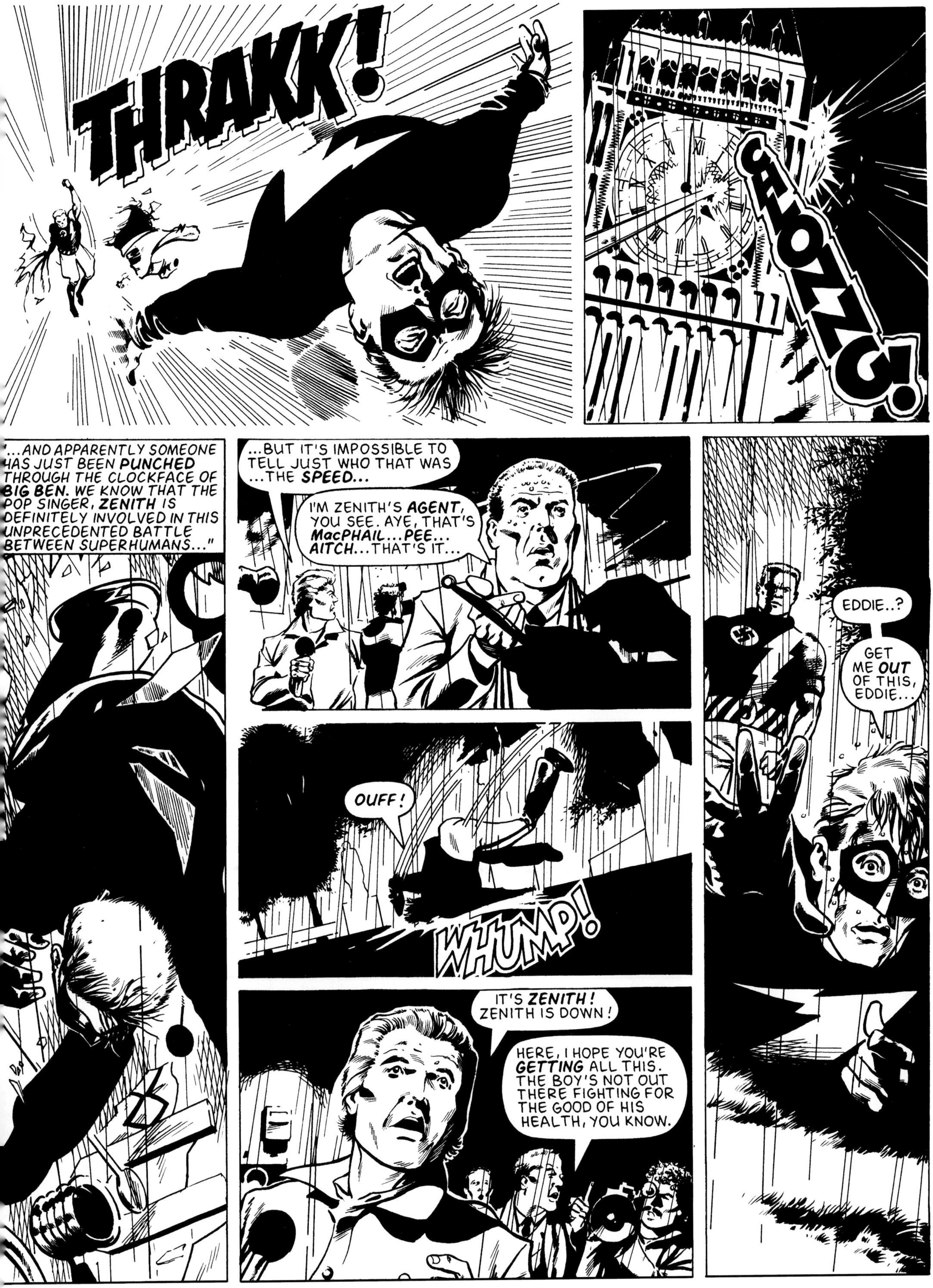

THRAKK!
CALONNG!
"...AND APPARENTLY SOMEONE HAS JUST BEEN PUNCHED THROUGH THE CLOCKFACE OF BIG BEN. WE KNOW THAT THE POP SINGER, ZENITH IS DEFINITELY INVOLVED IN THIS UNPRECEDENTED BATTLE BETWEEN SUPERHUMANS..."
...BUT IT'S IMPOSSIBLE TO TELL JUST WHO THAT WAS ...THE SPEED...
I'M ZENITH'S AGENT, YOU SEE. AYE, THAT'S MacPHAIL...PEE... AITCH...THAT'S IT...
OUFF!
WHUMP!
IT'S ZENITH! ZENITH IS DOWN!
HERE, I HOPE YOU'RE GETTING ALL THIS. THE BOY'S NOT OUT THERE FIGHTING FOR THE GOOD OF HIS HEALTH, YOU KNOW.
EDDIE..?
GET ME OUT OF THIS, EDDIE...

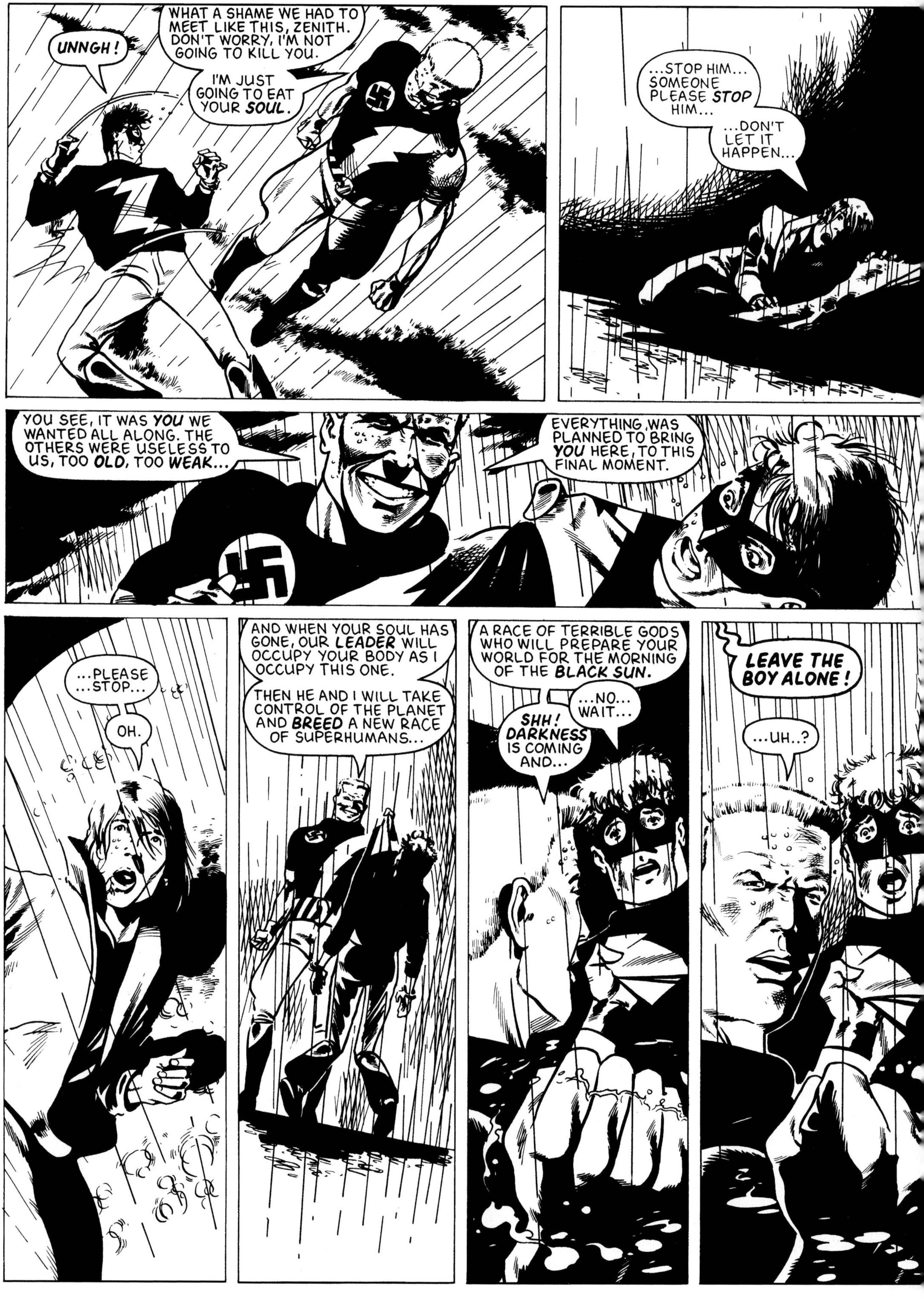
UNNGH!
WHAT A SHAME WE HAD TO MEET LIKE THIS, ZENITH. DON'T WORRY, I'M NOT GOING TO KILL YOU.
I'M JUST GOING TO EAT YOUR SOUL.
...STOP HIM... SOMEONE PLEASE STOP HIM...
...DON'T LET IT HAPPEN...
YOU SEE, IT WAS YOU WE WANTED ALL ALONG. THE OTHERS WERE USELESS TO US, TOO OLD, TOO WEAK...
EVERYTHING WAS PLANNED TO BRING YOU HERE, TO THIS FINAL MOMENT.
...PLEASE ...STOP...
OH.
AND WHEN YOUR SOUL HAS GONE, OUR LEADER WILL OCCUPY YOUR BODY AS I OCCUPY THIS ONE.
THEN HE AND I WILL TAKE CONTROL OF THE PLANET AND BREED A NEW RACE OF SUPERHUMANS...
A RACE OF TERRIBLE GODS WHO WILL PREPARE YOUR WORLD FOR THE MORNING OF THE BLACK SUN.
...NO... WAIT...
SHH! DARKNESS IS COMING AND...
LEAVE THE BOY ALONE!
...UH..?

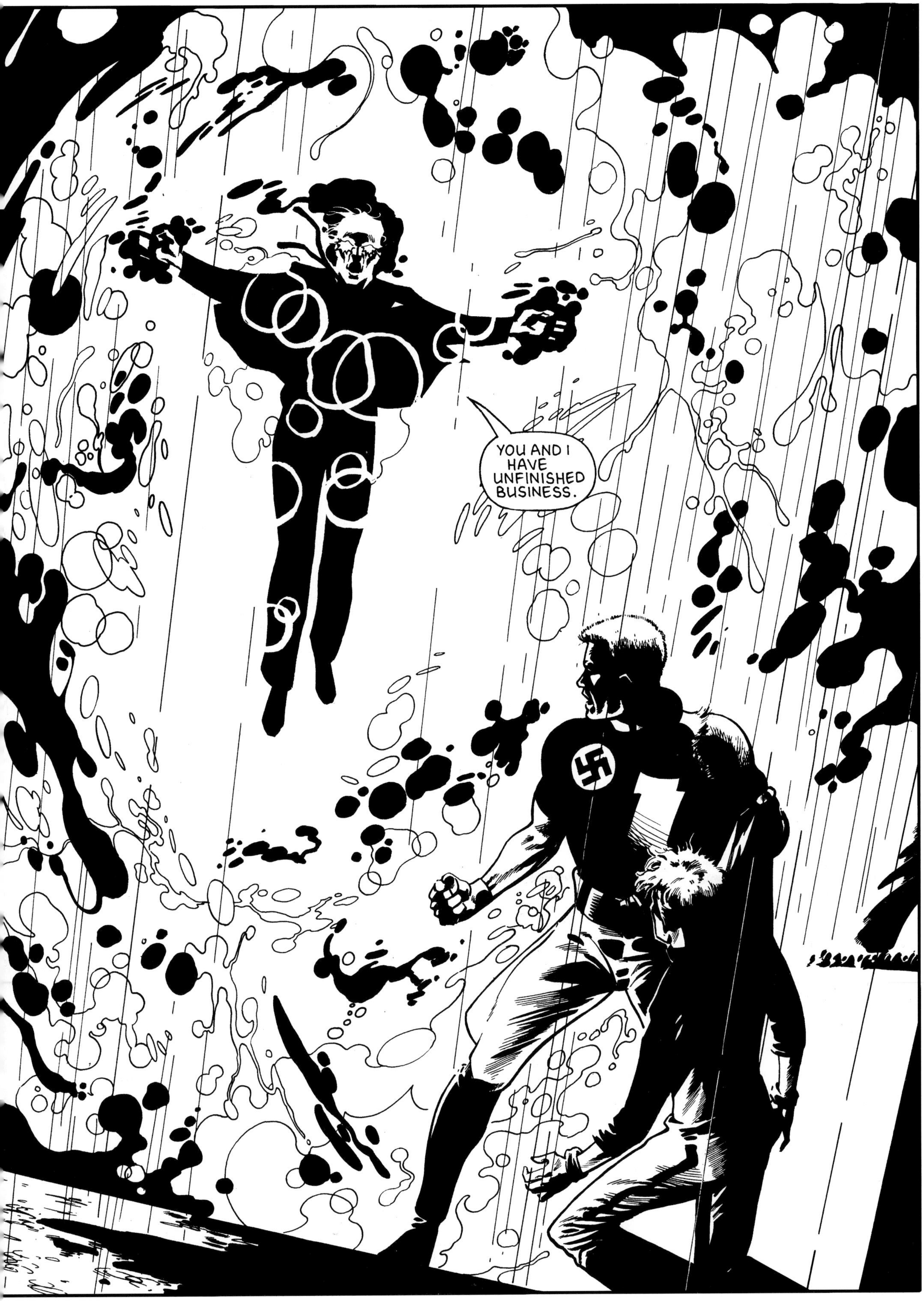
YOU AND I HAVE UNFINISHED BUSINESS.

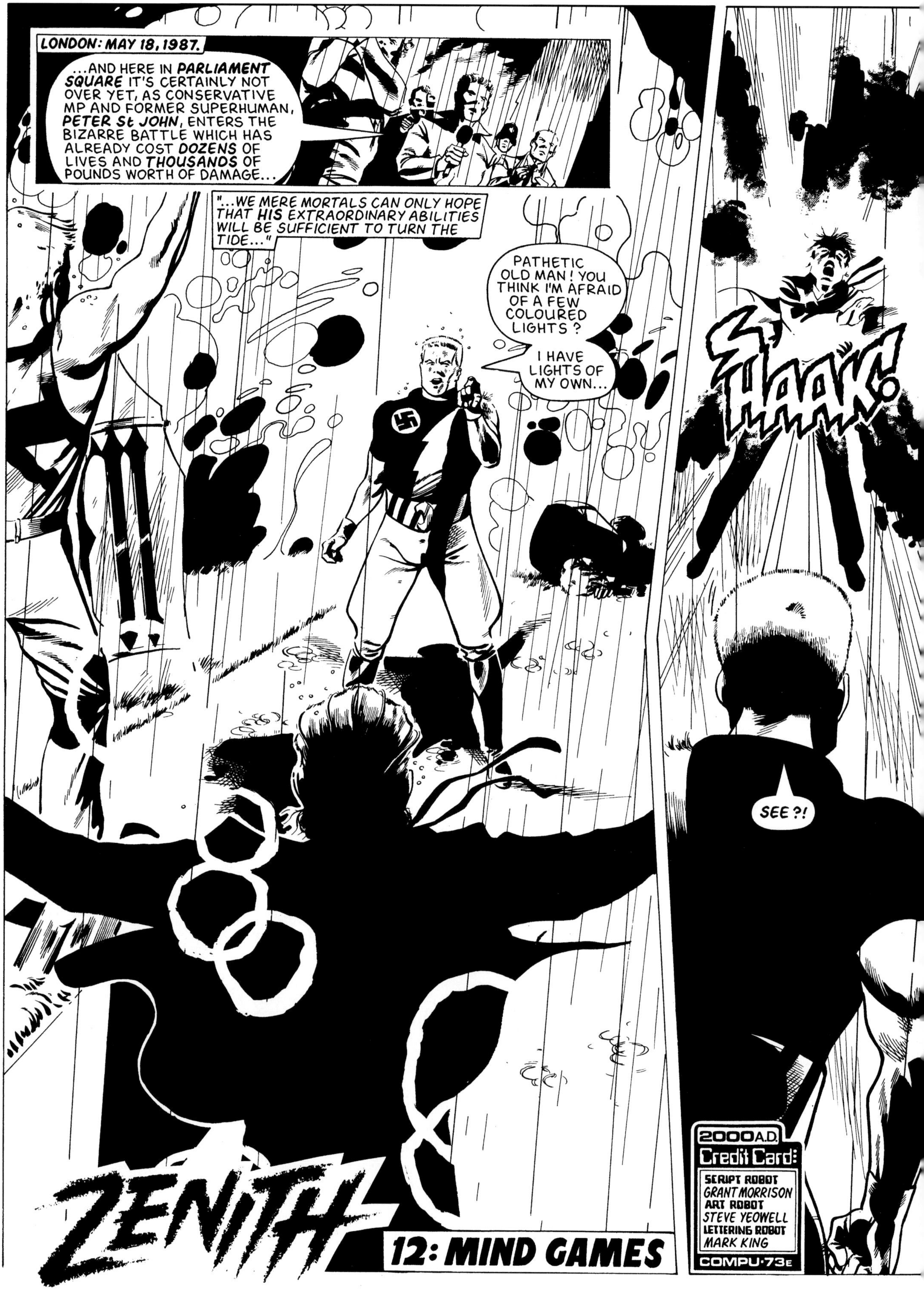
LONDON: MAY 18, 1987.
...AND HERE IN PARLIAMENT SQUARE IT'S CERTAINLY NOT OVER YET, AS CONSERVATIVE MP AND FORMER SUPERHUMAN, PETER St JOHN, ENTERS THE BIZARRE BATTLE WHICH HAS ALREADY COST DOZENS OF LIVES AND THOUSANDS OF POUNDS WORTH OF DAMAGE...
"...WE MERE MORTALS CAN ONLY HOPE THAT HIS EXTRAORDINARY ABILITIES WILL BE SUFFICIENT TO TURN THE TIDE..."
PATHETIC OLD MAN! YOU THINK I'M AFRAID OF A FEW COLOURED LIGHTS?
I HAVE LIGHTS OF MY OWN...
SHAAAK!
SEE?!
ZENITH
12: MIND GAMES
2000 A.D. Credit Card:
SCRIPT ROBOT GRANT MORRISON
ART ROBOT STEVE YEOWELL
LETTERING ROBOT MARK KING
COMPU·73E

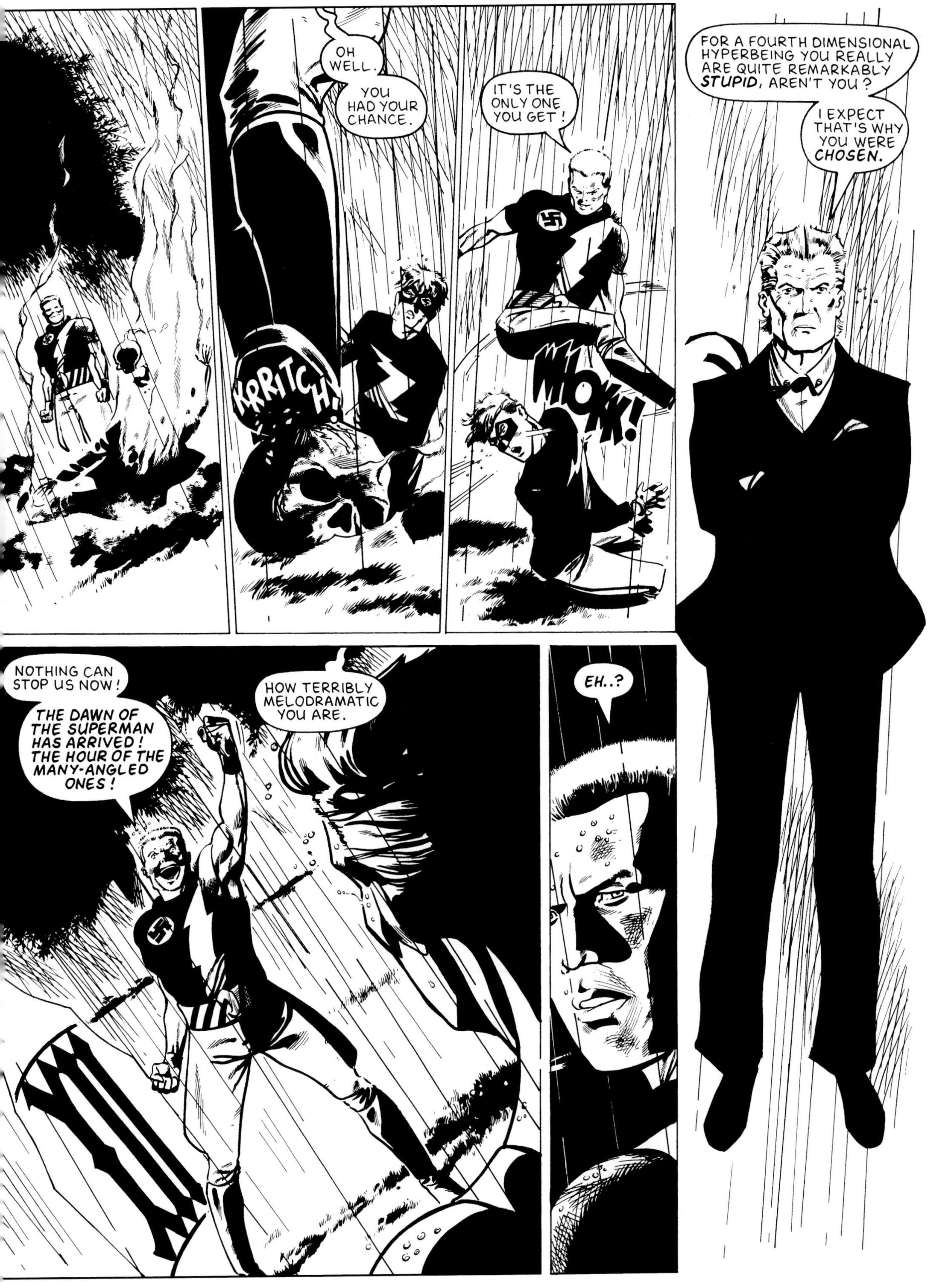
OH WELL.
YOU HAD YOUR CHANCE.
KRRITCH!
IT'S THE ONLY ONE YOU GET!
WOK!
FOR A FOURTH DIMENSIONAL HYPERBEING YOU REALLY ARE QUITE REMARKABLY STUPID, AREN'T YOU?
I EXPECT THAT'S WHY YOU WERE CHOSEN.
NOTHING CAN STOP US NOW!
THE DAWN OF THE SUPERMAN HAS ARRIVED! THE HOUR OF THE MANY-ANGLED ONES!
HOW TERRIBLY MELODRAMATIC YOU ARE.
EH..?

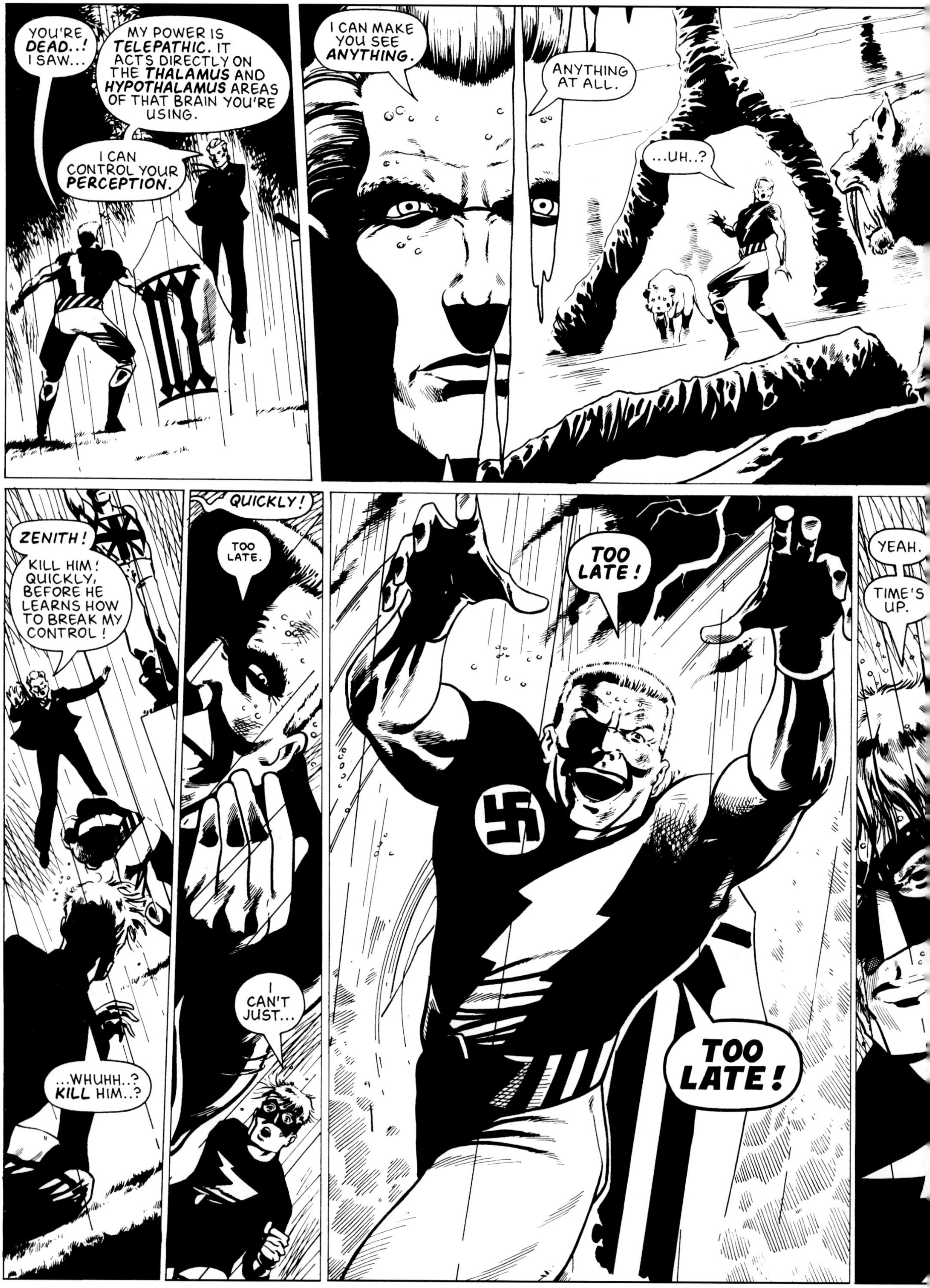
YOU'RE DEAD..! I SAW...
MY POWER IS TELEPATHIC. IT ACTS DIRECTLY ON THE THALAMUS AND HYPOTHALAMUS AREAS OF THAT BRAIN YOU'RE USING.
I CAN CONTROL YOUR PERCEPTION.
I CAN MAKE YOU SEE ANYTHING.
ANYTHING AT ALL.
...UH..?
ZENITH!
KILL HIM! QUICKLY, BEFORE HE LEARNS HOW TO BREAK MY CONTROL!
...WHUHH..? KILL HIM..?
QUICKLY!
TOO LATE.
I CAN'T JUST...
TOO LATE!
TOO LATE!
YEAH.
TIME'S UP.

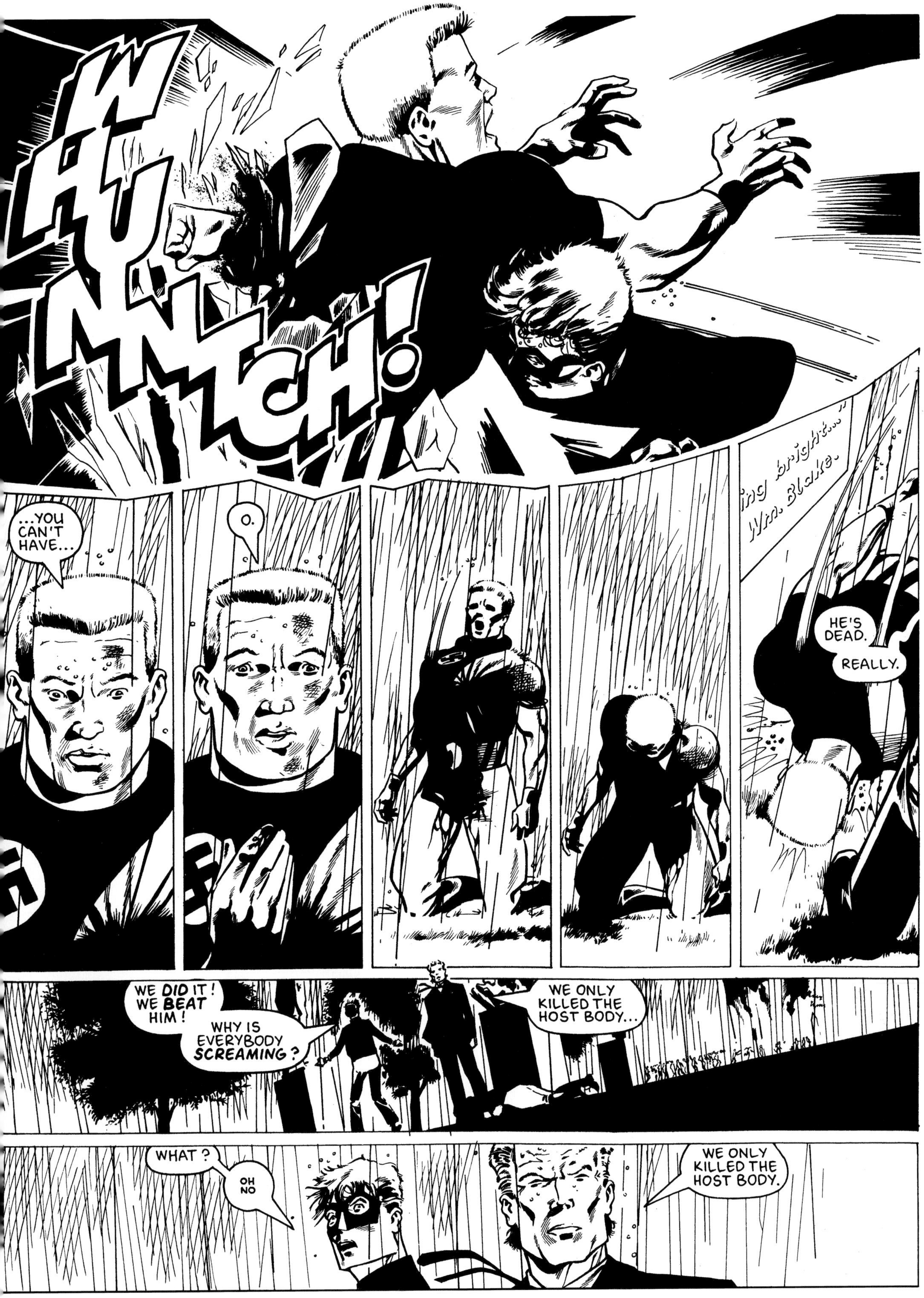
WHUNTCH!
ing bright..." Wm. Blake.
...YOU CAN'T HAVE...
O.
HE'S DEAD.
REALLY.
WE DID IT! WE BEAT HIM!
WHY IS EVERYBODY SCREAMING?
WE ONLY KILLED THE HOST BODY...
WHAT?
OH NO
WE ONLY KILLED THE HOST BODY.

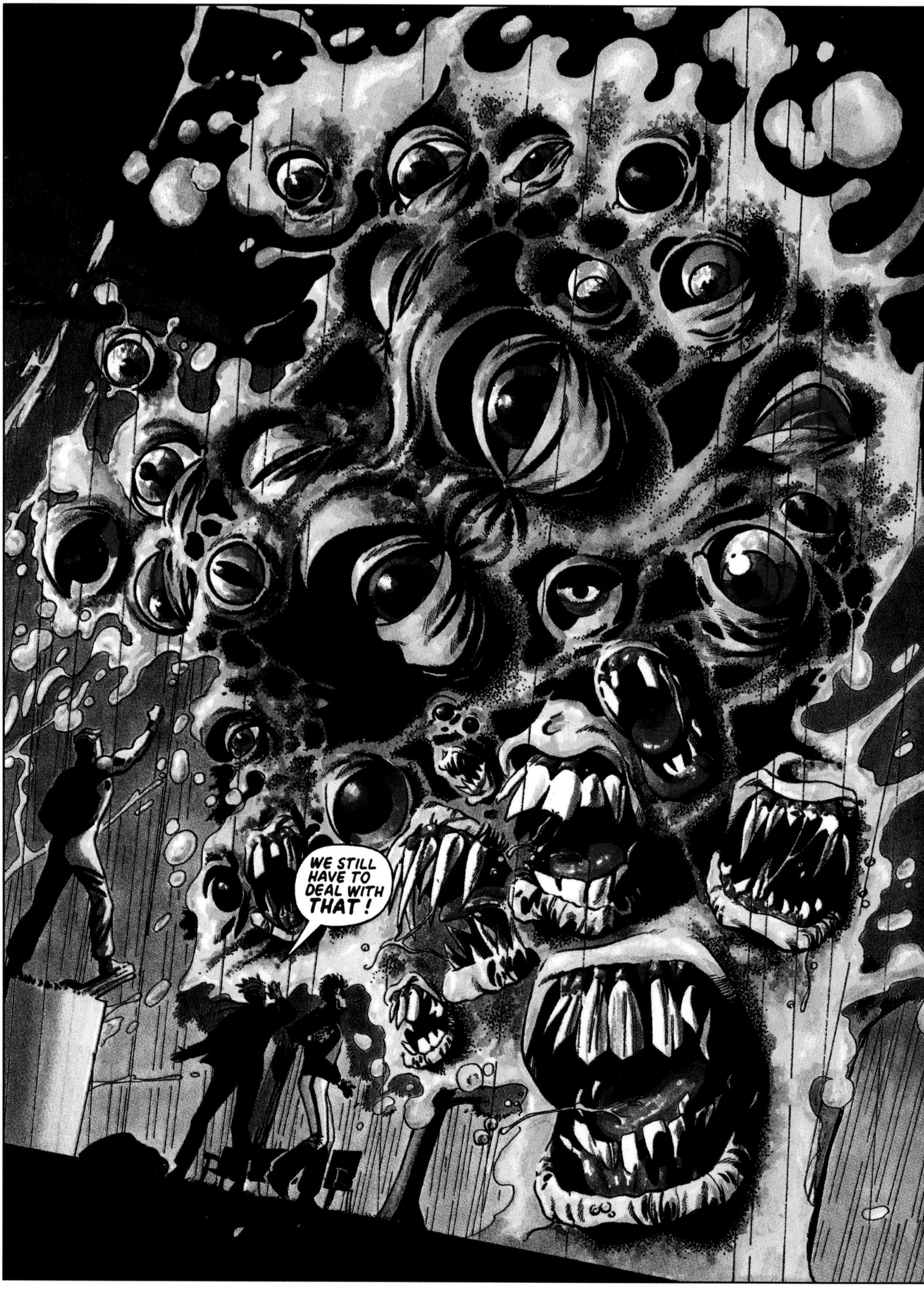
WE STILL HAVE TO DEAL WITH THAT!

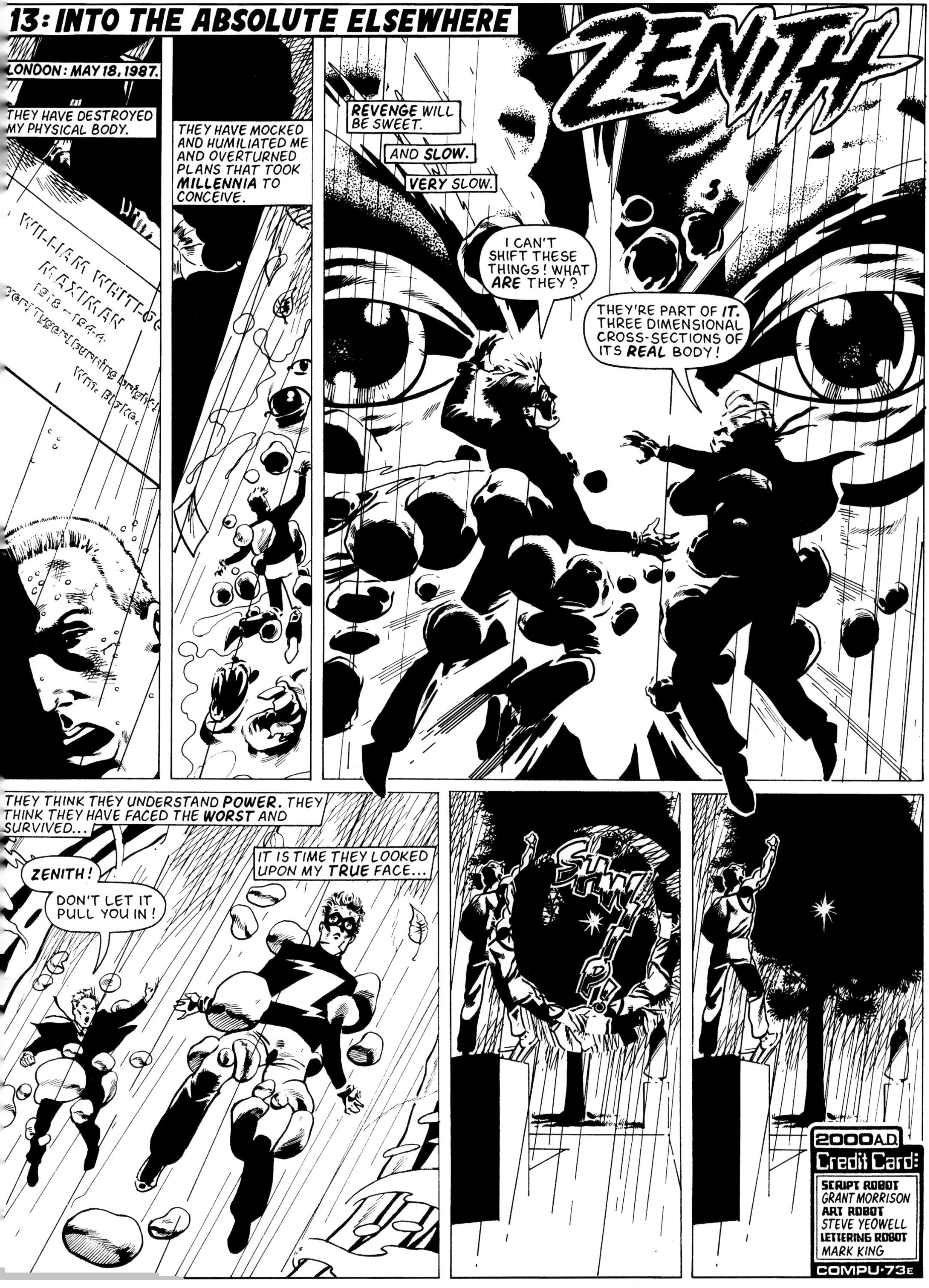

13: INTO THE ABSOLUTE ELSEWHERE
ZENITH
LONDON: MAY 18, 1987.
THEY HAVE DESTROYED MY PHYSICAL BODY.
MAXIMAN
1918 – 1944
Wm. Blake.
THEY HAVE MOCKED AND HUMILIATED ME AND OVERTURNED PLANS THAT TOOK MILLENNIA TO CONCEIVE.
REVENGE WILL BE SWEET.
AND SLOW.
VERY SLOW.
I CAN'T SHIFT THESE THINGS! WHAT ARE THEY?
THEY'RE PART OF IT. THREE DIMENSIONAL CROSS-SECTIONS OF ITS REAL BODY!
THEY THINK THEY UNDERSTAND POWER. THEY THINK THEY HAVE FACED THE WORST AND SURVIVED...
ZENITH!
DON'T LET IT PULL YOU IN!
IT IS TIME THEY LOOKED UPON MY TRUE FACE...
2000 A.D. Credit Card:
SCRIPT ROBOT
GRANT MORRISON
ART ROBOT
STEVE YEOWELL
LETTERING ROBOT
MARK KING
COMPU·73E

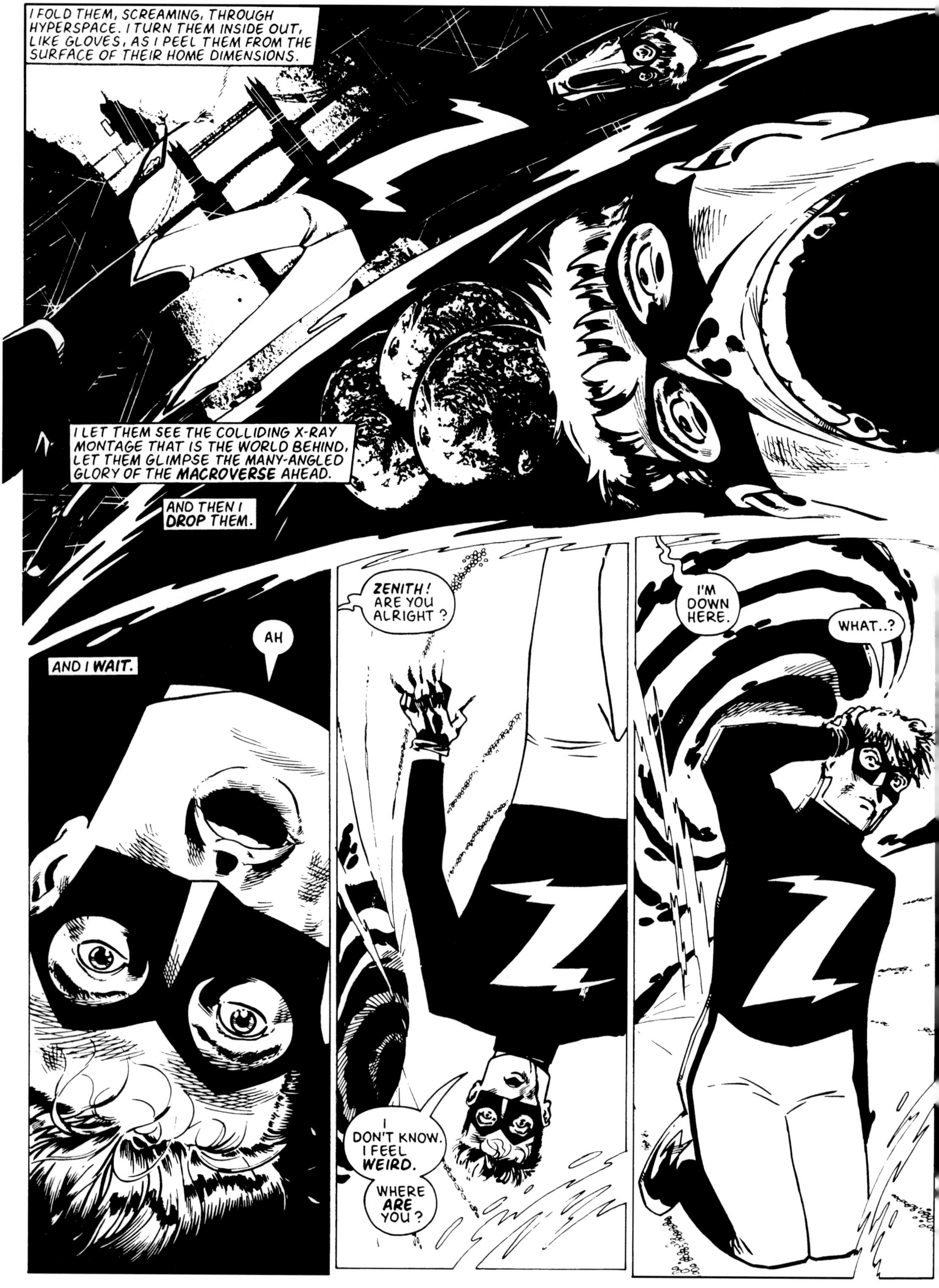
I FOLD THEM, SCREAMING, THROUGH HYPERSPACE. I TURN THEM INSIDE OUT, LIKE GLOVES, AS I PEEL THEM FROM THE SURFACE OF THEIR HOME DIMENSIONS.
I LET THEM SEE THE COLLIDING X-RAY MONTAGE THAT IS THE WORLD BEHIND, LET THEM GLIMPSE THE MANY-ANGLED GLORY OF THE MACROVERSE AHEAD.
AND THEN I DROP THEM.
AND I WAIT.
AH
ZENITH! ARE YOU ALRIGHT?
I DON'T KNOW. I FEEL WEIRD.
WHERE ARE YOU?
I'M DOWN HERE.
WHAT..?

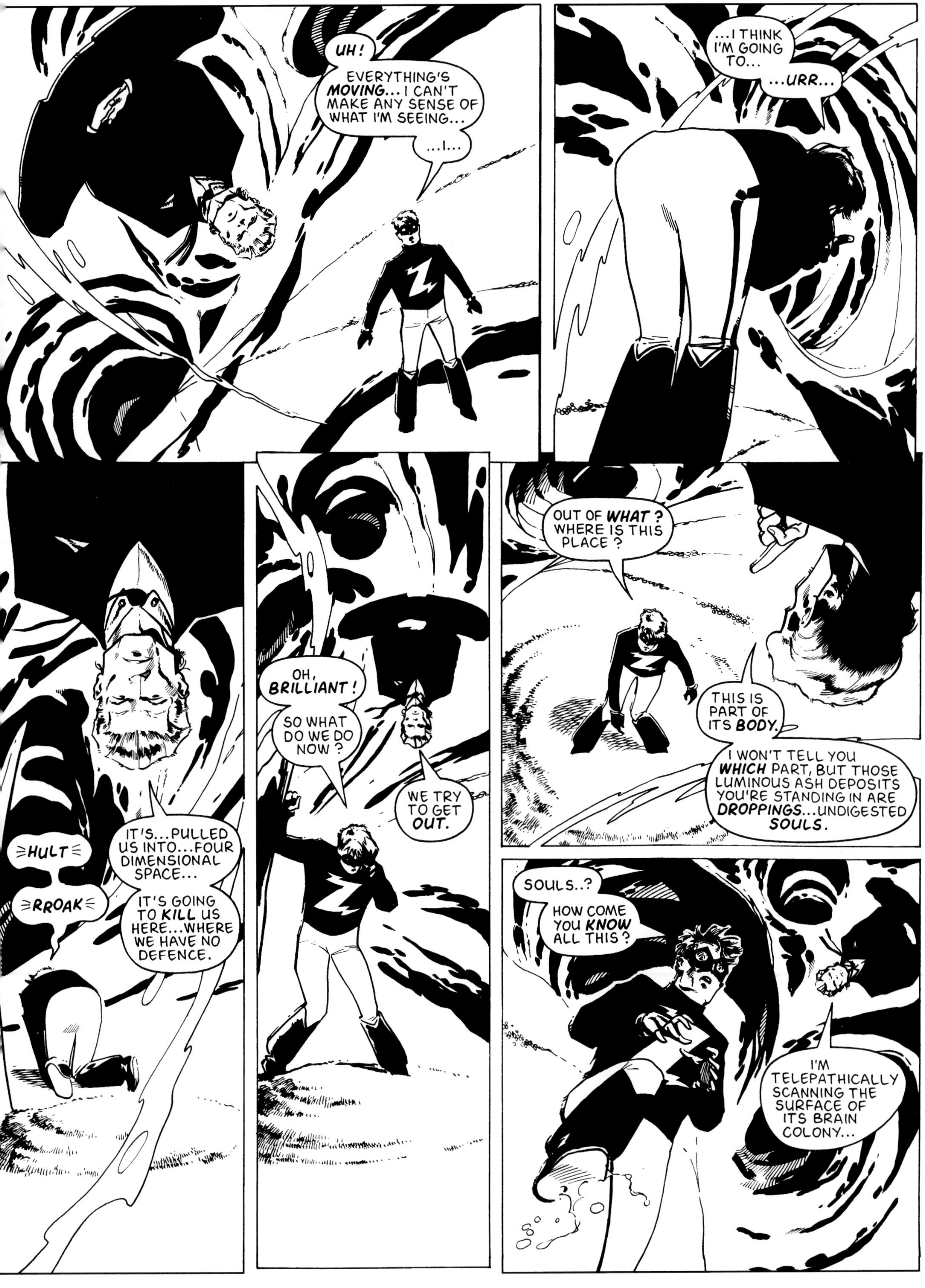
UH!
EVERYTHING'S **MOVING...** I CAN'T MAKE ANY SENSE OF WHAT I'M SEEING...
...I...
...I THINK I'M GOING TO...
...URR...
HULT
RROAK
IT'S...PULLED US INTO...FOUR DIMENSIONAL SPACE...
IT'S GOING TO **KILL** US HERE...WHERE WE HAVE NO DEFENCE.
OH, **BRILLIANT!**
SO WHAT DO WE DO NOW?
WE TRY TO GET **OUT.**
OUT OF **WHAT?** WHERE IS THIS PLACE?
THIS IS PART OF ITS **BODY.**
I WON'T TELL YOU **WHICH** PART, BUT THOSE LUMINOUS ASH DEPOSITS YOU'RE STANDING IN ARE **DROPPINGS**...UNDIGESTED **SOULS.**
SOULS..?
HOW COME YOU **KNOW** ALL THIS?
I'M TELEPATHICALLY SCANNING THE SURFACE OF ITS BRAIN COLONY...

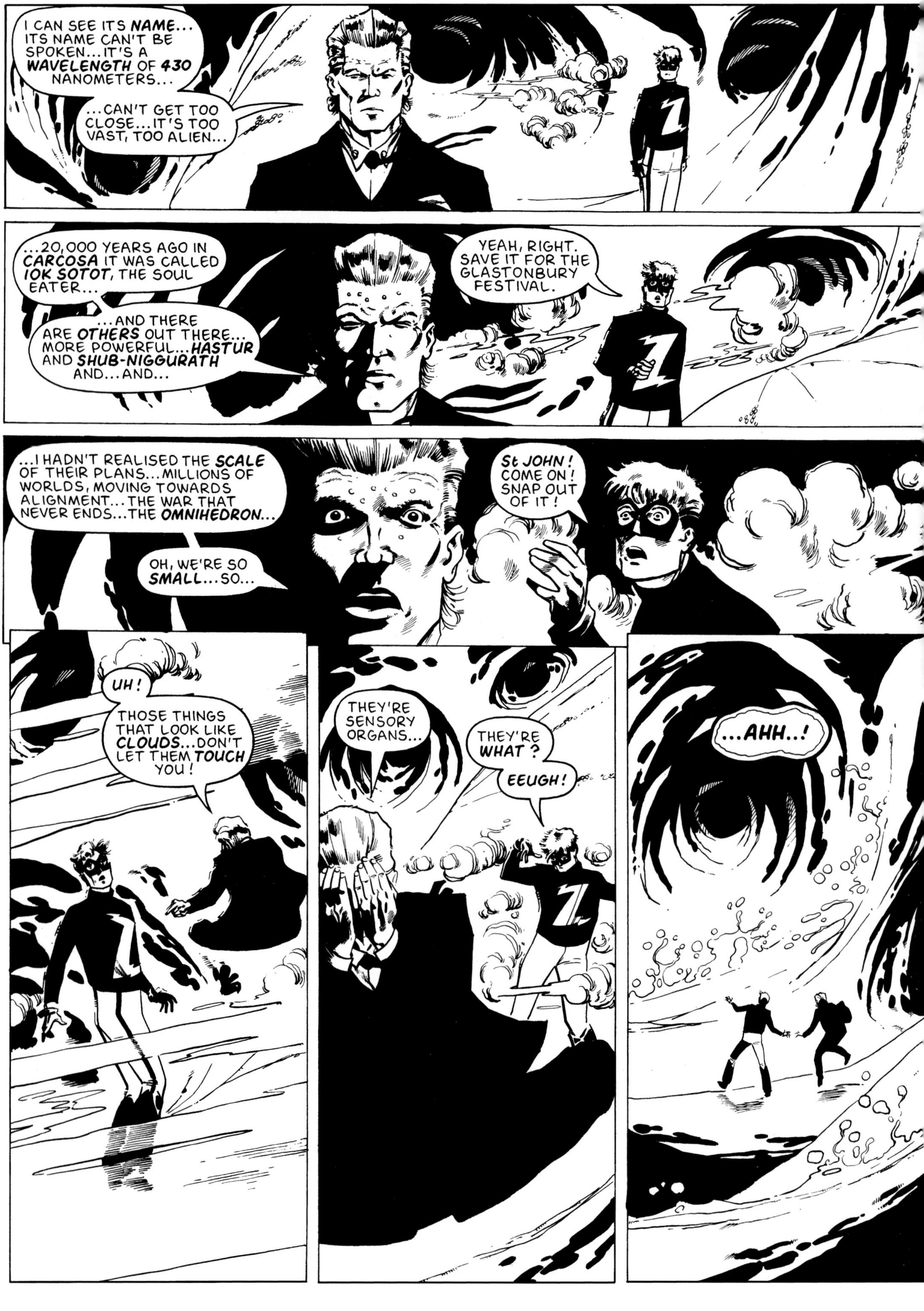
I CAN SEE ITS NAME... ITS NAME CAN'T BE SPOKEN... IT'S A WAVELENGTH OF 430 NANOMETERS...
...CAN'T GET TOO CLOSE... IT'S TOO VAST, TOO ALIEN...
...20,000 YEARS AGO IN CARCOSA IT WAS CALLED IOK SOTOT, THE SOUL EATER...
...AND THERE ARE OTHERS OUT THERE... MORE POWERFUL... HASTUR AND SHUB-NIGGURATH AND... AND...
YEAH, RIGHT. SAVE IT FOR THE GLASTONBURY FESTIVAL.
...I HADN'T REALISED THE SCALE OF THEIR PLANS... MILLIONS OF WORLDS, MOVING TOWARDS ALIGNMENT... THE WAR THAT NEVER ENDS... THE OMNIHEDRON...
OH, WE'RE SO SMALL... SO...
St JOHN! COME ON! SNAP OUT OF IT!
UH!
THOSE THINGS THAT LOOK LIKE CLOUDS... DON'T LET THEM TOUCH YOU!
THEY'RE SENSORY ORGANS...
THEY'RE WHAT?
EEUGH!
...AHH..!

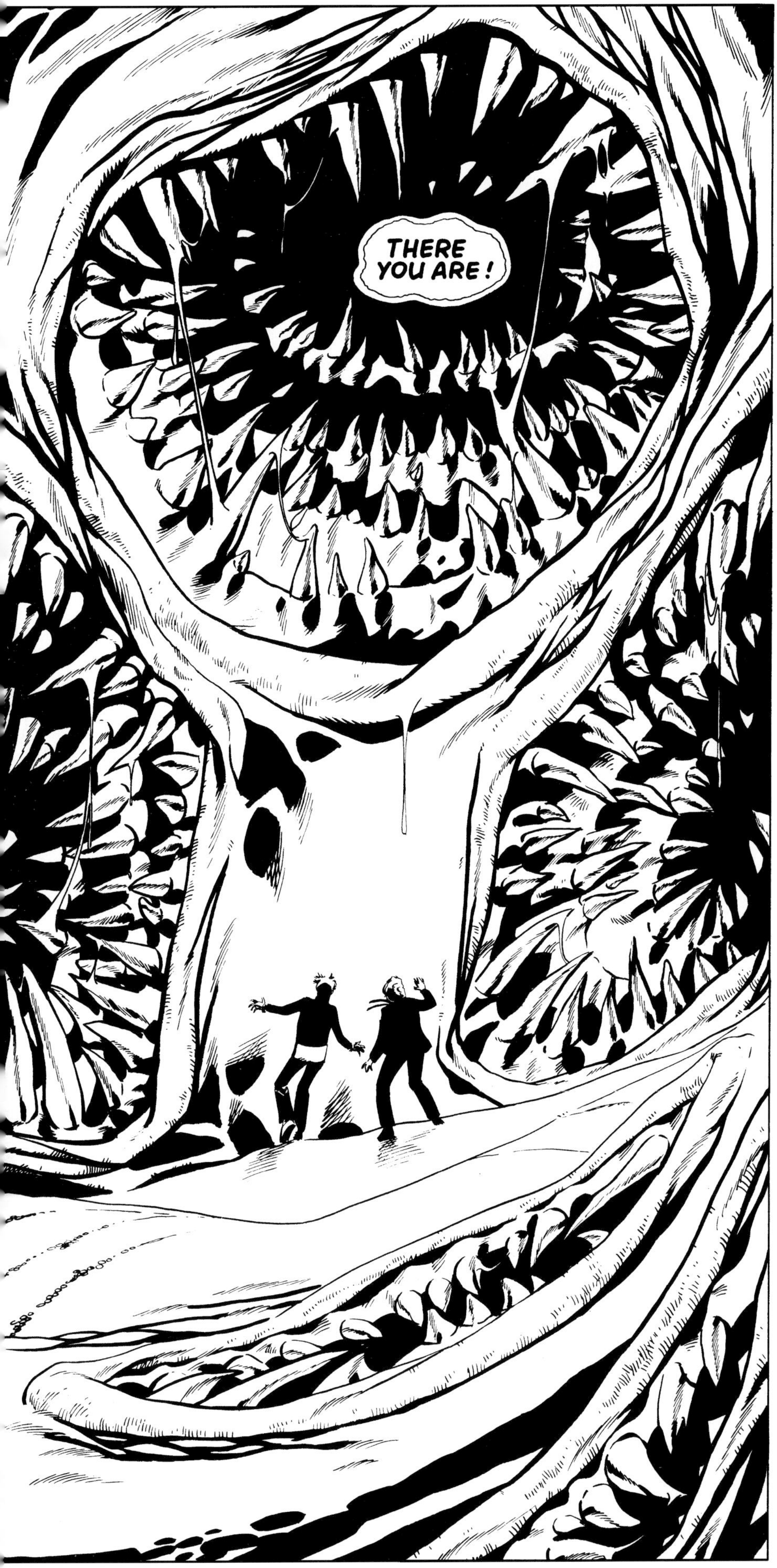
THERE YOU ARE!

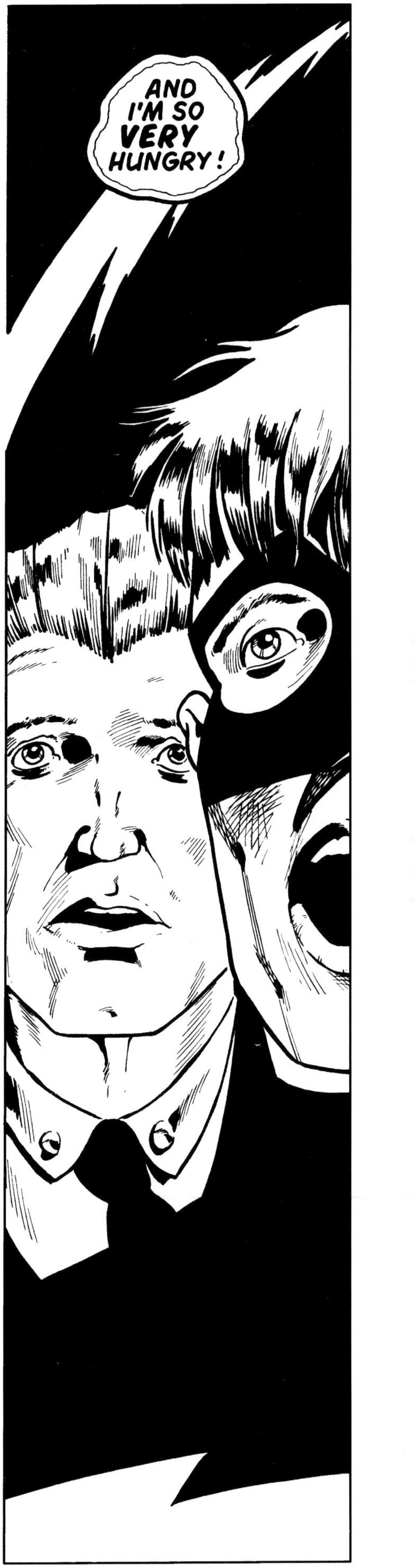
AND I'M SO VERY HUNGRY!

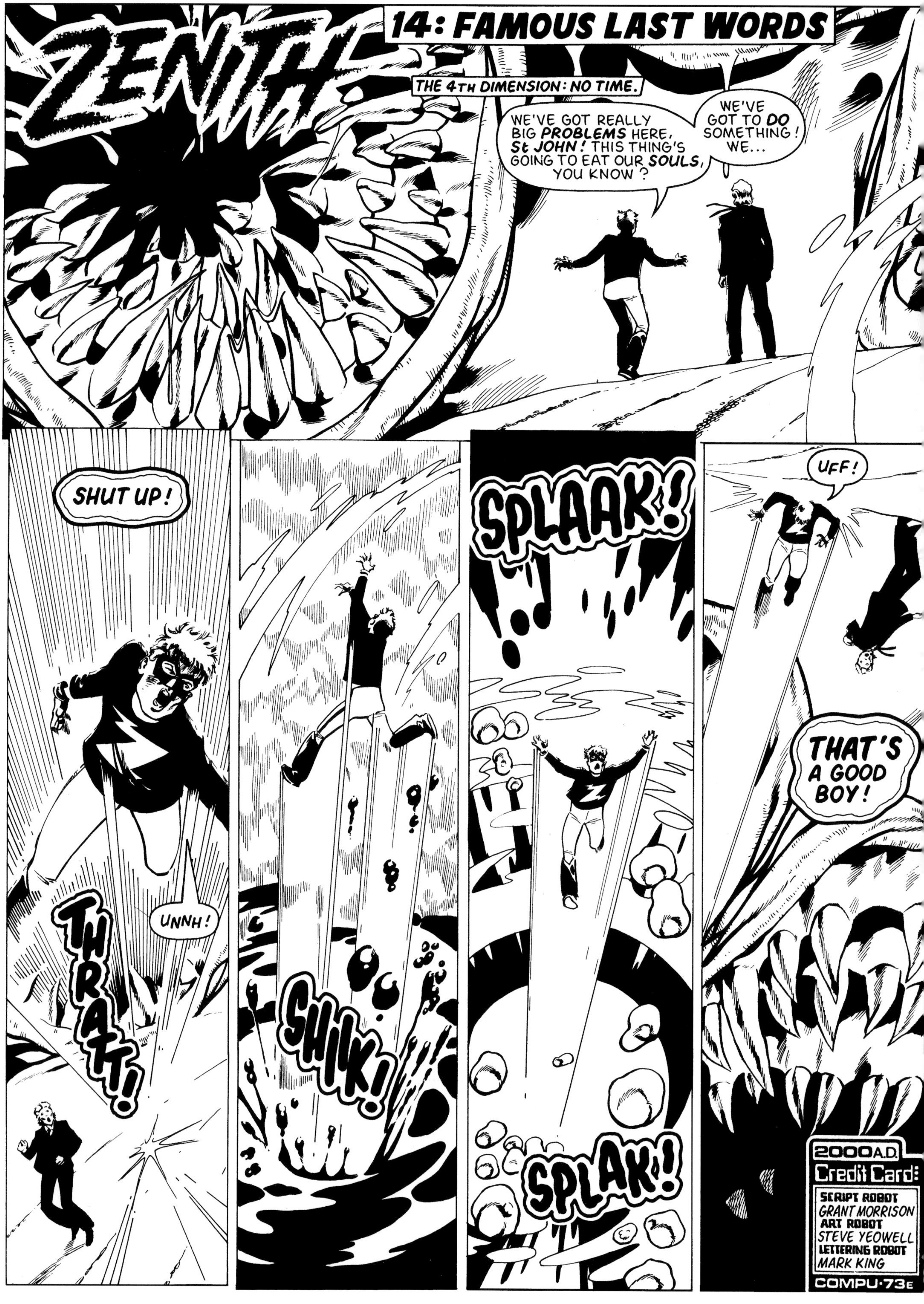
ZENITH
14: FAMOUS LAST WORDS
THE 4TH DIMENSION: NO TIME.
WE'VE GOT REALLY BIG PROBLEMS HERE, St JOHN! THIS THING'S GOING TO EAT OUR SOULS, YOU KNOW?
WE'VE GOT TO DO SOMETHING! WE...
SHUT UP!
UNNH!
THRATT!
SHLIK!
SPLAAK!
SPLAK!
UFF!
THAT'S A GOOD BOY!
2000 A.D.
Credit Card:
SCRIPT ROBOT
GRANT MORRISON
ART ROBOT
STEVE YEOWELL
LETTERING ROBOT
MARK KING
COMPU-73E

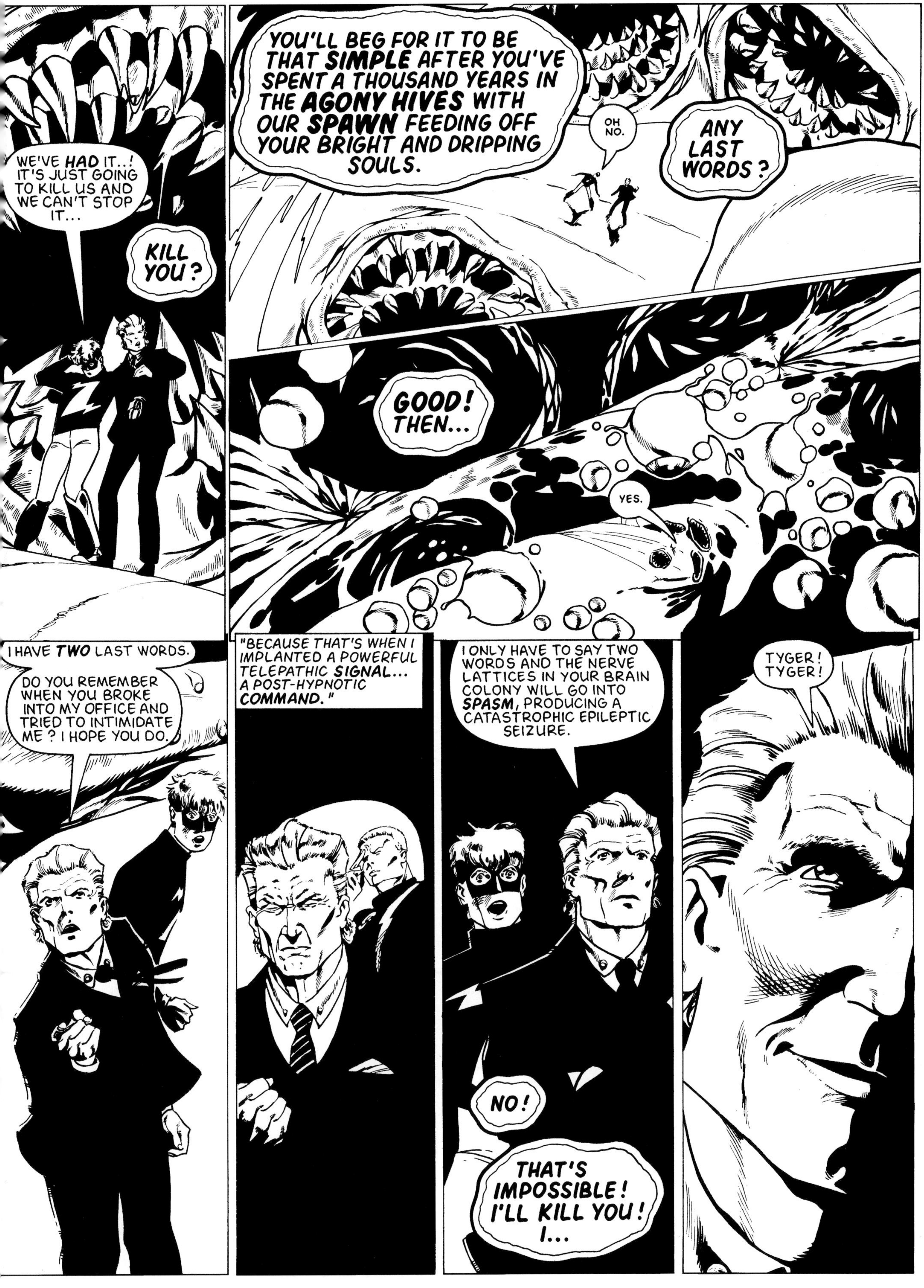
WE'VE HAD IT..! IT'S JUST GOING TO KILL US AND WE CAN'T STOP IT...
KILL YOU?
YOU'LL BEG FOR IT TO BE THAT SIMPLE AFTER YOU'VE SPENT A THOUSAND YEARS IN THE AGONY HIVES WITH OUR SPAWN FEEDING OFF YOUR BRIGHT AND DRIPPING SOULS.
OH NO.
ANY LAST WORDS?
GOOD! THEN...
YES.
I HAVE TWO LAST WORDS.
DO YOU REMEMBER WHEN YOU BROKE INTO MY OFFICE AND TRIED TO INTIMIDATE ME? I HOPE YOU DO.
"BECAUSE THAT'S WHEN I IMPLANTED A POWERFUL TELEPATHIC SIGNAL... A POST-HYPNOTIC COMMAND."
I ONLY HAVE TO SAY TWO WORDS AND THE NERVE LATTICES IN YOUR BRAIN COLONY WILL GO INTO SPASM, PRODUCING A CATASTROPHIC EPILEPTIC SEIZURE.
NO!
THAT'S IMPOSSIBLE! I'LL KILL YOU! I...
TYGER! TYGER!

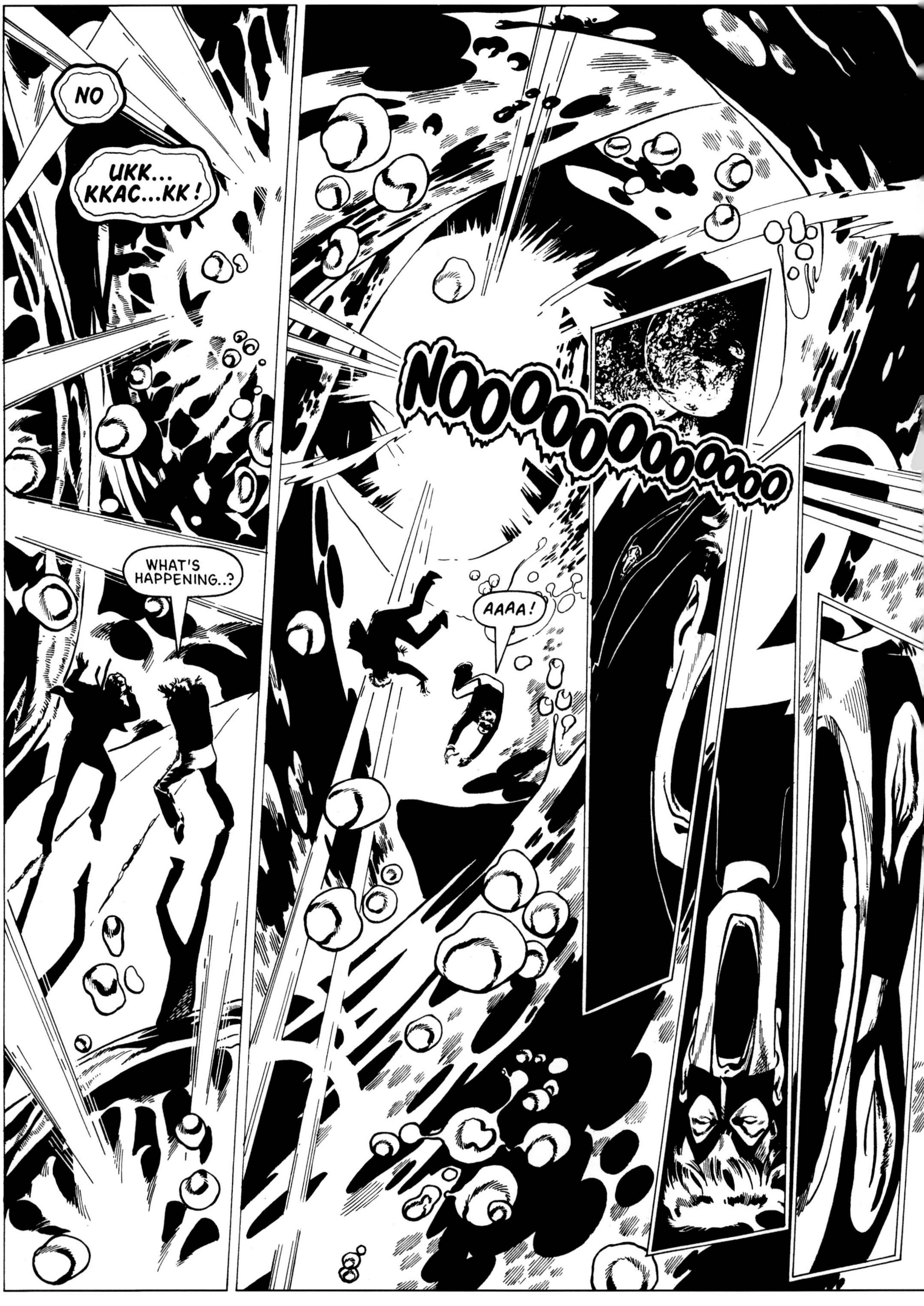
NO
UKK... KKAC...KK!
NOOOOOOOOOOOOO
WHAT'S HAPPENING..?
AAAA!

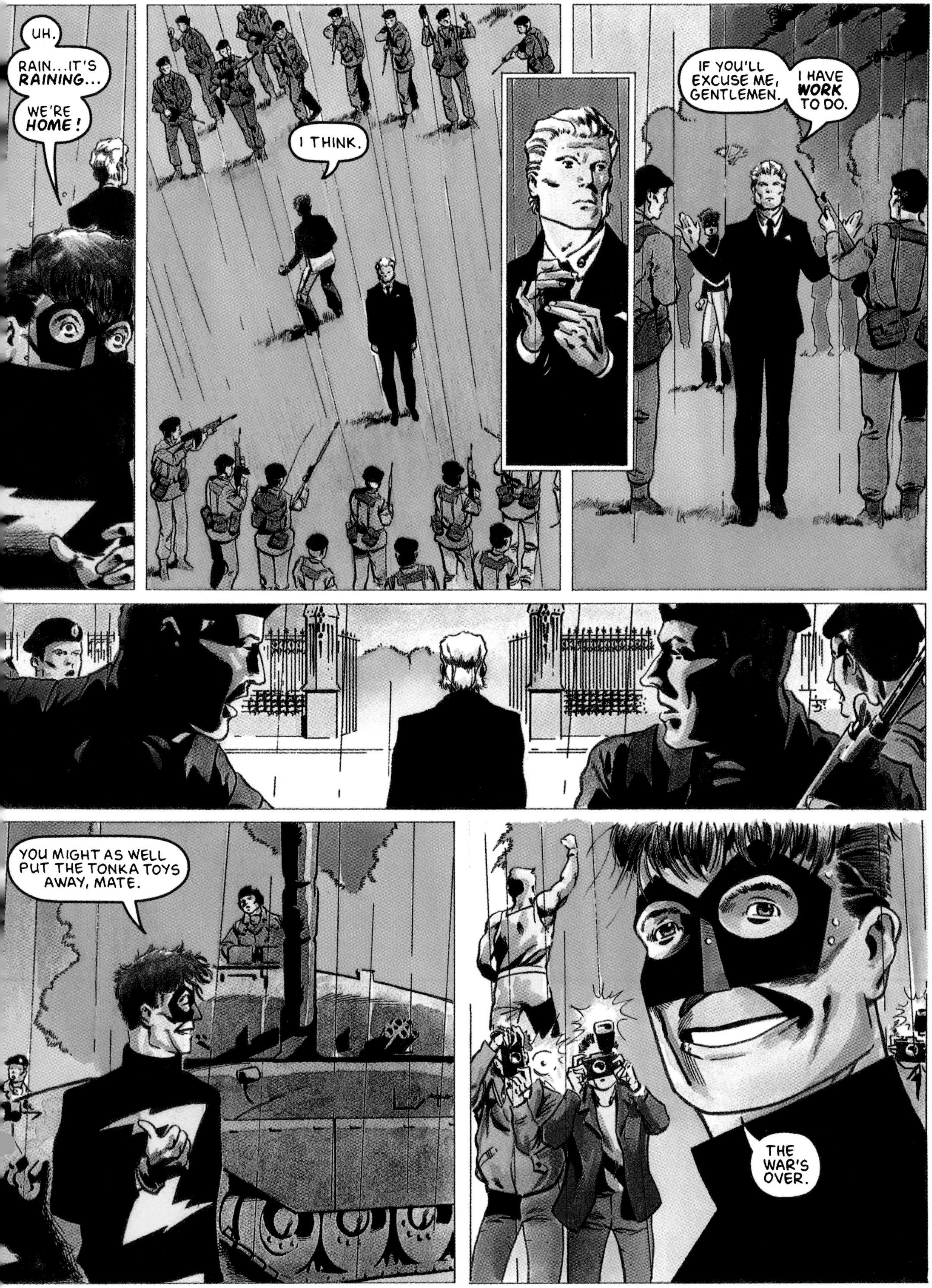
UH.
RAIN...IT'S RAINING...
WE'RE HOME!
I THINK.
IF YOU'LL EXCUSE ME, GENTLEMEN.
I HAVE WORK TO DO.
YOU MIGHT AS WELL PUT THE TONKA TOYS AWAY, MATE.
THE WAR'S OVER.

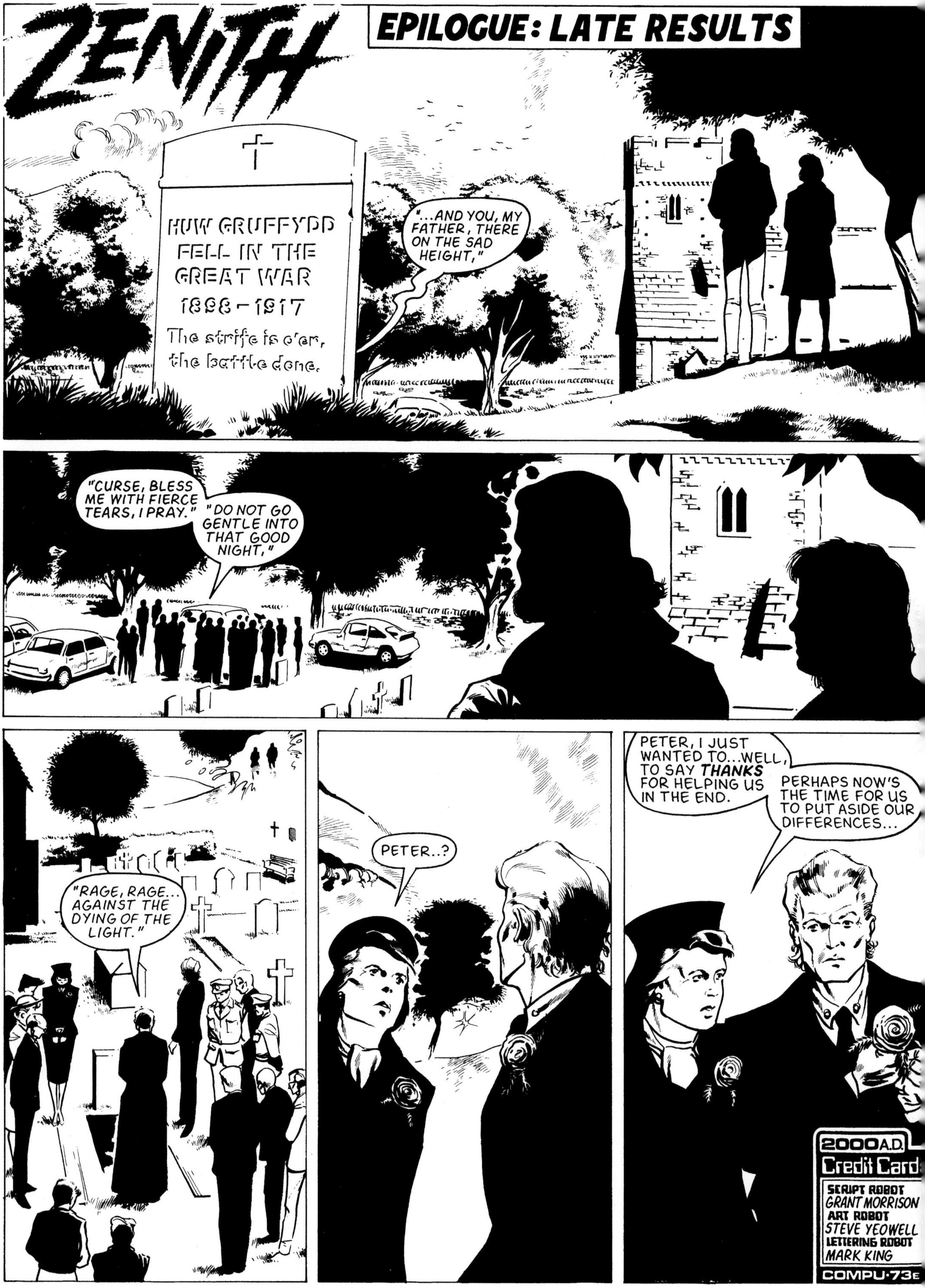
ZENITH
EPILOGUE: LATE RESULTS
HUW GRUFFYDD FELL IN THE GREAT WAR 1898-1917 The strife is o'er, the battle done.
"...AND YOU, MY FATHER, THERE ON THE SAD HEIGHT,"
"CURSE, BLESS ME WITH FIERCE TEARS, I PRAY."
"DO NOT GO GENTLE INTO THAT GOOD NIGHT,"
"RAGE, RAGE... AGAINST THE DYING OF THE LIGHT."
PETER..?
PETER, I JUST WANTED TO...WELL, TO SAY THANKS FOR HELPING US IN THE END.
PERHAPS NOW'S THE TIME FOR US TO PUT ASIDE OUR DIFFERENCES...
2000 A.D. Credit Card
SCRIPT ROBOT GRANT MORRISON
ART ROBOT STEVE YEOWELL
LETTERING ROBOT MARK KING
COMPU-73E

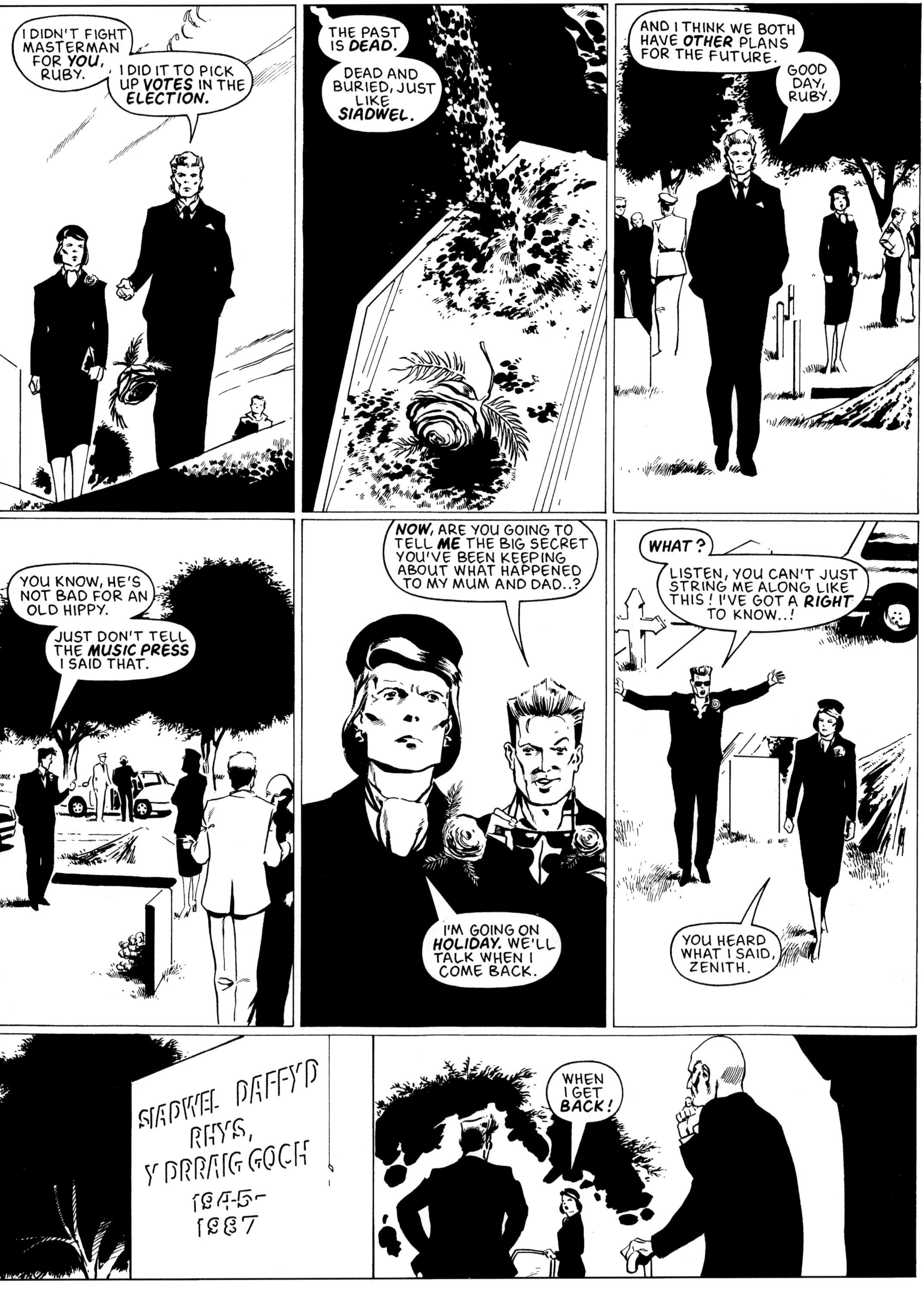
I DIDN'T FIGHT MASTERMAN FOR YOU, RUBY.
I DID IT TO PICK UP VOTES IN THE ELECTION.
THE PAST IS DEAD.
DEAD AND BURIED, JUST LIKE SIADWEL.
AND I THINK WE BOTH HAVE OTHER PLANS FOR THE FUTURE.
GOOD DAY, RUBY.
YOU KNOW, HE'S NOT BAD FOR AN OLD HIPPY.
JUST DON'T TELL THE MUSIC PRESS I SAID THAT.
NOW, ARE YOU GOING TO TELL ME THE BIG SECRET YOU'VE BEEN KEEPING ABOUT WHAT HAPPENED TO MY MUM AND DAD..?
I'M GOING ON HOLIDAY. WE'LL TALK WHEN I COME BACK.
WHAT ?
LISTEN, YOU CAN'T JUST STRING ME ALONG LIKE THIS ! I'VE GOT A RIGHT TO KNOW..!
YOU HEARD WHAT I SAID, ZENITH.
SIADWEL DAFFYD RHYS, Y DRRAIG GOCH 1945- 1987
WHEN I GET BACK!

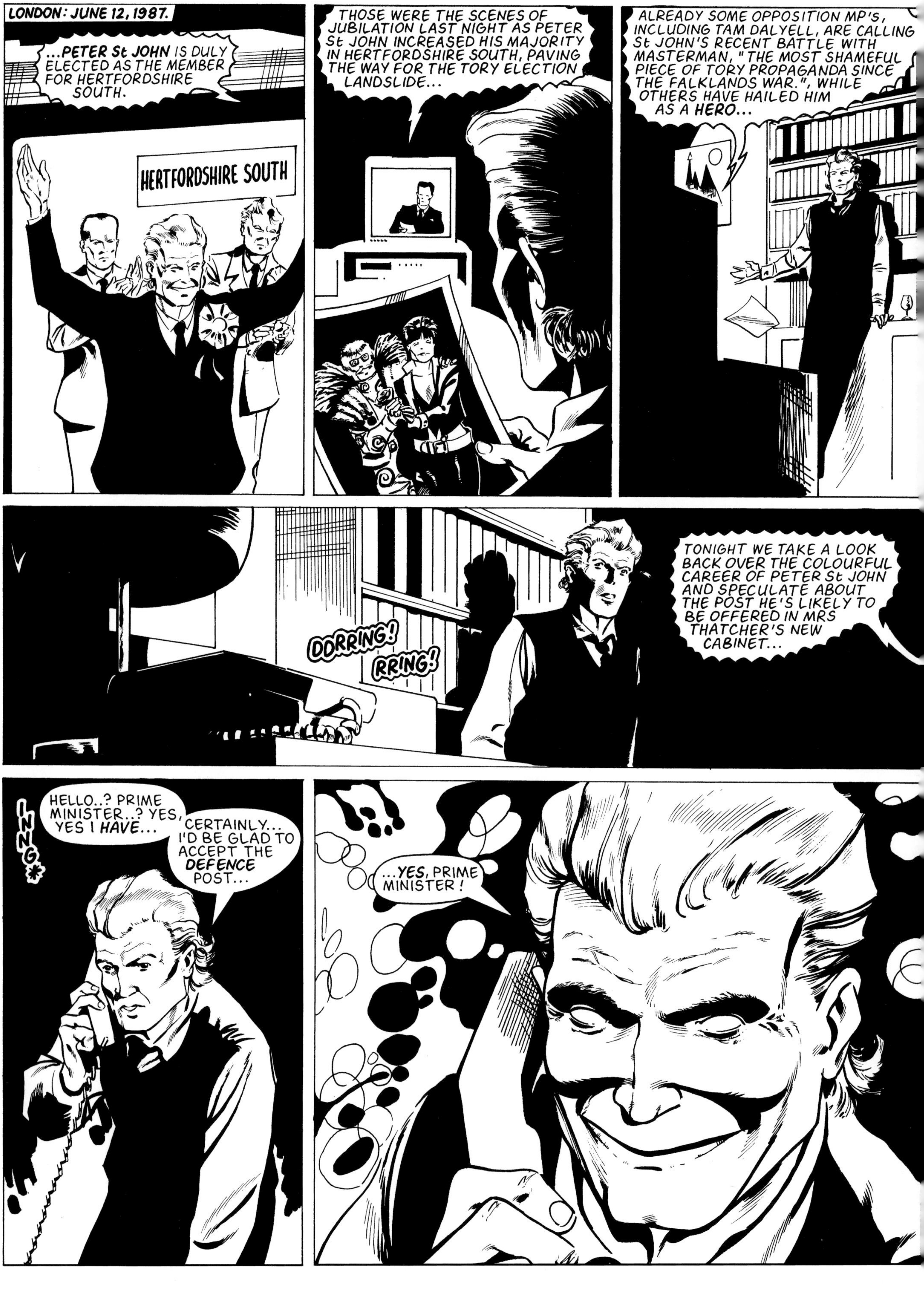
LONDON: JUNE 12, 1987.
...PETER St JOHN IS DULY ELECTED AS THE MEMBER FOR HERTFORDSHIRE SOUTH.
HERTFORDSHIRE SOUTH
THOSE WERE THE SCENES OF JUBILATION LAST NIGHT AS PETER St JOHN INCREASED HIS MAJORITY IN HERTFORDSHIRE SOUTH, PAVING THE WAY FOR THE TORY ELECTION LANDSLIDE...
ALREADY SOME OPPOSITION MP'S, INCLUDING TAM DALYELL, ARE CALLING St JOHN'S RECENT BATTLE WITH MASTERMAN, "THE MOST SHAMEFUL PIECE OF TORY PROPAGANDA SINCE THE FALKLANDS WAR.", WHILE OTHERS HAVE HAILED HIM AS A HERO...
TONIGHT WE TAKE A LOOK BACK OVER THE COLOURFUL CAREER OF PETER St JOHN AND SPECULATE ABOUT THE POST HE'S LIKELY TO BE OFFERED IN MRS THATCHER'S NEW CABINET...
DORRING!
RRING!
INNG*
HELLO..? PRIME MINISTER..? YES, YES I HAVE...
CERTAINLY... I'D BE GLAD TO ACCEPT THE DEFENCE POST...
...YES, PRIME MINISTER!

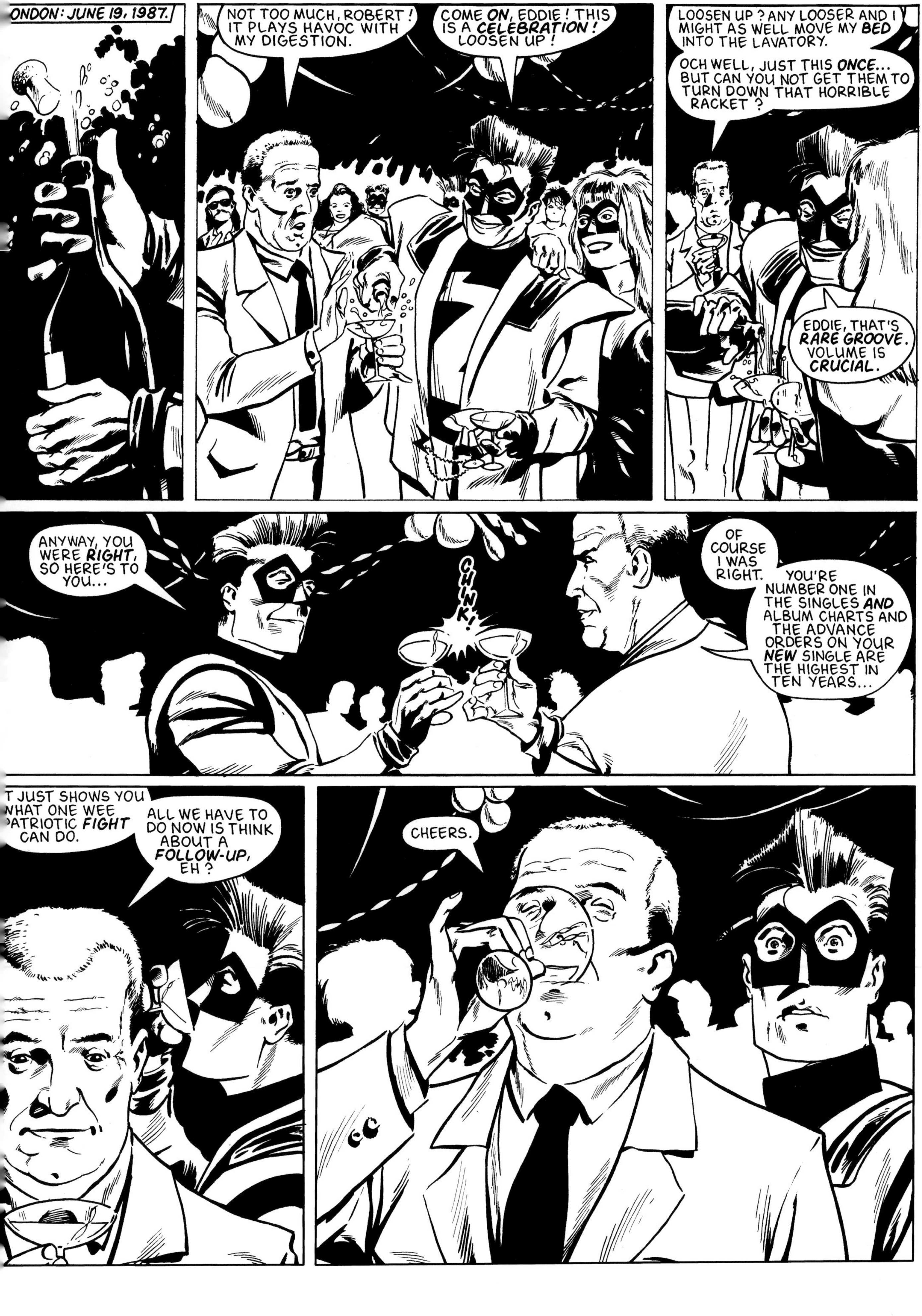
ONDON: JUNE 19, 1987.
NOT TOO MUCH, ROBERT! IT PLAYS HAVOC WITH MY DIGESTION.
COME ON, EDDIE! THIS IS A CELEBRATION! LOOSEN UP!
LOOSEN UP? ANY LOOSER AND I MIGHT AS WELL MOVE MY BED INTO THE LAVATORY.
OCH WELL, JUST THIS ONCE... BUT CAN YOU NOT GET THEM TO TURN DOWN THAT HORRIBLE RACKET?
EDDIE, THAT'S RARE GROOVE. VOLUME IS CRUCIAL.
ANYWAY, YOU WERE RIGHT, SO HERE'S TO YOU...
CHINK!
OF COURSE I WAS RIGHT.
YOU'RE NUMBER ONE IN THE SINGLES AND ALBUM CHARTS AND THE ADVANCE ORDERS ON YOUR NEW SINGLE ARE THE HIGHEST IN TEN YEARS...
T JUST SHOWS YOU WHAT ONE WEE PATRIOTIC FIGHT CAN DO.
ALL WE HAVE TO DO NOW IS THINK ABOUT A FOLLOW-UP, EH?
CHEERS.

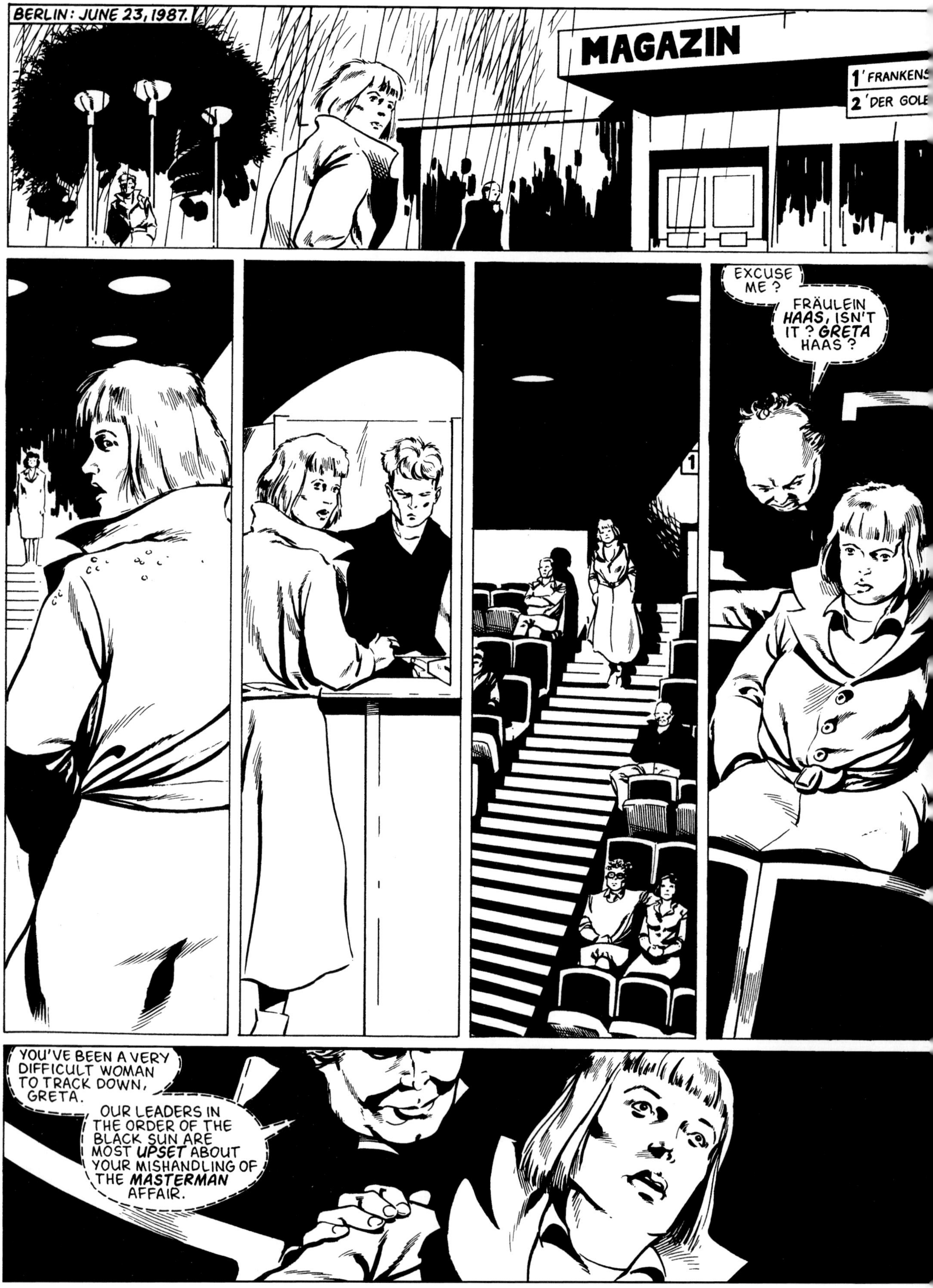
BERLIN: JUNE 23, 1987.
MAGAZIN
1 'FRANKENS
2 'DER GOLE
1
EXCUSE ME ?
FRÄULEIN HAAS, ISN'T IT ? GRETA HAAS ?
YOU'VE BEEN A VERY DIFFICULT WOMAN TO TRACK DOWN, GRETA.
OUR LEADERS IN THE ORDER OF THE BLACK SUN ARE MOST UPSET ABOUT YOUR MISHANDLING OF THE MASTERMAN AFFAIR.

THEY'VE ALSO ASKED ME TO CONVEY THEIR SYMPATHY, FOLLOWING YOUR TRAGIC *DEATH*.

WHAT DO YOU MEAN..? I'M NOT...

SHH!

SO YOUNG. SO SUDDEN. SO SAD.

THE *BOMB'S* IN YOUR POCKET.

WHAT..?

...OH NO... HELP ME...

SHH!

...SOMEONE PLEASE...

SHH!

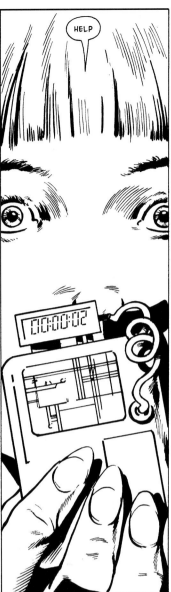

HELP

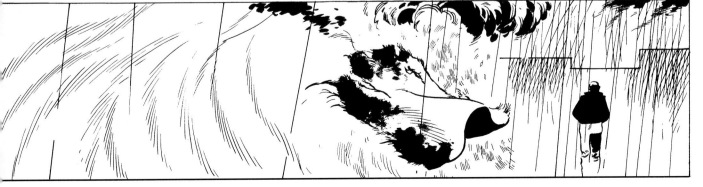

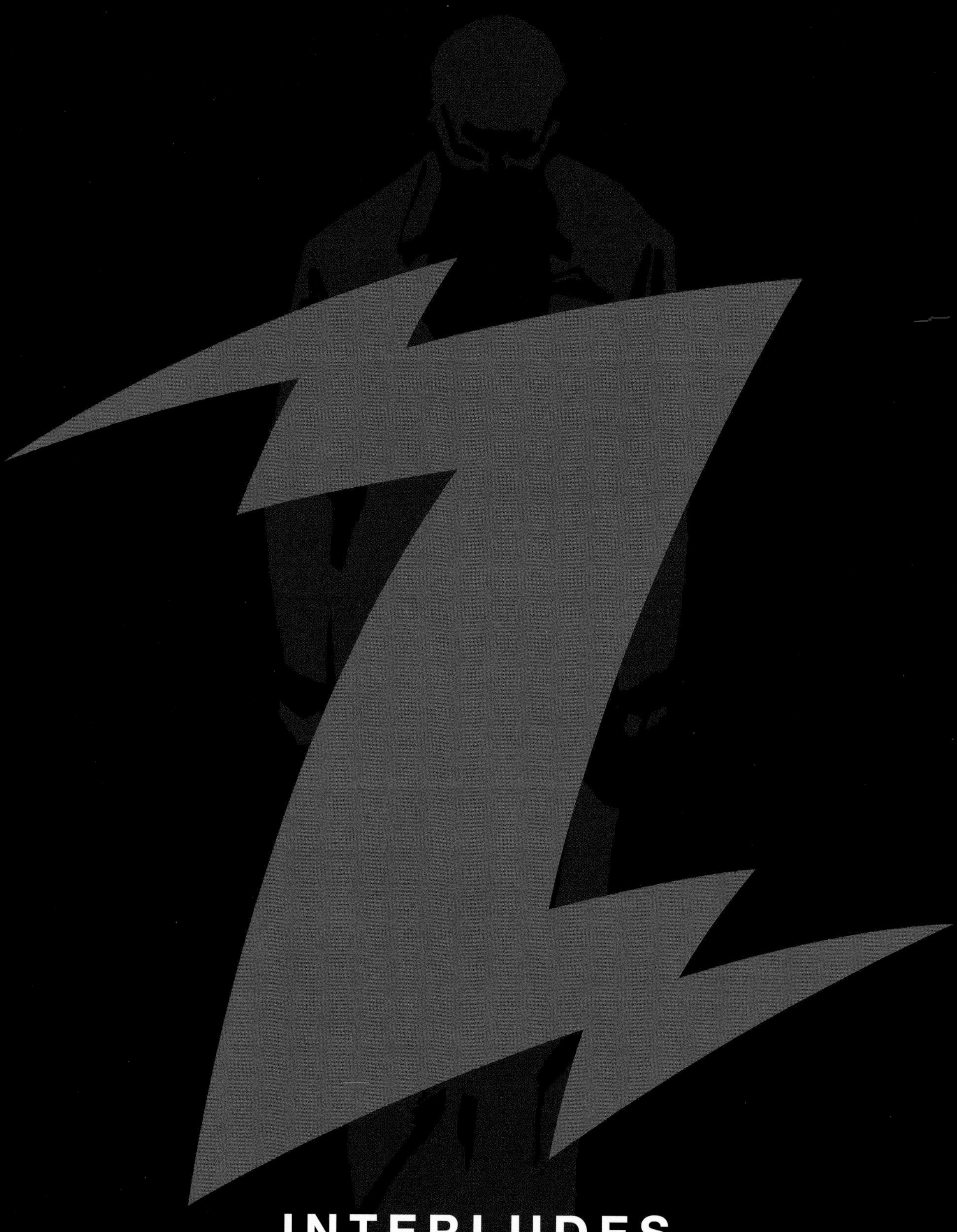

INTERLUDES

WHITLOCK // PEYNE

Script: Grant Morrison
Art: Steve Yeowell
Letters: Mark King

Originally published in *2000 AD* Progs 558-559

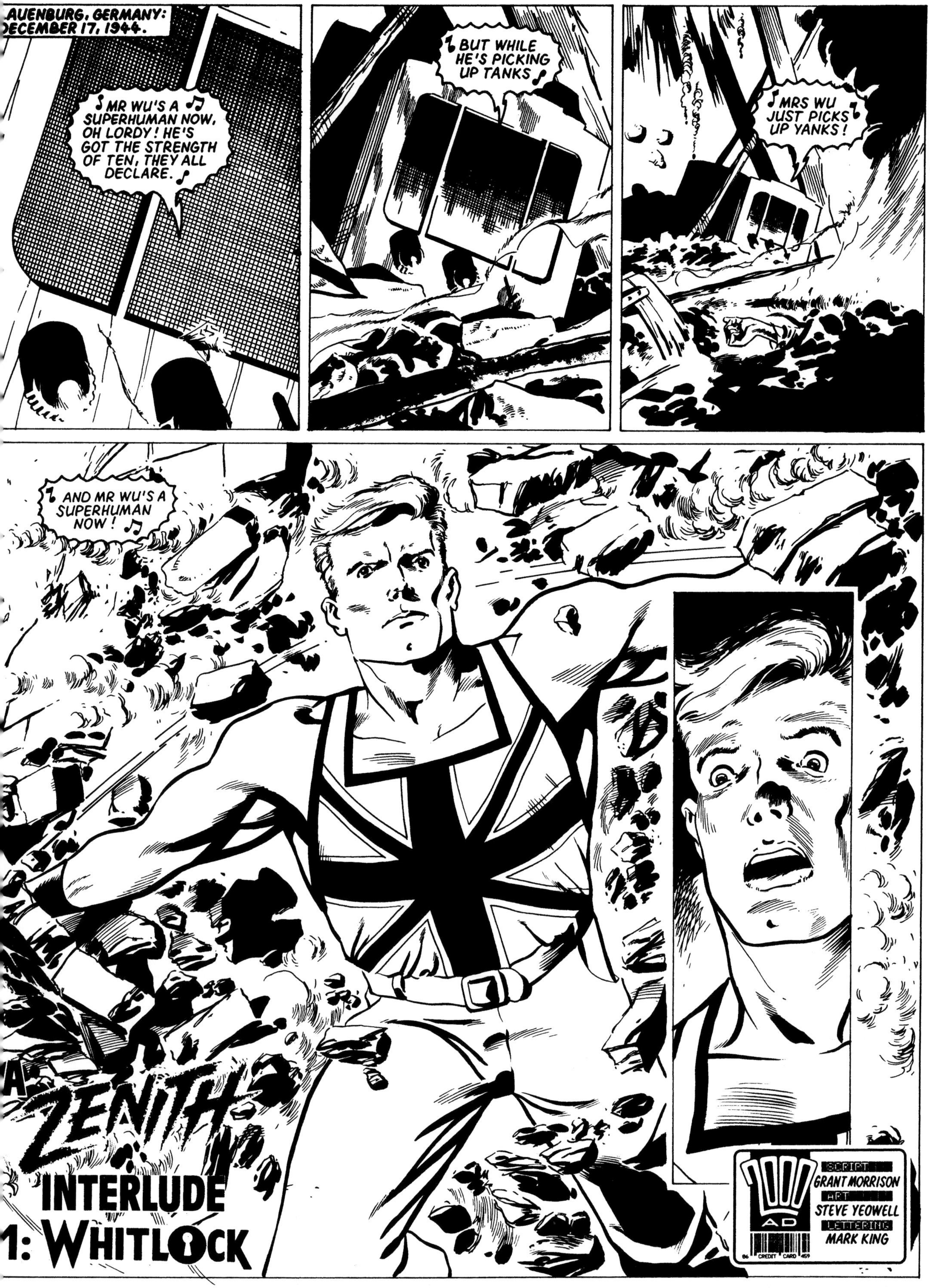

LAUENBURG, GERMANY: DECEMBER 17, 1944.
MR WU'S A SUPERHUMAN NOW, OH LORDY! HE'S GOT THE STRENGTH OF TEN, THEY ALL DECLARE.
BUT WHILE HE'S PICKING UP TANKS
MRS WU JUST PICKS UP YANKS!
AND MR WU'S A SUPERHUMAN NOW!
A ZENITH
INTERLUDE 1: WHITLOCK
2000 AD
SCRIPT GRANT MORRISON
ART STEVE YEOWELL
LETTERING MARK KING

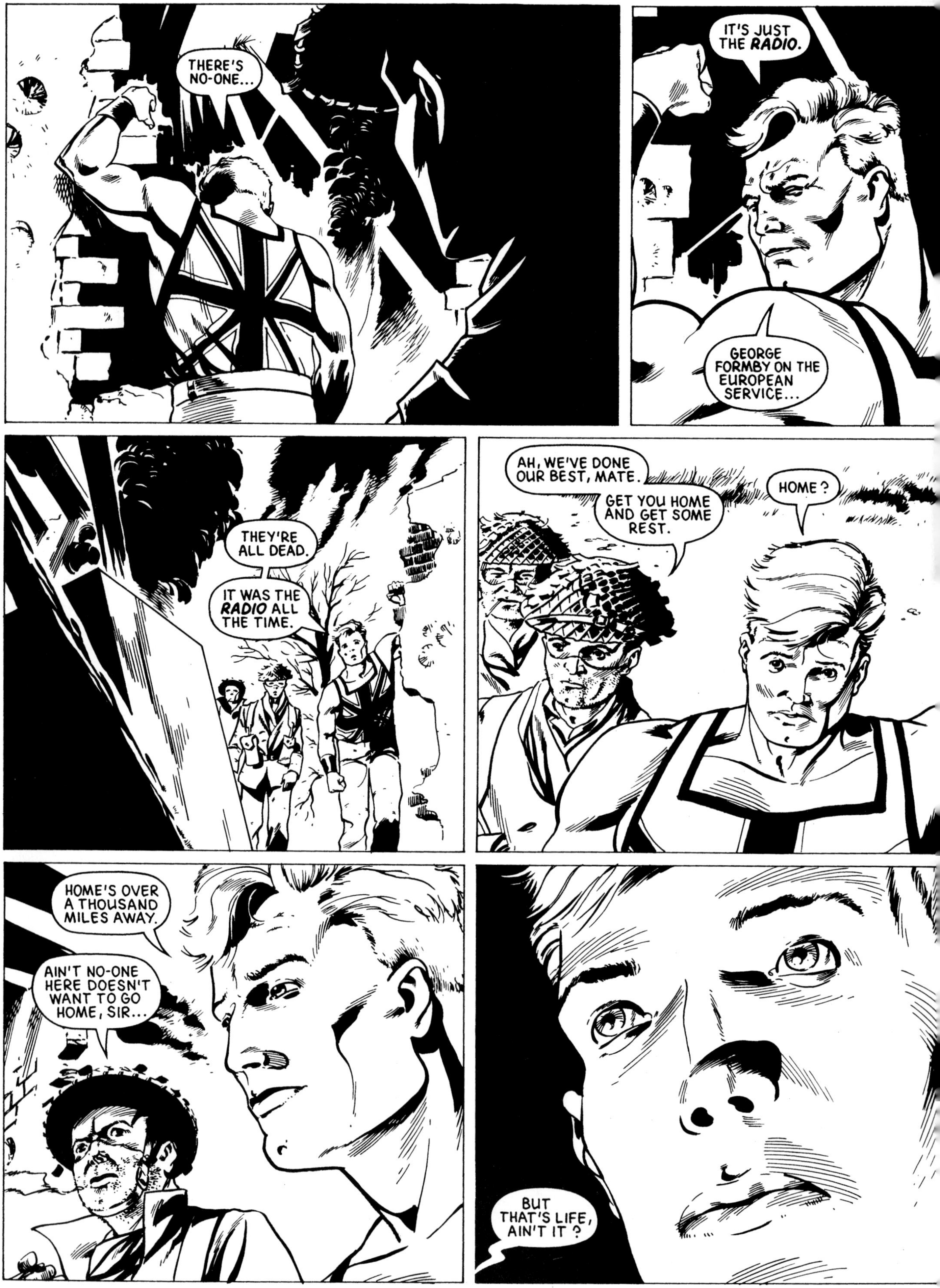
THERE'S NO-ONE...
IT'S JUST THE RADIO.
GEORGE FORMBY ON THE EUROPEAN SERVICE...
THEY'RE ALL DEAD.
IT WAS THE RADIO ALL THE TIME.
AH, WE'VE DONE OUR BEST, MATE.
GET YOU HOME AND GET SOME REST.
HOME?
HOME'S OVER A THOUSAND MILES AWAY.
AIN'T NO-ONE HERE DOESN'T WANT TO GO HOME, SIR...
BUT THAT'S LIFE, AIN'T IT?

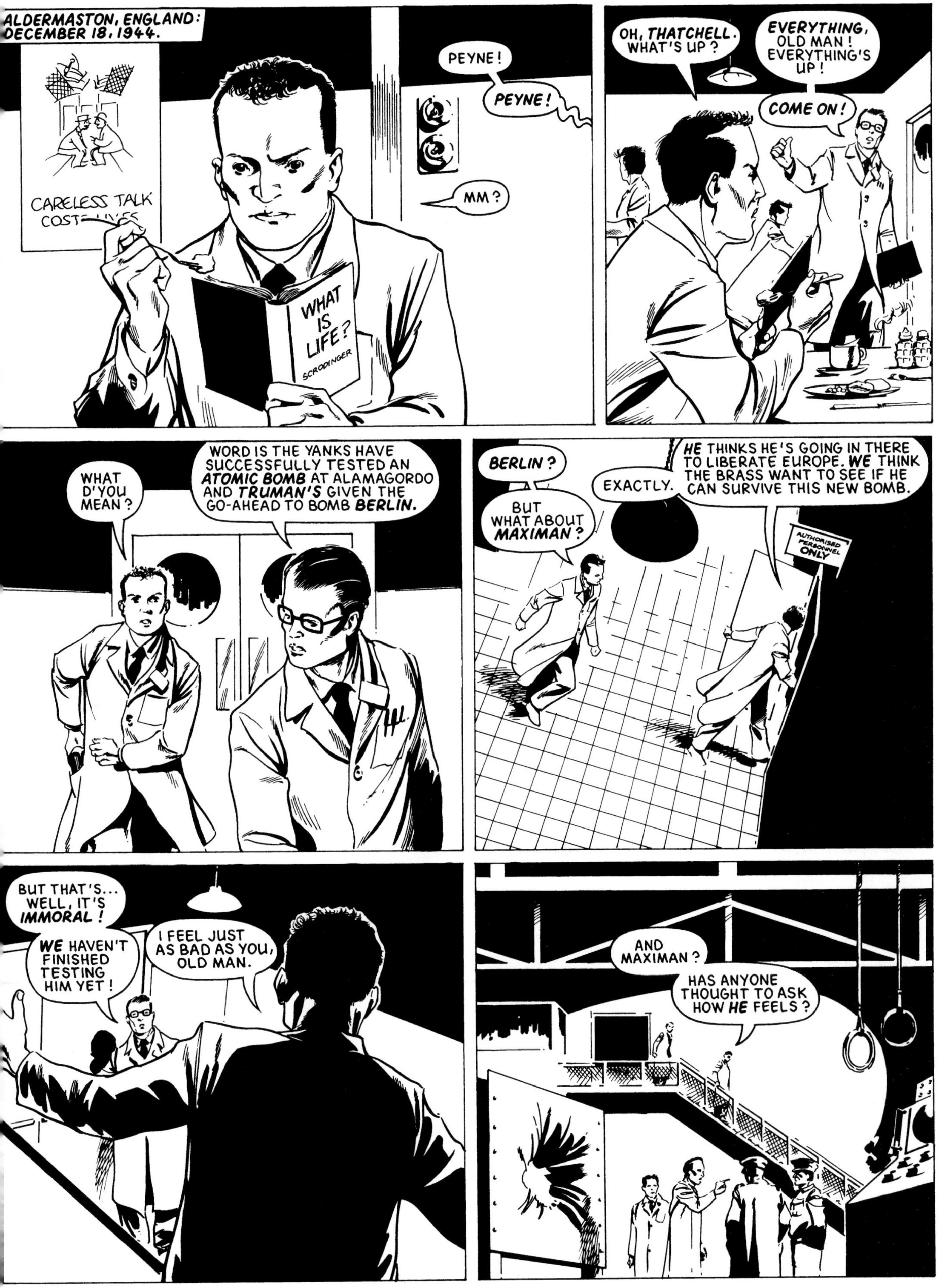
ALDERMASTON, ENGLAND: DECEMBER 18, 1944.
CARELESS TALK COSTS LIVES
PEYNE!
PEYNE!
MM?
WHAT IS LIFE? SCRODINGER
OH, THATCHELL. WHAT'S UP?
EVERYTHING, OLD MAN! EVERYTHING'S UP!
COME ON!
WHAT D'YOU MEAN?
WORD IS THE YANKS HAVE SUCCESSFULLY TESTED AN ATOMIC BOMB AT ALAMAGORDO AND TRUMAN'S GIVEN THE GO-AHEAD TO BOMB BERLIN.
BERLIN?
BUT WHAT ABOUT MAXIMAN?
EXACTLY.
HE THINKS HE'S GOING IN THERE TO LIBERATE EUROPE. WE THINK THE BRASS WANT TO SEE IF HE CAN SURVIVE THIS NEW BOMB.
AUTHORISED PERSONNEL ONLY
BUT THAT'S... WELL, IT'S IMMORAL!
WE HAVEN'T FINISHED TESTING HIM YET!
I FEEL JUST AS BAD AS YOU, OLD MAN.
AND MAXIMAN?
HAS ANYONE THOUGHT TO ASK HOW HE FEELS?

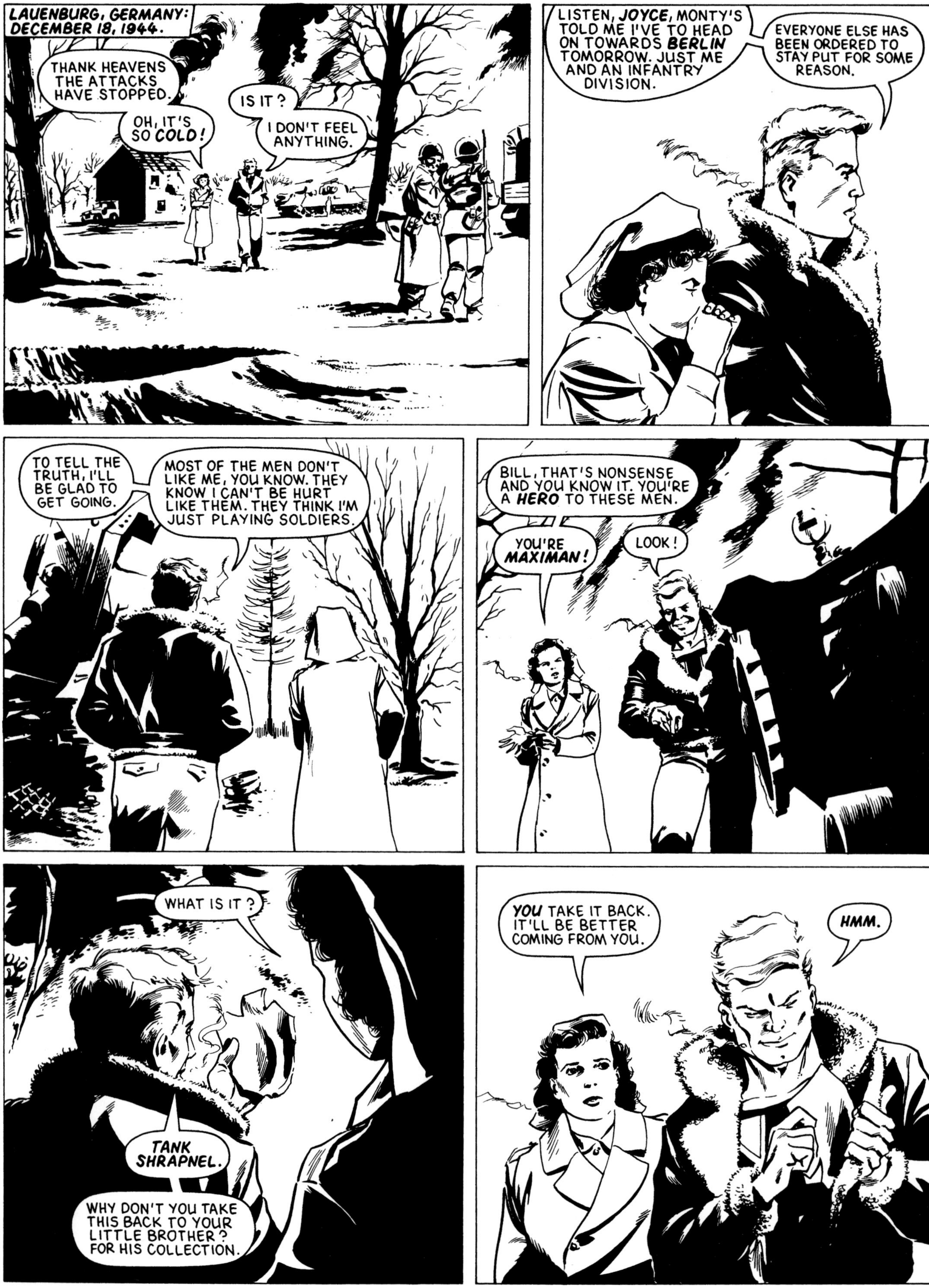
LAUENBURG, GERMANY: DECEMBER 18, 1944.
THANK HEAVENS THE ATTACKS HAVE STOPPED.
OH, IT'S SO COLD!
IS IT?
I DON'T FEEL ANYTHING.
LISTEN, JOYCE, MONTY'S TOLD ME I'VE TO HEAD ON TOWARDS BERLIN TOMORROW. JUST ME AND AN INFANTRY DIVISION.
EVERYONE ELSE HAS BEEN ORDERED TO STAY PUT FOR SOME REASON.
TO TELL THE TRUTH, I'LL BE GLAD TO GET GOING.
MOST OF THE MEN DON'T LIKE ME, YOU KNOW. THEY KNOW I CAN'T BE HURT LIKE THEM. THEY THINK I'M JUST PLAYING SOLDIERS.
BILL, THAT'S NONSENSE AND YOU KNOW IT. YOU'RE A HERO TO THESE MEN.
YOU'RE MAXIMAN!
LOOK!
WHAT IS IT?
TANK SHRAPNEL.
WHY DON'T YOU TAKE THIS BACK TO YOUR LITTLE BROTHER? FOR HIS COLLECTION.
YOU TAKE IT BACK. IT'LL BE BETTER COMING FROM YOU.
HMM.

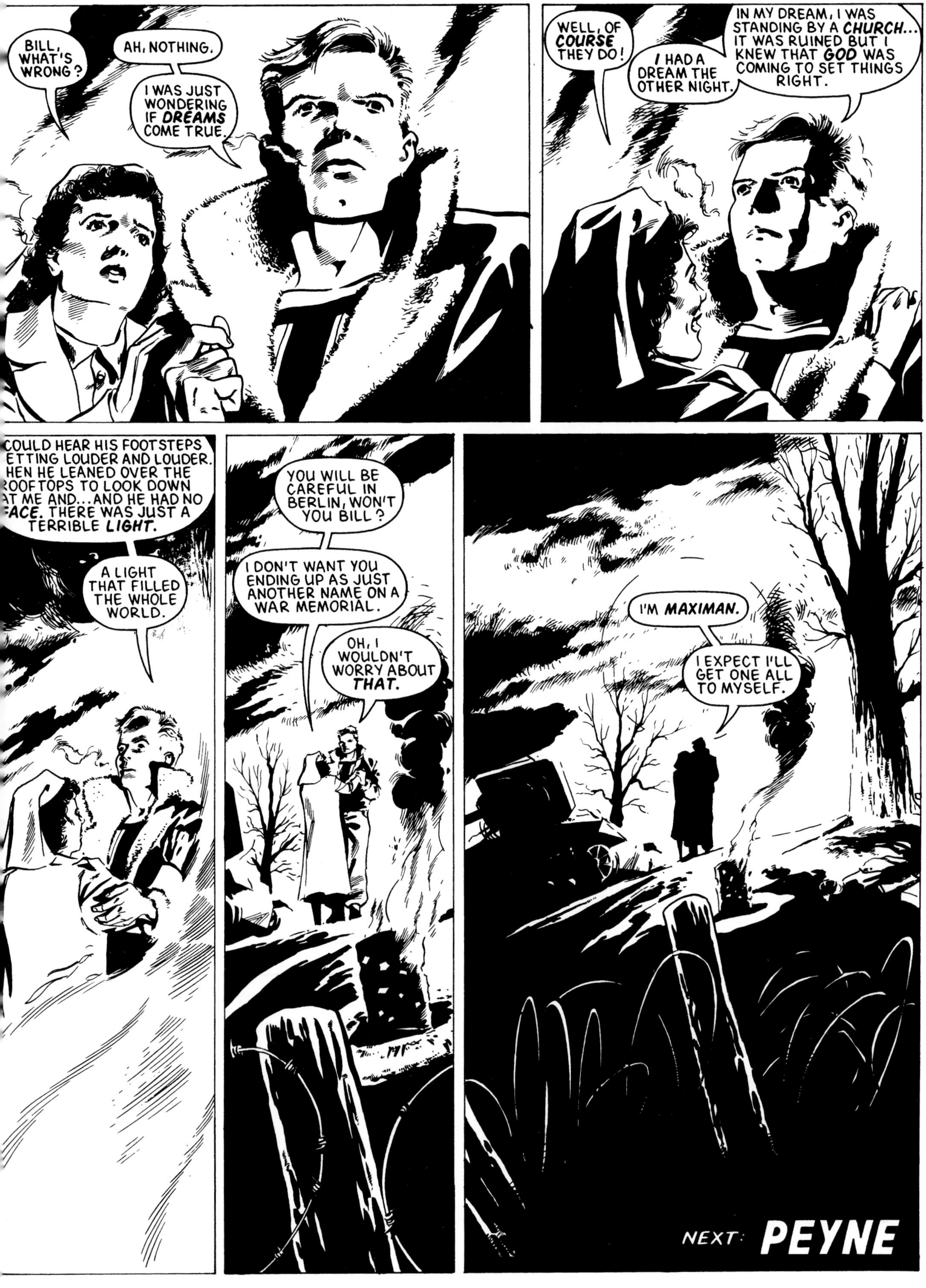

BILL, WHAT'S WRONG?
AH, NOTHING.
I WAS JUST WONDERING IF DREAMS COME TRUE.
WELL, OF COURSE THEY DO!
I HAD A DREAM THE OTHER NIGHT.
IN MY DREAM, I WAS STANDING BY A CHURCH... IT WAS RUINED BUT I KNEW THAT GOD WAS COMING TO SET THINGS RIGHT.
COULD HEAR HIS FOOTSTEPS ETTING LOUDER AND LOUDER. HEN HE LEANED OVER THE OOFTOPS TO LOOK DOWN AT ME AND... AND HE HAD NO FACE. THERE WAS JUST A TERRIBLE LIGHT.
A LIGHT THAT FILLED THE WHOLE WORLD.
YOU WILL BE CAREFUL IN BERLIN, WON'T YOU BILL?
I DON'T WANT YOU ENDING UP AS JUST ANOTHER NAME ON A WAR MEMORIAL.
OH, I WOULDN'T WORRY ABOUT THAT.
I'M MAXIMAN.
I EXPECT I'LL GET ONE ALL TO MYSELF.
NEXT: PEYNE

Extracts from *"SEIZING THE FIRE"*, by Dr MICHAEL PEYNE (Unpublished):

IN FEBRUARY **1945**, FOLLOWING THE SURRENDER OF **JAPAN**, A MEMORIAL SERVICE WAS HELD FOR **MAXIMAN**.

THE HYPOCRISY OF THE WHOLE SORRY CHARADE TURNED MY STOMACH.

CHURCHILL KNEW THE AMERICANS HAD DEVELOPED THE ATOM BOMB, KNEW THAT THEY PLANNED TO USE IT ON BERLIN.

AND STILL HE SENT MAXIMAN TO HIS DEATH — CONSIGNING AN **ANGEL** TO THE FIRES OF HELL.

I **HATED** MANKIND. I HATED OUR PETTINESS, OUR GREED, OUR IGNORANT CRUELTY.

I DREAMED OF A PURER WORLD.

AND I VOWED THEN AND THERE TO **BUILD** THAT WORLD.

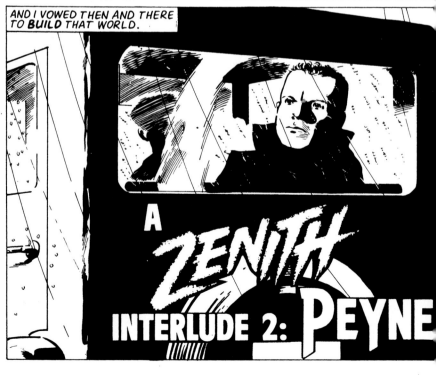

A **ZENITH**

INTERLUDE 2: **PEYNE**

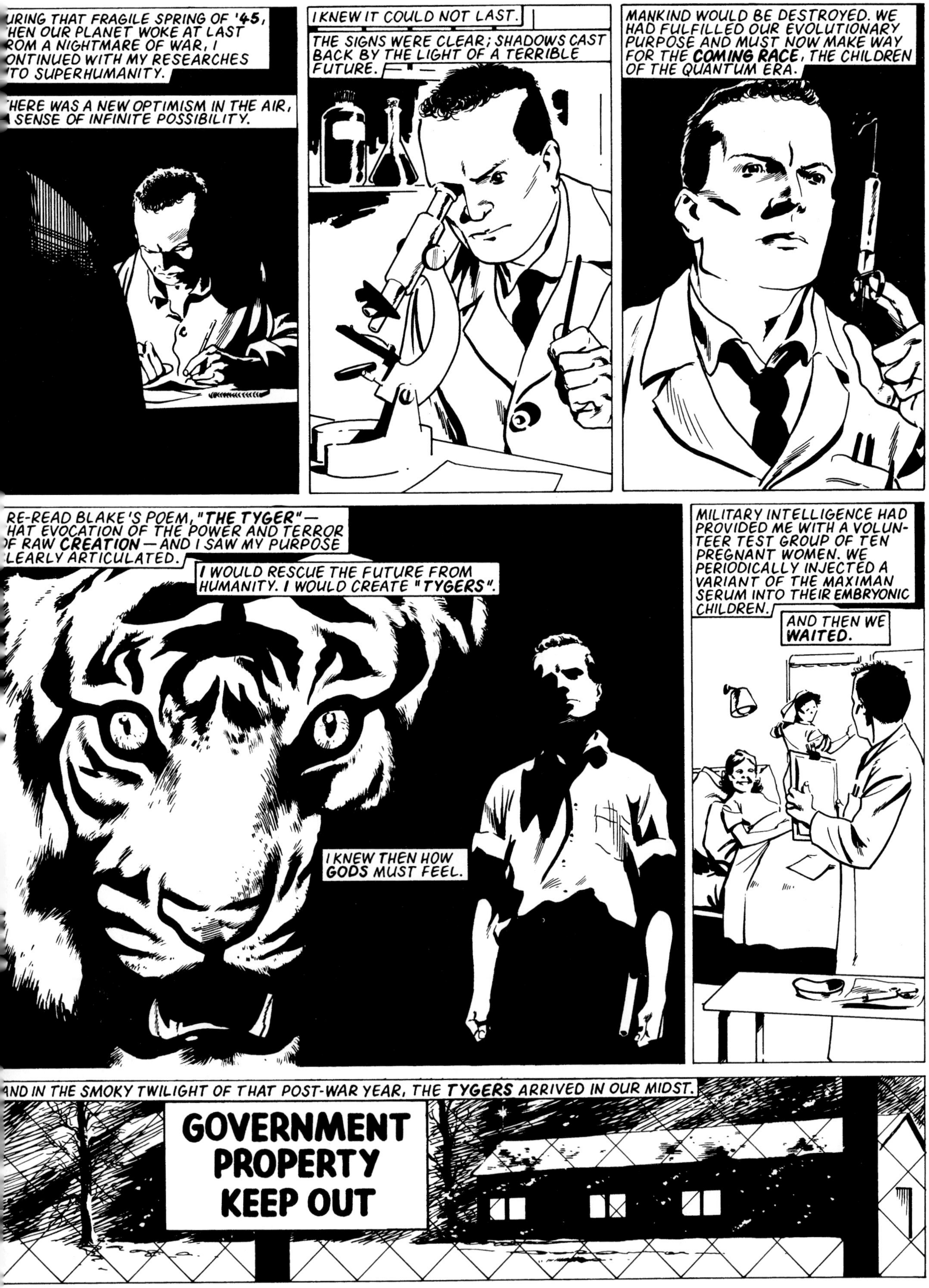
URING THAT FRAGILE SPRING OF '45, HEN OUR PLANET WOKE AT LAST ROM A NIGHTMARE OF WAR, I ONTINUED WITH MY RESEARCHES ITO SUPERHUMANITY.
THERE WAS A NEW OPTIMISM IN THE AIR, A SENSE OF INFINITE POSSIBILITY.
I KNEW IT COULD NOT LAST.
THE SIGNS WERE CLEAR; SHADOWS CAST BACK BY THE LIGHT OF A TERRIBLE FUTURE.
MANKIND WOULD BE DESTROYED. WE HAD FULFILLED OUR EVOLUTIONARY PURPOSE AND MUST NOW MAKE WAY FOR THE COMING RACE, THE CHILDREN OF THE QUANTUM ERA.
RE-READ BLAKE'S POEM, "THE TYGER"— HAT EVOCATION OF THE POWER AND TERROR OF RAW CREATION—AND I SAW MY PURPOSE LEARLY ARTICULATED.
I WOULD RESCUE THE FUTURE FROM HUMANITY. I WOULD CREATE "TYGERS".
I KNEW THEN HOW GODS MUST FEEL.
MILITARY INTELLIGENCE HAD PROVIDED ME WITH A VOLUNTEER TEST GROUP OF TEN PREGNANT WOMEN. WE PERIODICALLY INJECTED A VARIANT OF THE MAXIMAN SERUM INTO THEIR EMBRYONIC CHILDREN.
AND THEN WE WAITED.
AND IN THE SMOKY TWILIGHT OF THAT POST-WAR YEAR, THE TYGERS ARRIVED IN OUR MIDST.
GOVERNMENT PROPERTY KEEP OUT

THE FIRST TWO, FOX AND RIDGEWAY, WERE GIRLS.

THE THIRD, A SEXLESS ABOMINATION, WAS MERCIFULLY STILLBORN.

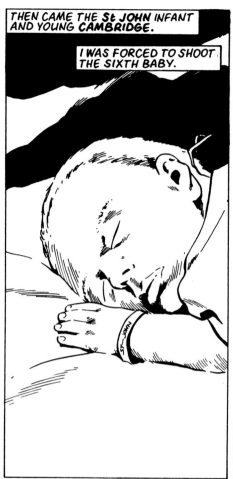

THEN CAME THE St JOHN INFANT AND YOUNG CAMBRIDGE.

I WAS FORCED TO SHOOT THE SIXTH BABY.

IT WAS AN APPALLING, SKINLESS CREATURE WITH A DOZEN MOUTHS THAT WHIMPERED AND BIT THE MIDWIVES.

NERVOUSLY, WE AWAITE THE NEXT FOUR BIRTHS

RHYS, McDOWELL AND MOON ARRIVED IN PINK AND PERFECT HEALTH.

AND THEN THE FINAL CHILD EXPLODED INTO THE WORLD.

I CAN STILL REMEMBER THE FEAR THAT TOOK ME WHEN IT ROSE UP IN A STORM OF SHAPES, SPEAKING IN TONGUES.

GOD KNOWS I TRIED TO KILL IT BUT IT SIMPLY WOULD NOT DIE.

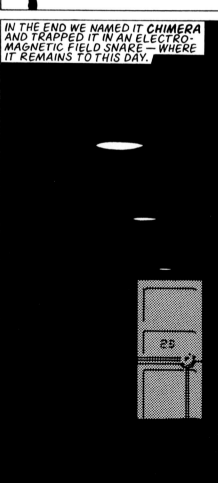

IN THE END WE NAMED IT CHIMERA AND TRAPPED IT IN AN ELECTRO-MAGNETIC FIELD SNARE — WHERE IT REMAINS TO THIS DAY.

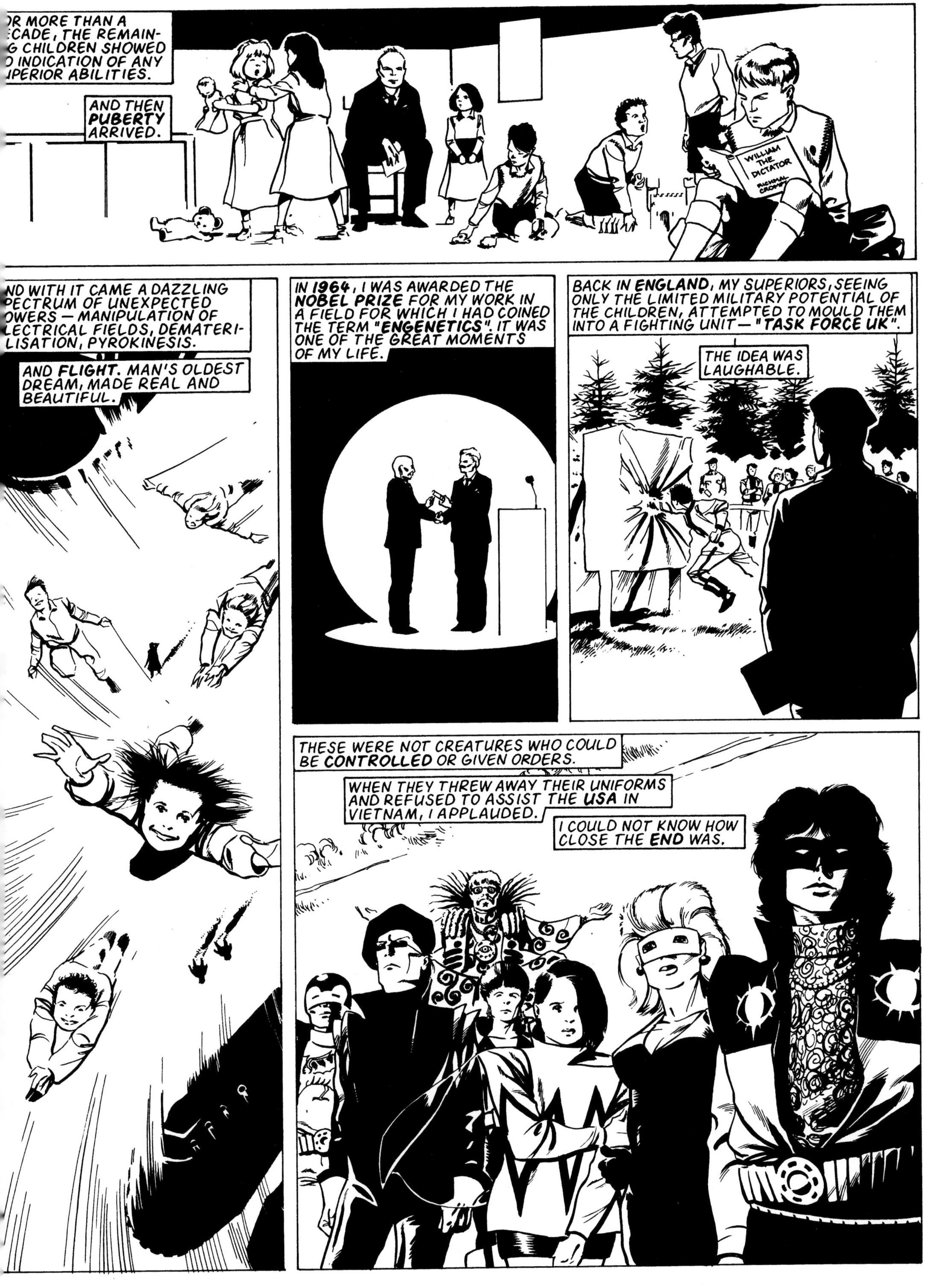

OR MORE THAN A DECADE, THE REMAINING CHILDREN SHOWED NO INDICATION OF ANY SUPERIOR ABILITIES.
AND THEN PUBERTY ARRIVED.
WILLIAM THE DICTATOR
ND WITH IT CAME A DAZZLING SPECTRUM OF UNEXPECTED POWERS — MANIPULATION OF ELECTRICAL FIELDS, DEMATERIALISATION, PYROKINESIS.
AND FLIGHT. MAN'S OLDEST DREAM, MADE REAL AND BEAUTIFUL.
IN 1964, I WAS AWARDED THE NOBEL PRIZE FOR MY WORK IN A FIELD FOR WHICH I HAD COINED THE TERM "ENGENETICS". IT WAS ONE OF THE GREAT MOMENTS OF MY LIFE.
BACK IN ENGLAND, MY SUPERIORS, SEEING ONLY THE LIMITED MILITARY POTENTIAL OF THE CHILDREN, ATTEMPTED TO MOULD THEM INTO A FIGHTING UNIT — "TASK FORCE UK".
THE IDEA WAS LAUGHABLE.
THESE WERE NOT CREATURES WHO COULD BE CONTROLLED OR GIVEN ORDERS.
WHEN THEY THREW AWAY THEIR UNIFORMS AND REFUSED TO ASSIST THE USA IN VIETNAM, I APPLAUDED.
I COULD NOT KNOW HOW CLOSE THE END WAS.

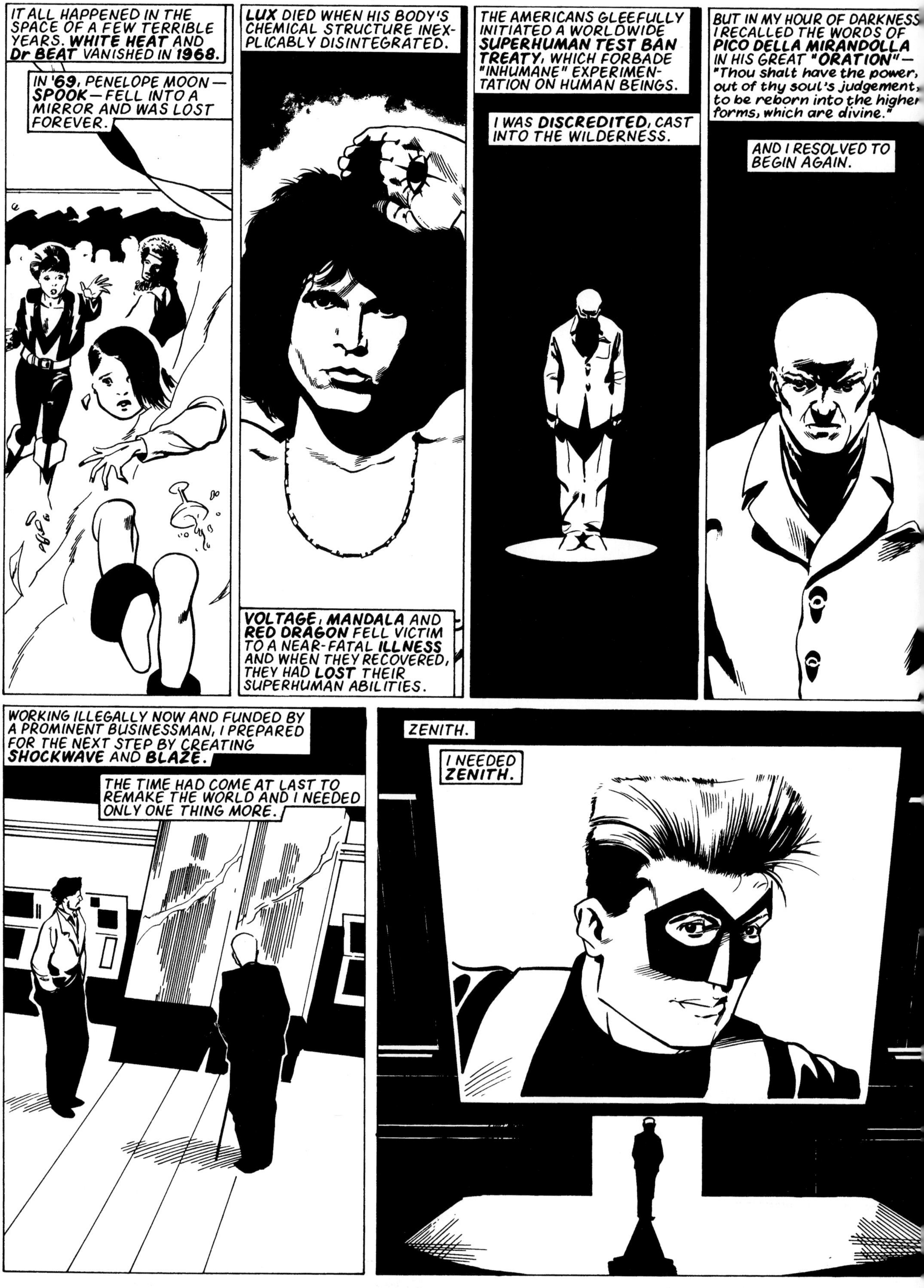

IT ALL HAPPENED IN THE SPACE OF A FEW TERRIBLE YEARS. WHITE HEAT AND Dr BEAT VANISHED IN 1968.
IN '69, PENELOPE MOON — SPOOK — FELL INTO A MIRROR AND WAS LOST FOREVER.
LUX DIED WHEN HIS BODY'S CHEMICAL STRUCTURE INEXPLICABLY DISINTEGRATED.
VOLTAGE, MANDALA AND RED DRAGON FELL VICTIM TO A NEAR-FATAL ILLNESS AND WHEN THEY RECOVERED, THEY HAD LOST THEIR SUPERHUMAN ABILITIES.
THE AMERICANS GLEEFULLY INITIATED A WORLDWIDE SUPERHUMAN TEST BAN TREATY, WHICH FORBADE "INHUMANE" EXPERIMENTATION ON HUMAN BEINGS.
I WAS DISCREDITED, CAST INTO THE WILDERNESS.
BUT IN MY HOUR OF DARKNESS I RECALLED THE WORDS OF PICO DELLA MIRANDOLLA IN HIS GREAT "ORATION" — "Thou shalt have the power, out of thy soul's judgement, to be reborn into the higher forms, which are divine."
AND I RESOLVED TO BEGIN AGAIN.
WORKING ILLEGALLY NOW AND FUNDED BY A PROMINENT BUSINESSMAN, I PREPARED FOR THE NEXT STEP BY CREATING SHOCKWAVE AND BLAZE.
THE TIME HAD COME AT LAST TO REMAKE THE WORLD AND I NEEDED ONLY ONE THING MORE.
ZENITH.
I NEEDED ZENITH.

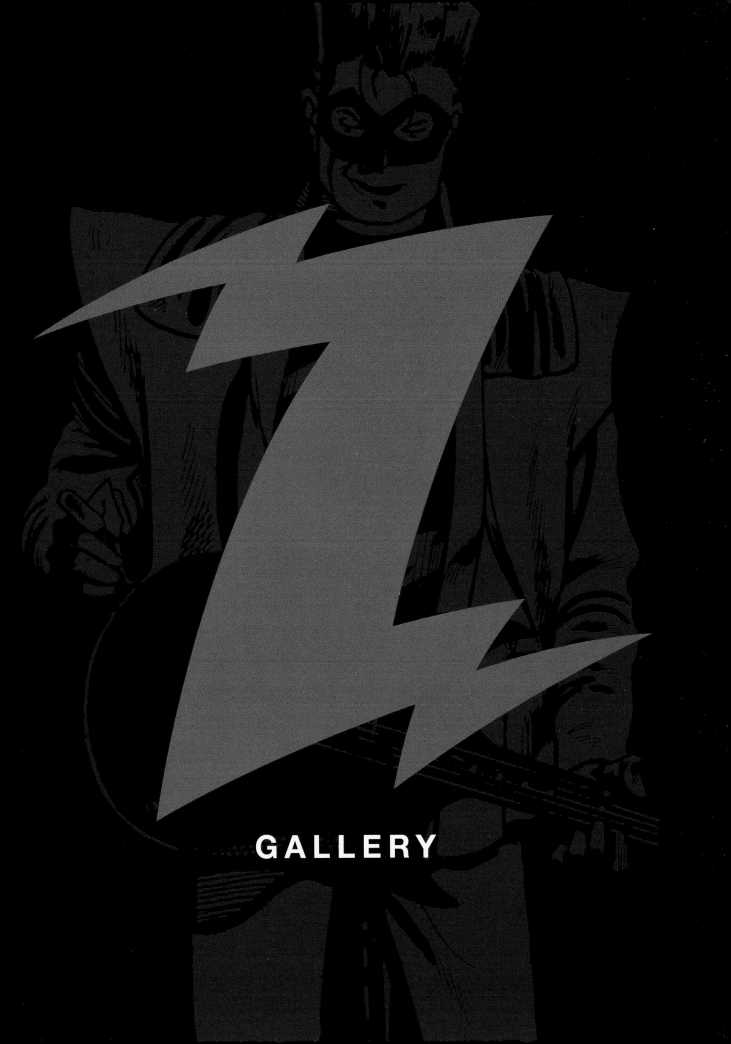

GALLERY

2000 AD Prog 535: Cover by **Steve Dillon**

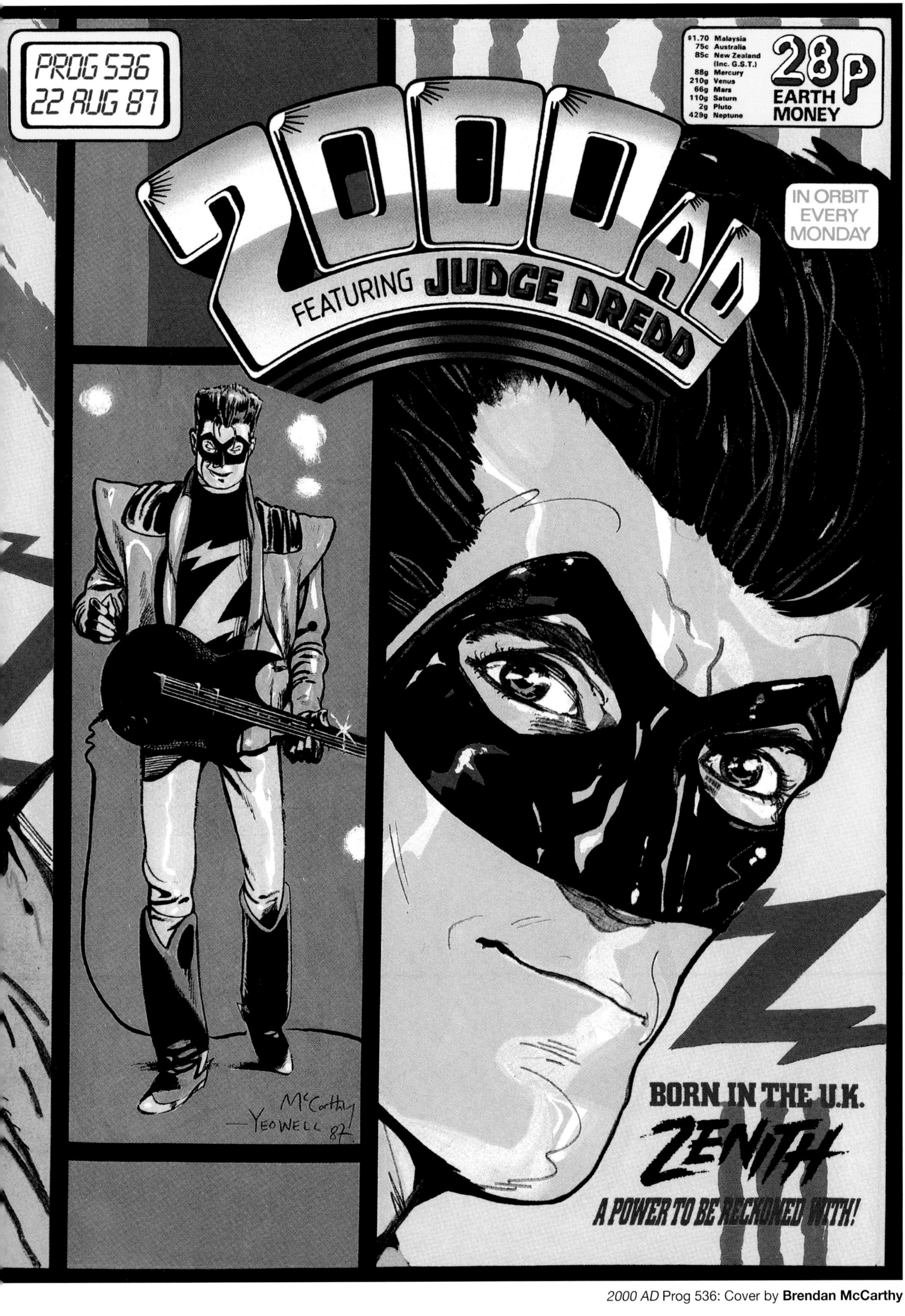
PROG 536
22 AUG 87
$1.70 Malaysia
75c Australia
85c New Zealand (Inc. G.S.T.)
88g Mercury
210g Venus
66g Mars
110g Saturn
2g Pluto
429g Neptune
28p
EARTH MONEY
2000 AD
FEATURING JUDGE DREDD
IN ORBIT EVERY MONDAY
McCarthy
Yeowell 87
BORN IN THE U.K.
ZENITH
A POWER TO BE RECKONED WITH!

2000 AD Prog 536: Cover by **Brendan McCarthy**

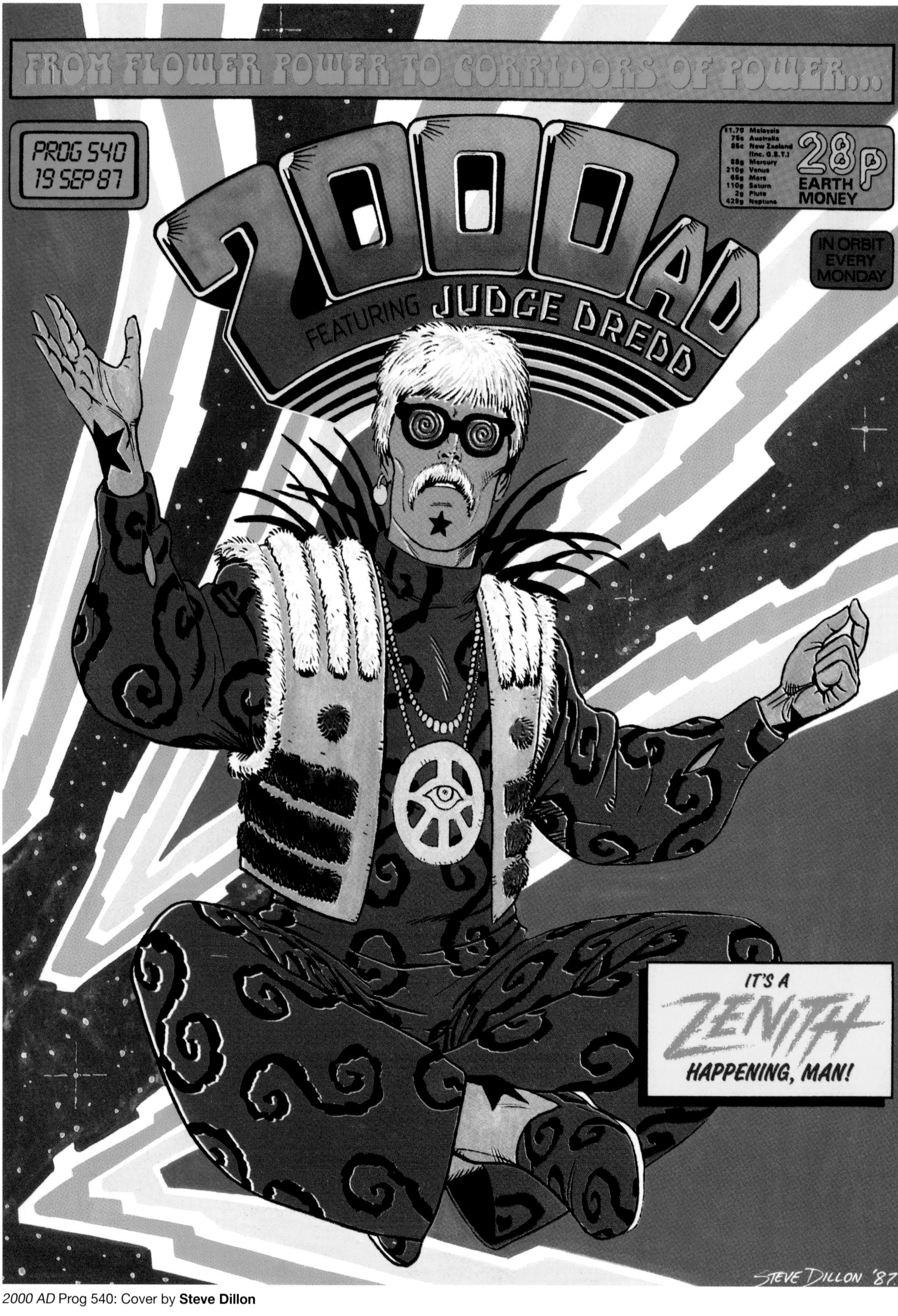
FROM FLOWER POWER TO CORRIDORS OF POWER...
PROG 540
19 SEP 87
2000 AD
FEATURING JUDGE DREDD
28p
EARTH MONEY
IN ORBIT EVERY MONDAY
IT'S A
ZENITH
HAPPENING, MAN!
STEVE DILLON '87.

2000 AD Prog 540: Cover by **Steve Dillon**

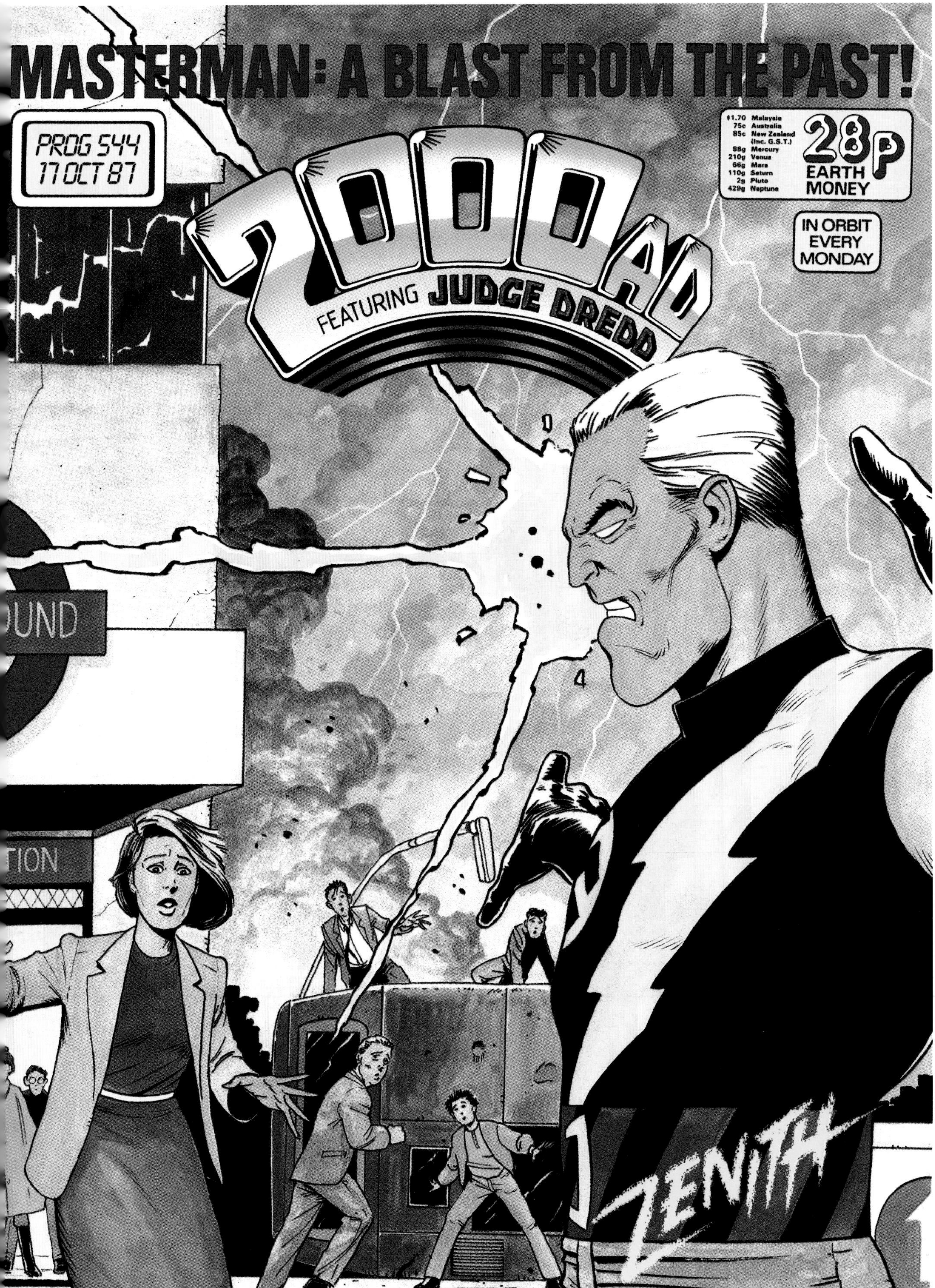
MASTERMAN: A BLAST FROM THE PAST!
PROG 544
17 OCT 87
2000 AD
FEATURING JUDGE DREDD
$1.70 Malaysia
75c Australia
85c New Zealand (inc. G.S.T.)
88g Mercury
210g Venus
66g Mars
110g Saturn
2g Pluto
429g Neptune
28p
EARTH MONEY
IN ORBIT EVERY MONDAY
UND
TION
ZENITH

2000 AD Prog 544: Cover by **Steve Dillon**

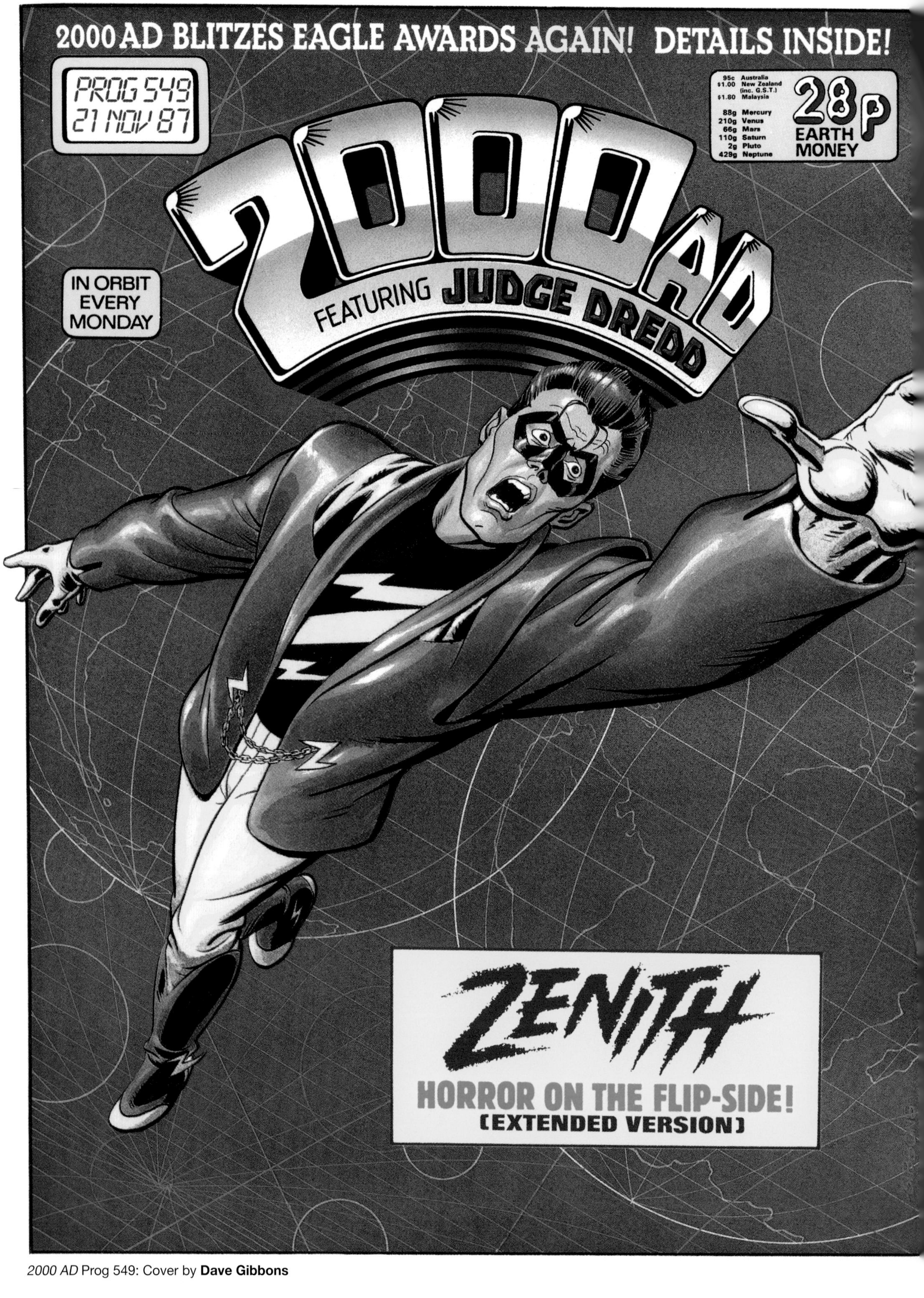

2000 AD BLITZES EAGLE AWARDS AGAIN! DETAILS INSIDE!
PROG 549
21 NOV 87
95c Australia
$1.00 New Zealand (inc. G.S.T.)
$1.80 Malaysia
88g Mercury
210g Venus
66g Mars
110g Saturn
2g Pluto
429g Neptune
28p
EARTH MONEY
2000 AD
FEATURING JUDGE DREDD
IN ORBIT EVERY MONDAY
ZENITH
HORROR ON THE FLIP-SIDE!
[EXTENDED VERSION]

2000 AD Prog 549: Cover by **Dave Gibbons**

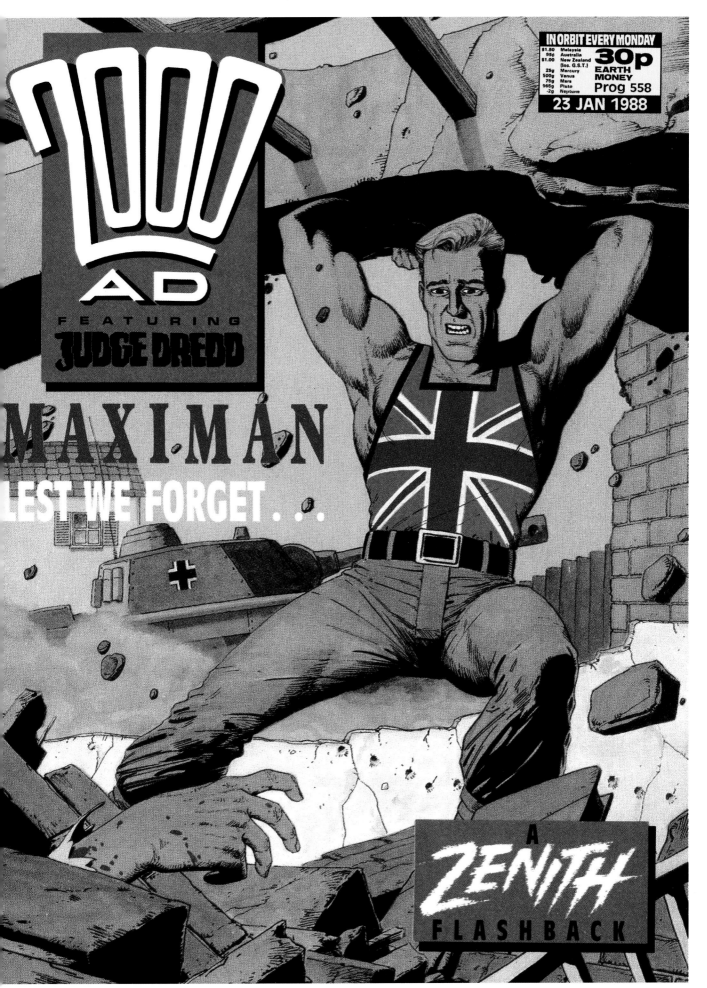

IN ORBIT EVERY MONDAY

$1.80 Malaysia
95c Australia
$1.00 New Zealand
(Inc. G.S.T.)
25g Mercury
500g Venus
75g Mars
965g Pluto
-2g Neptune

30p
EARTH
MONEY
Prog 558
23 JAN 1988

2000 AD
AD
FEATURING
Judge Dredd

MAXIMAN

LEST WE FORGET. . .

A
ZENITH
FLASHBACK

2000 AD Prog 558: Cover by **Steve Dillon**

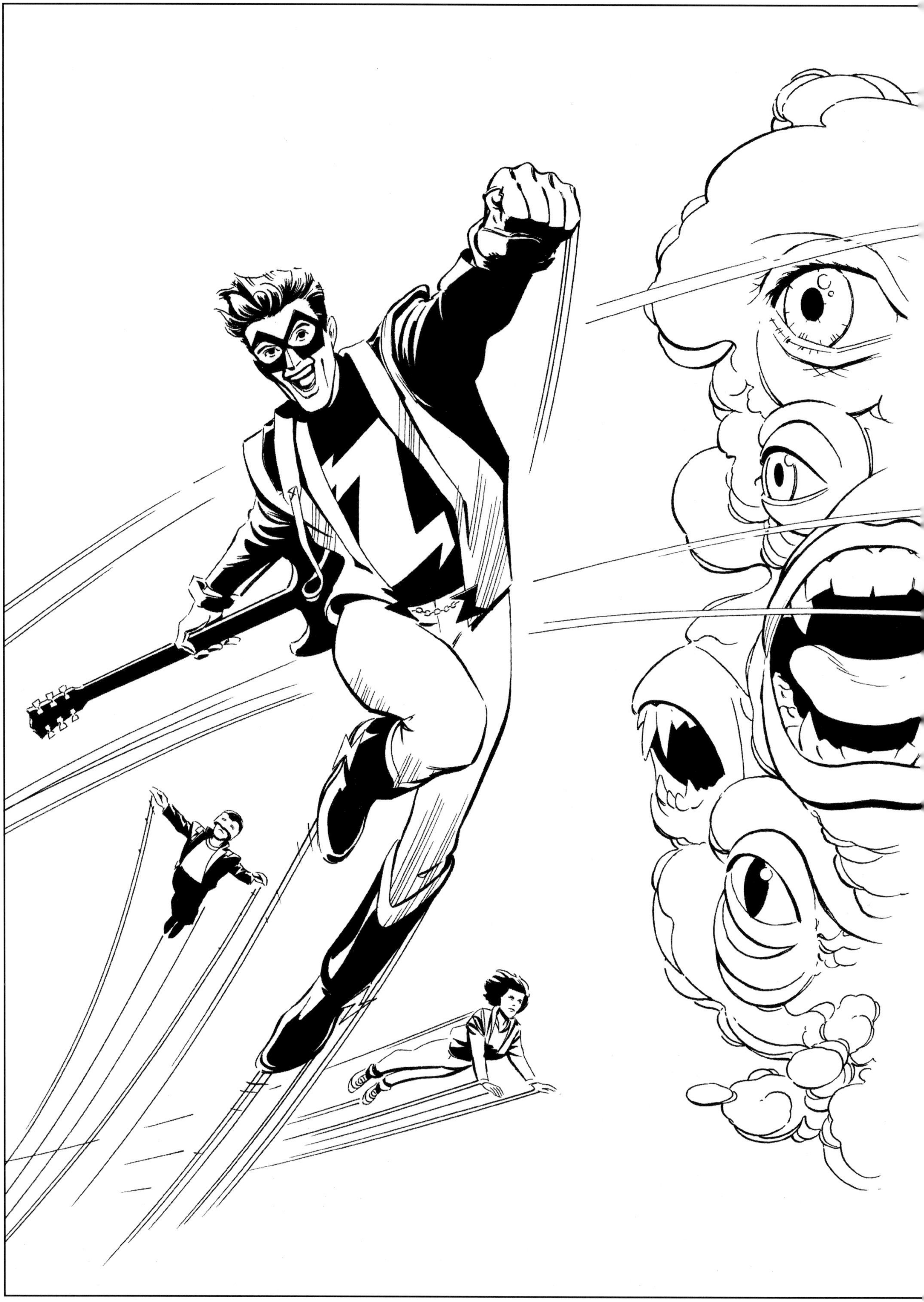

Zenith Phase 1: Cover by **Steve Yeowell**

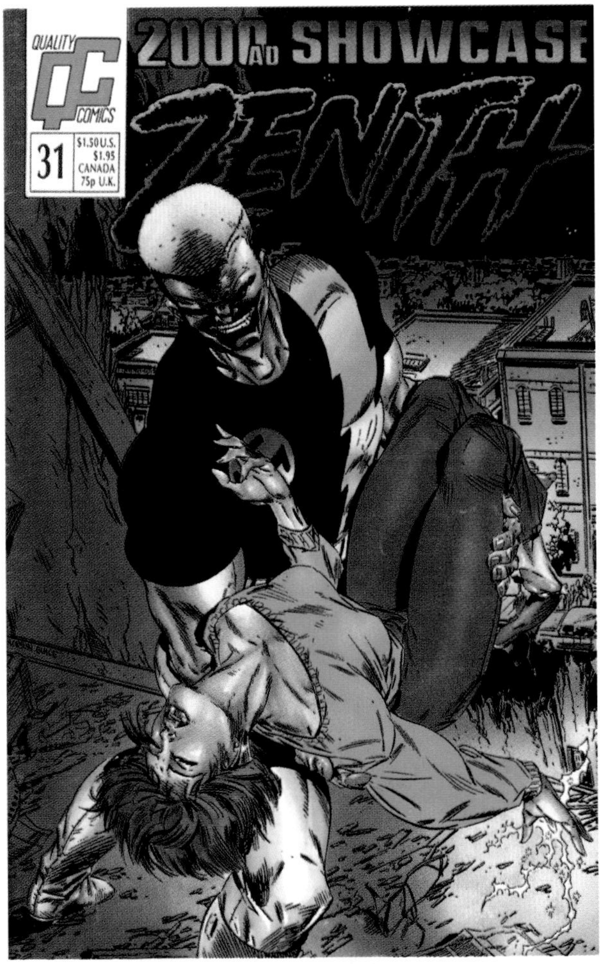
2000 AD SHOWCASE
QUALITY
COMICS
31
$1.50 U.S.
$1.95
CANADA
75p U.K.
ZENITH

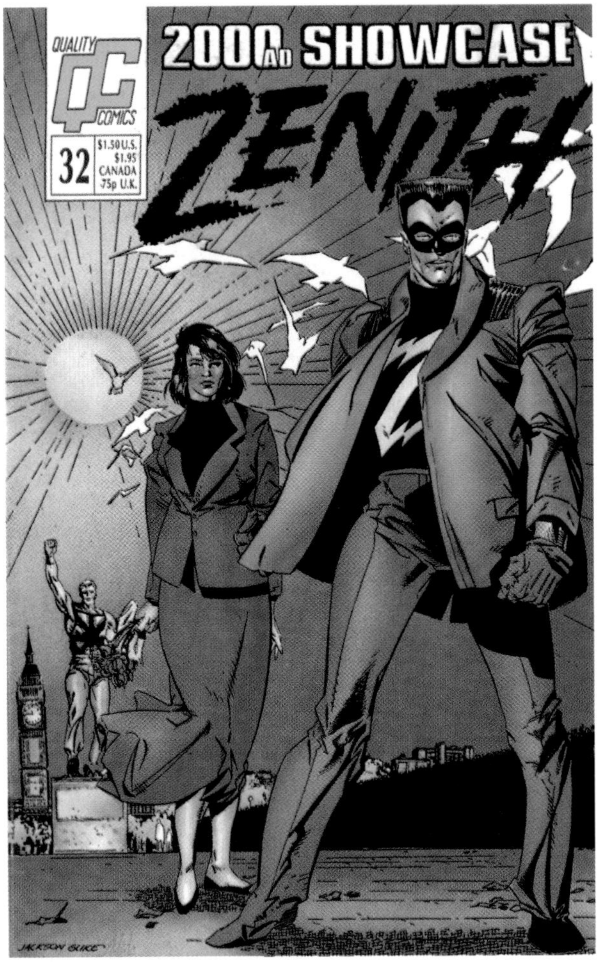
2000 AD SHOWCASE
QUALITY
COMICS
32
$1.50 U.S.
$1.95
CANADA
75p U.K.
ZENITH
JACKSON GUICE

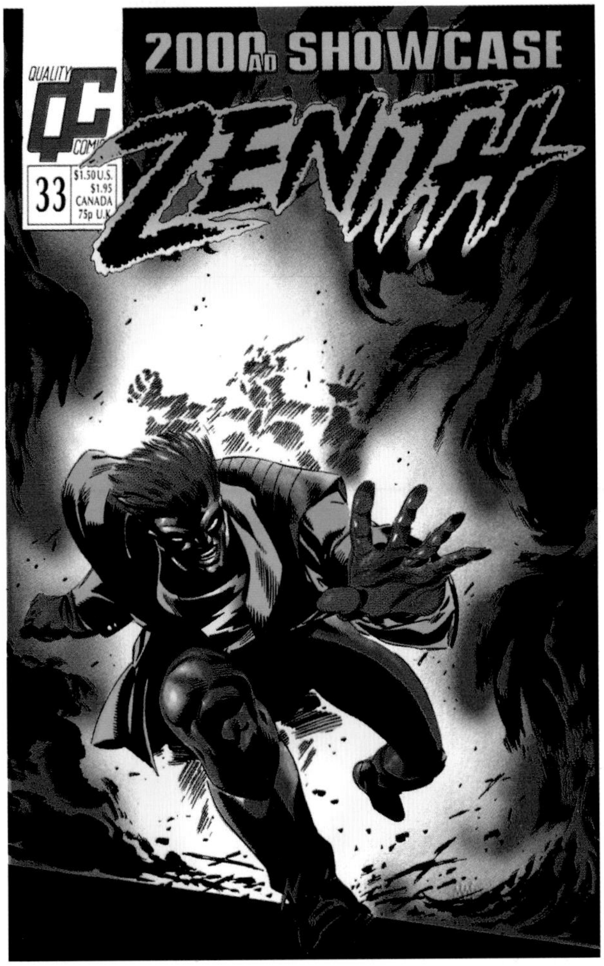
2000 AD SHOWCASE
QUALITY
COMICS
33
$1.50 U.S.
$1.95
CANADA
75p U.K.
ZENITH

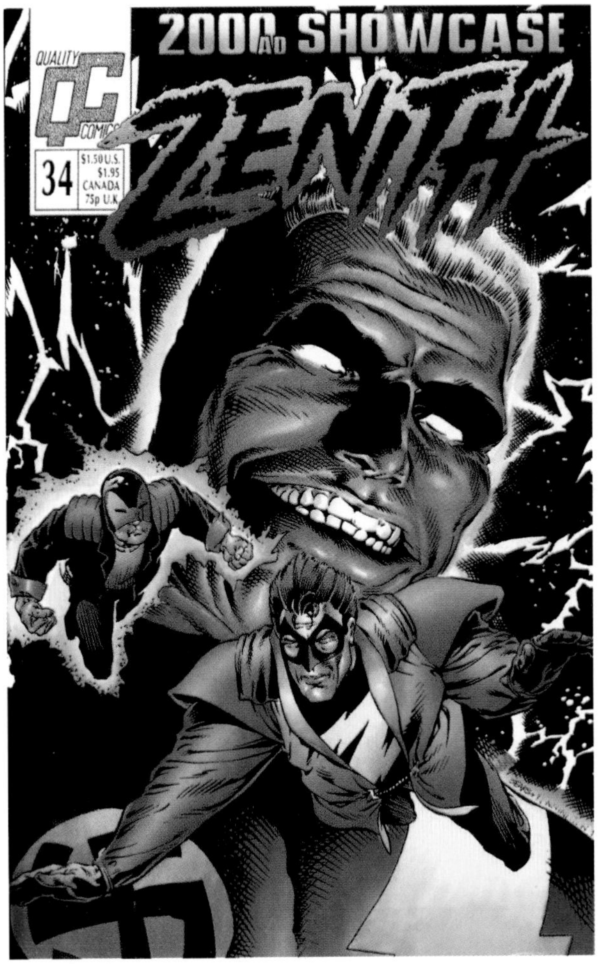
2000 AD SHOWCASE
QUALITY
COMICS
34
$1.50 U.S.
$1.95
CANADA
75p U.K.
ZENITH

Quality Comics Covers

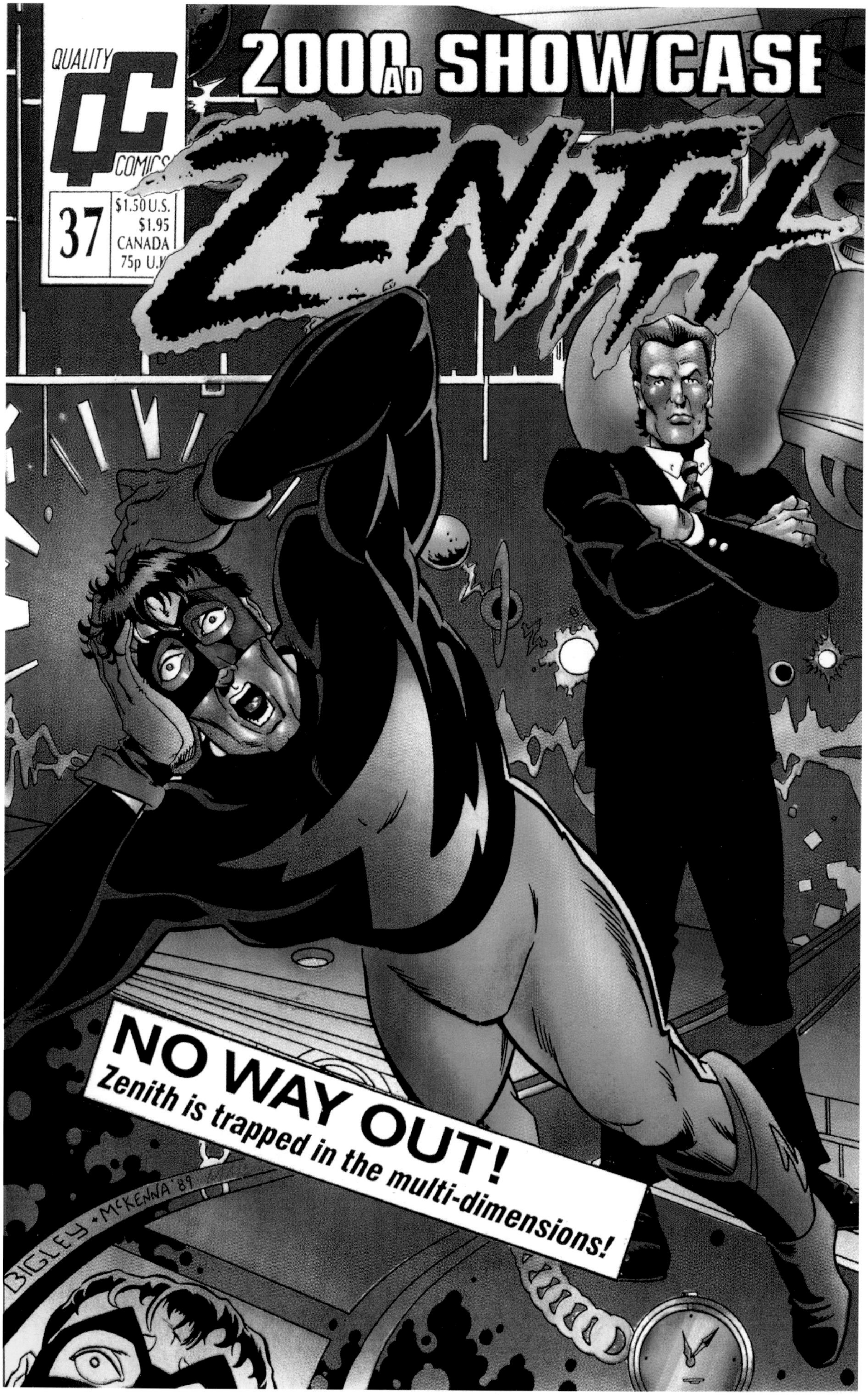
QUALITY
QC
COMICS
37
$1.50 U.S.
$1.95
CANADA
75p U.K.
2000 AD SHOWCASE
ZENITH
NO WAY OUT!
Zenith is trapped in the multi-dimensions!
BIGLEY • McKENNA '89

Quality Comics 37

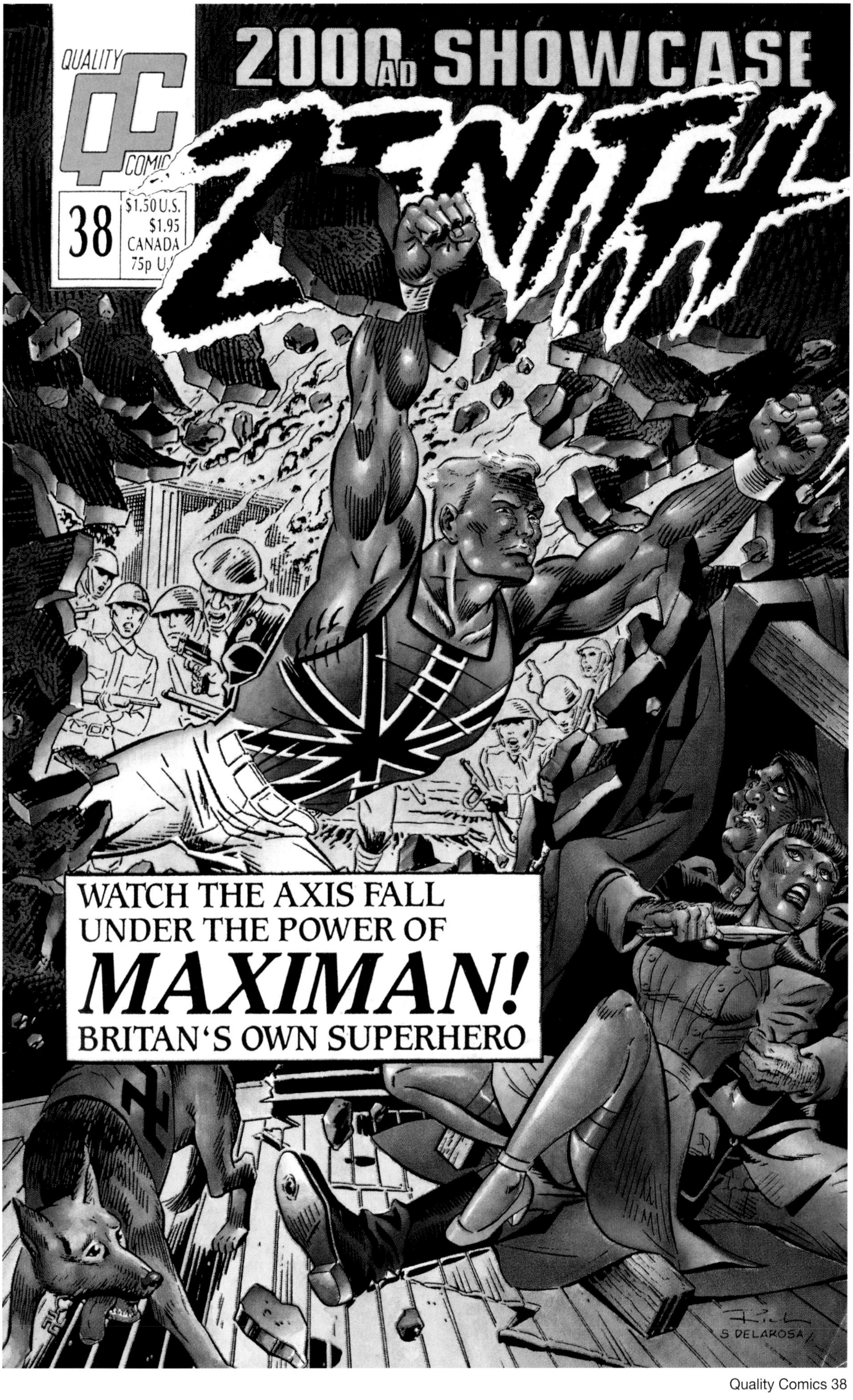
QUALITY
QC
COMICS
38
$1.50 U.S.
$1.95
CANADA
75p U.K.
2000 AD SHOWCASE
ZENITH
WATCH THE AXIS FALL
UNDER THE POWER OF
MAXIMAN!
BRITAN'S OWN SUPERHERO
S DELAROSA

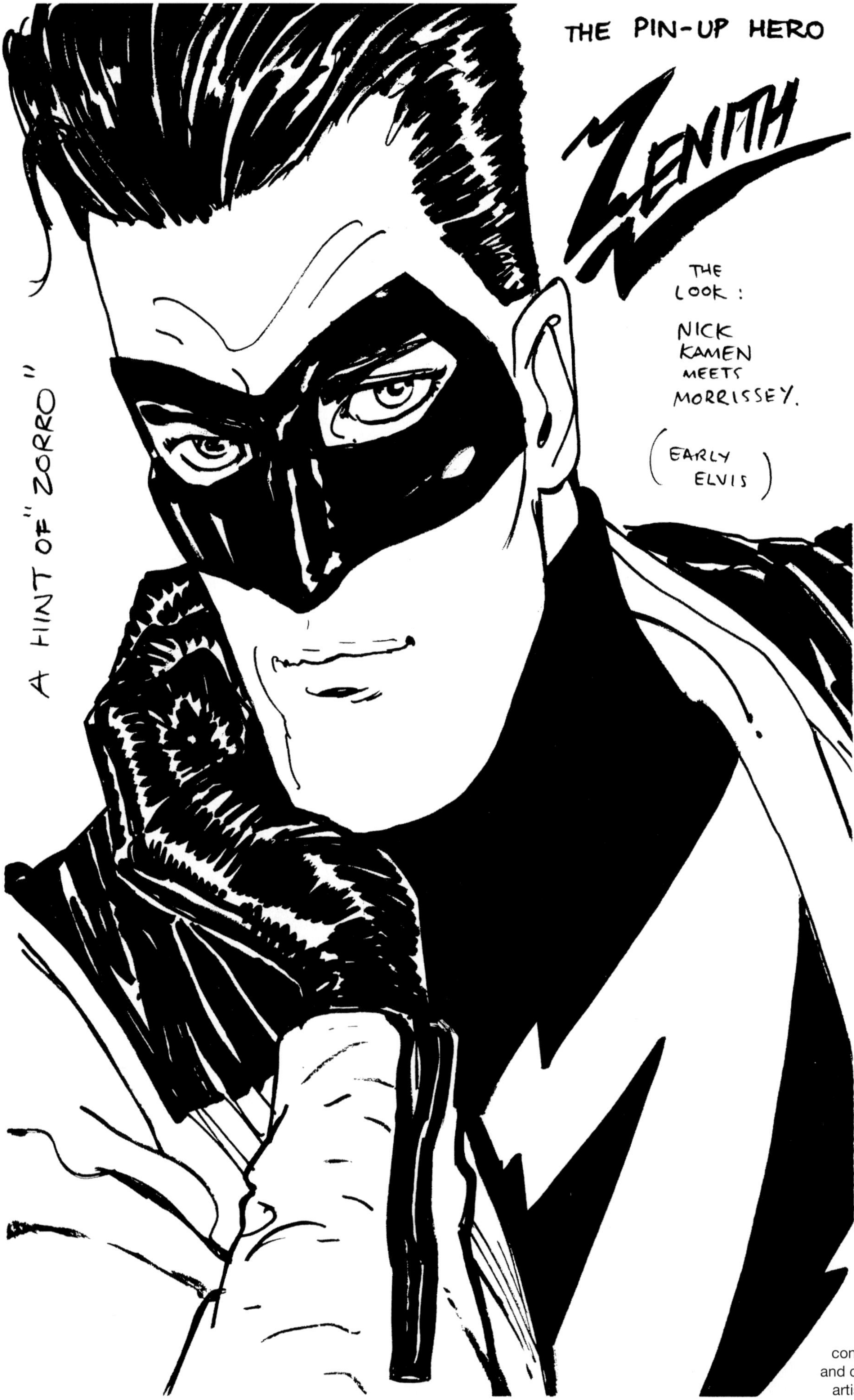
THE PIN-UP HERO
ZENITH
THE LOOK :
NICK KAMEN MEETS MORRISSEY.
(EARLY ELVIS)
A HINT OF "ZORRO"

The following 5 page
contain concept sketche
and character designs fro
artist **Brendan McCarth**

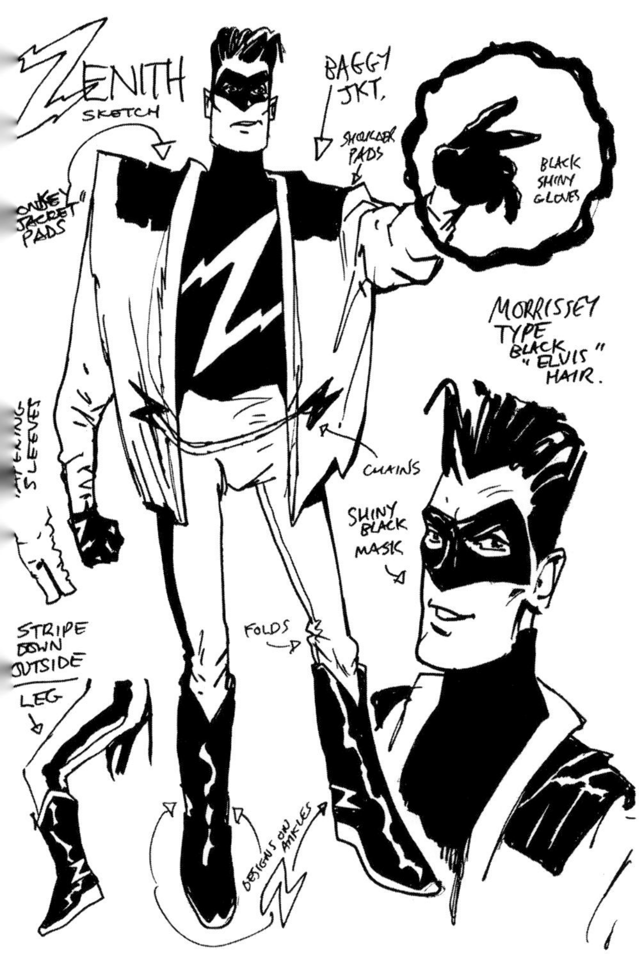
ZENITH
SKETCH
BAGGY JKT.
SHOULDER PADS
BLACK SHINY GLOVES
JACKET PADS
MORRISSEY TYPE BLACK "ELVIS" HAIR.
SLEEVES
CHAINS
SHINY BLACK MASK
STRIPE DOWN OUTSIDE LEG
FOLDS
DESIGNS ON ANKLES

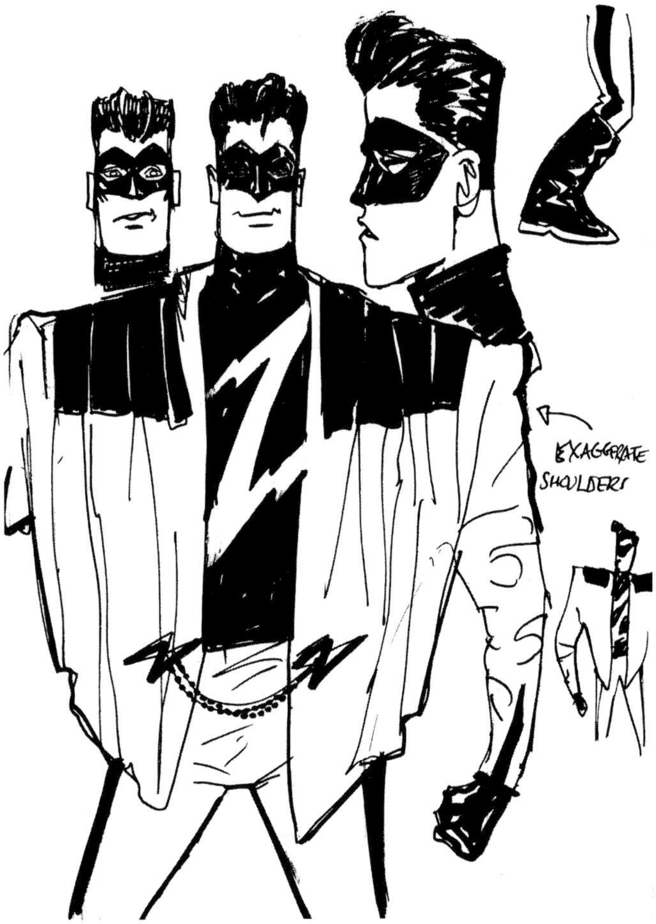
EXAGGERATE SHOULDERS

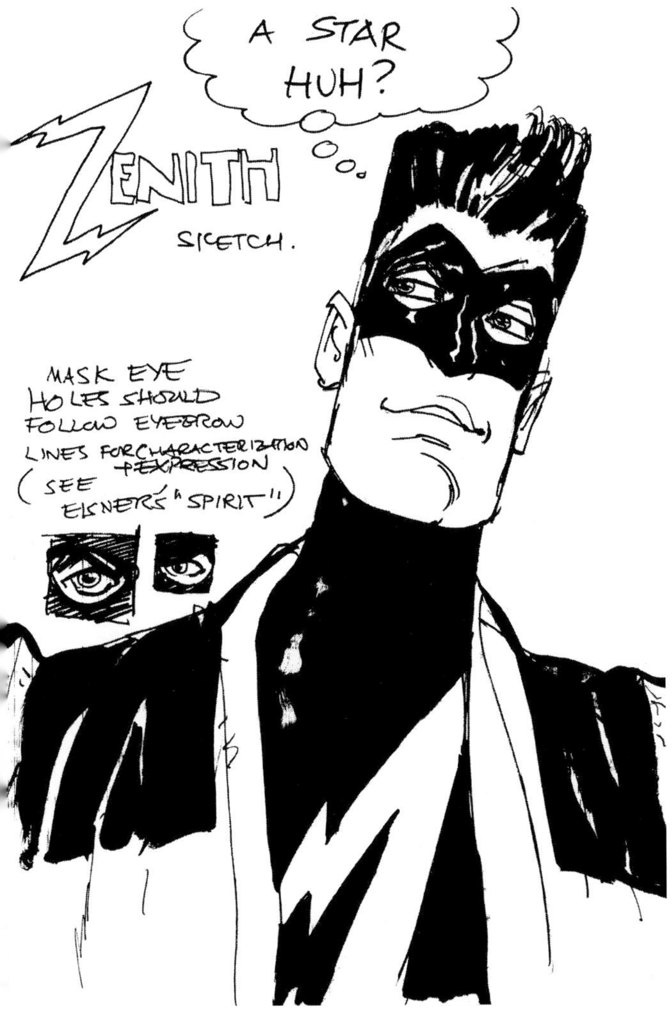
A STAR HUH?
ZENITH
SKETCH.
MASK EYE HOLES SHOULD FOLLOW EYEBROW LINES FOR CHARACTERIZATION + EXPRESSION (SEE EISNER'S "SPIRIT")

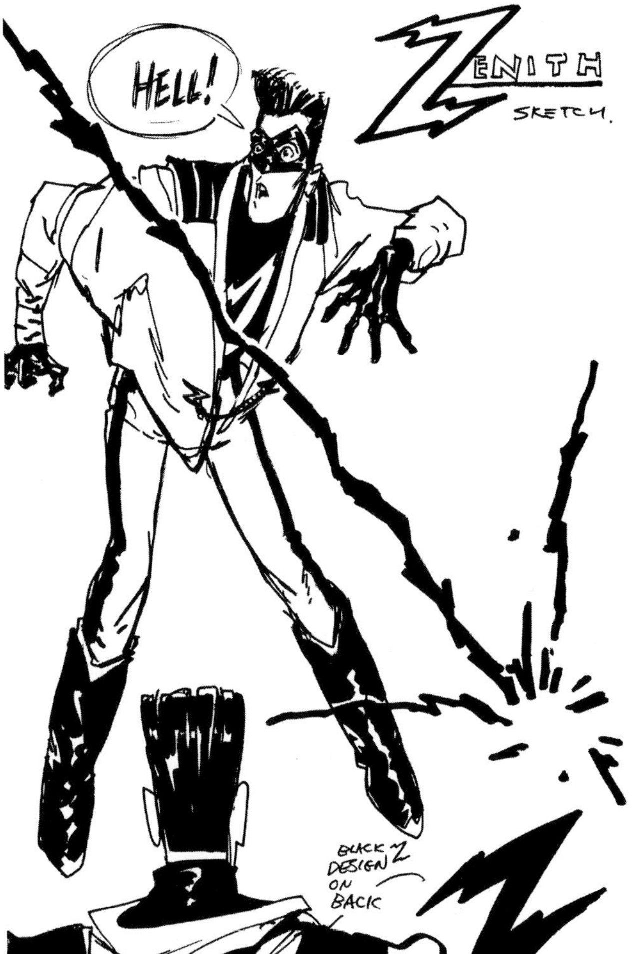
HELL!
ZENITH
SKETCH.
BLACK Z DESIGN ON BACK

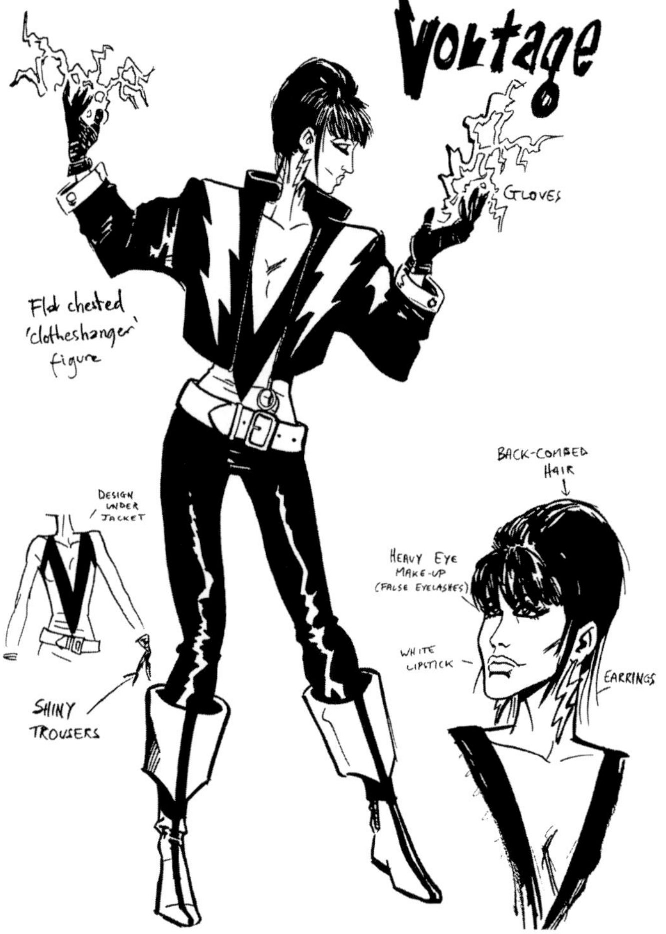
Voltage
GLOVES
Flat chested
'clotheshanger'
figure
DESIGN UNDER JACKET
SHINY TROUSERS
BACK-COMBED HAIR
HEAVY EYE MAKE-UP (FALSE EYELASHES)
WHITE LIPSTICK
EARRINGS

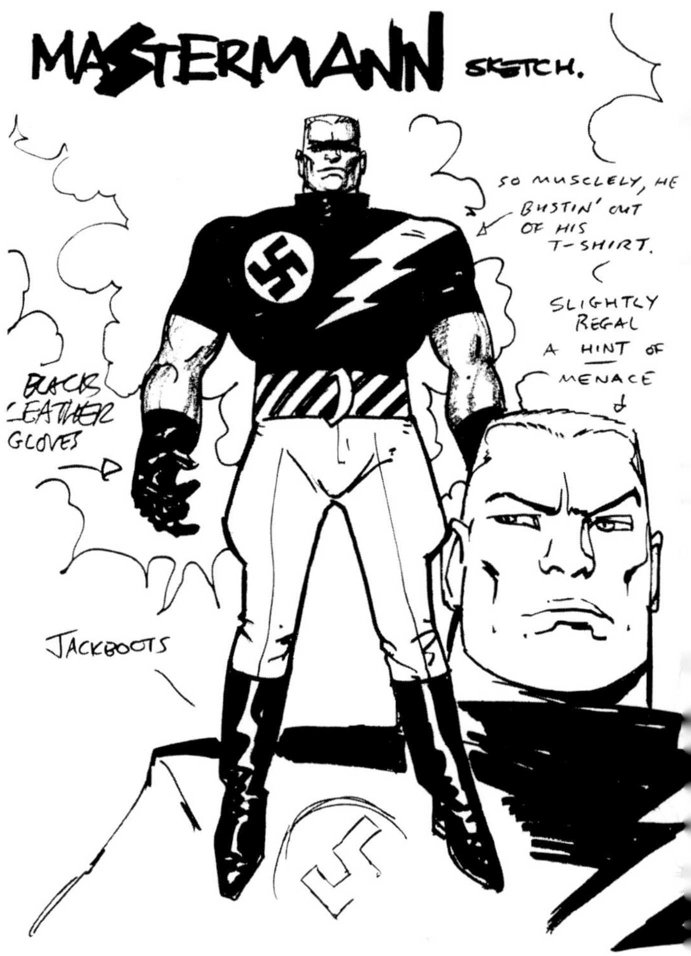
MASTERMANN SKETCH.
SO MUSCLELY, HE BUSTIN' OUT OF HIS T-SHIRT.
SLIGHTLY REGAL
A HINT OF MENACE
BLACK LEATHER GLOVES
JACKBOOTS

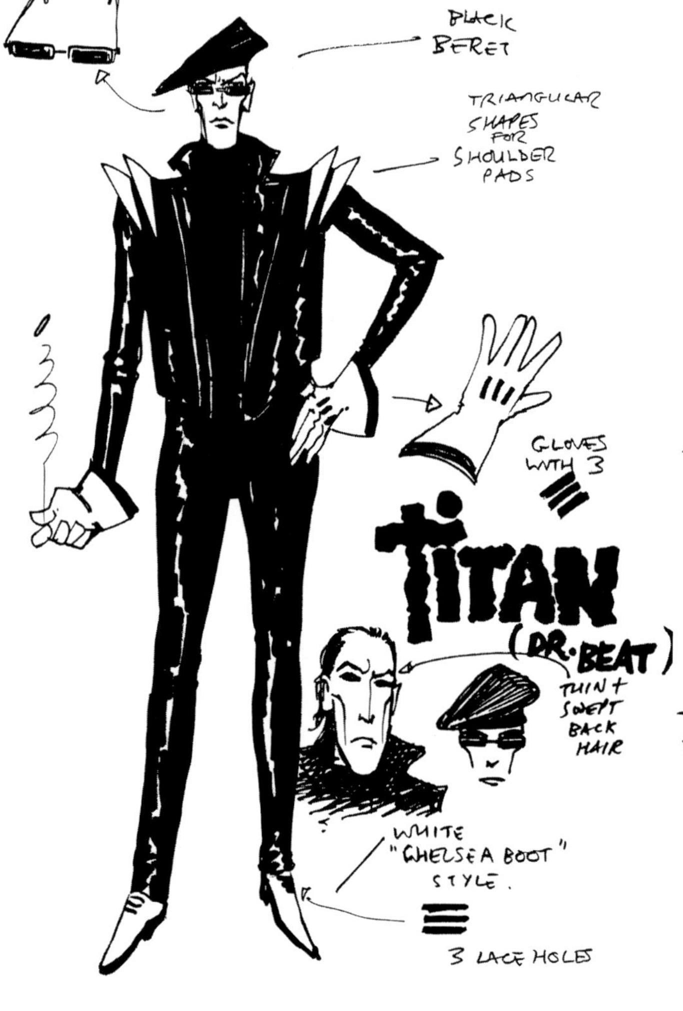
BLACK BERET
TRIANGULAR SHAPES FOR SHOULDER PADS
GLOVES WITH 3
TITAN
(DR. BEAT)
THIN + SWEPT BACK HAIR
WHITE "CHELSEA BOOT" STYLE.
3 LACE HOLES

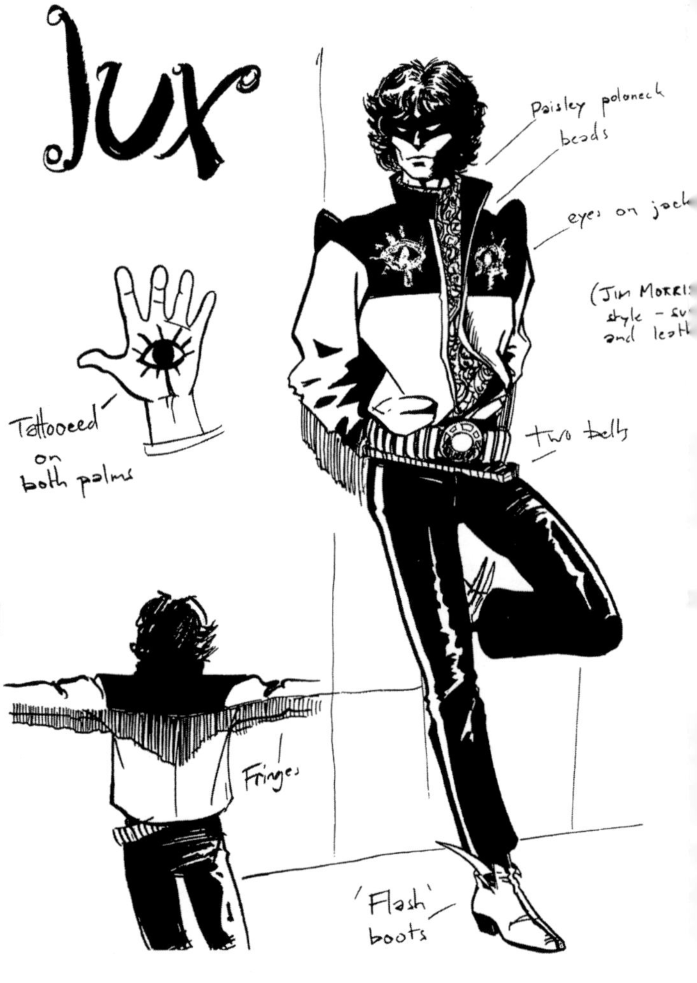
JUX
Paisley poloneck
beads
eyes on jack
(JIM MORRIS
style – su
and leath
Tattooed on both palms
Two belts
Fringes
'Flash' boots

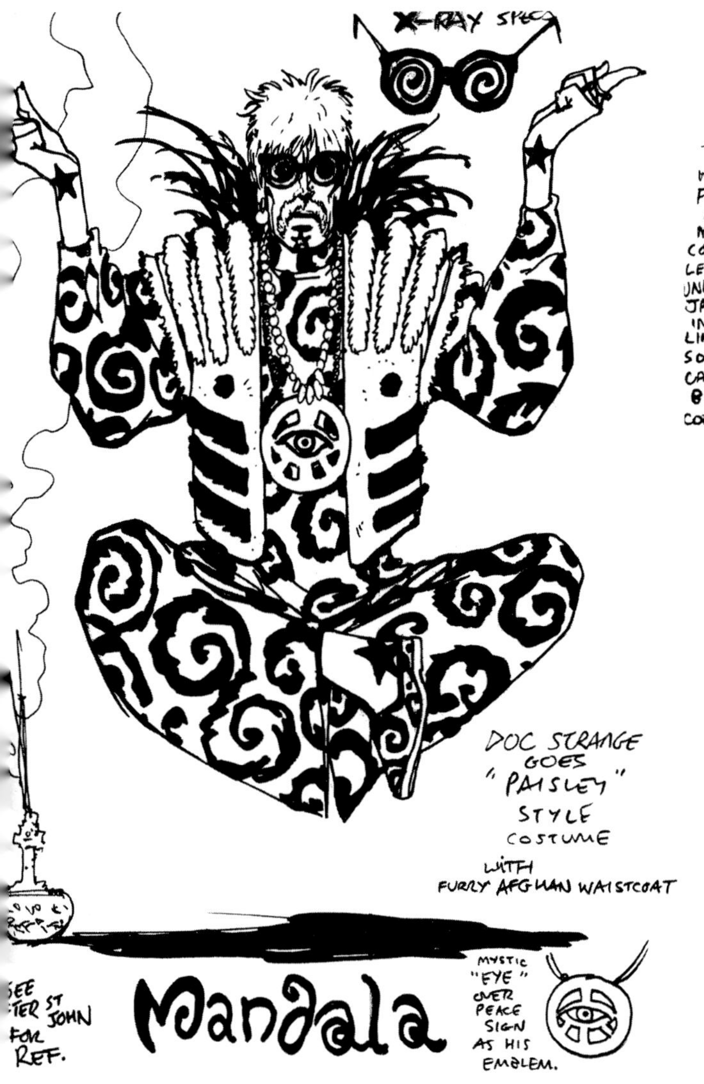
X-RAY SPECS
DOC STRANGE GOES "PAISLEY" STYLE COSTUME
WITH FURRY AFGHAN WAISTCOAT
Mandala
SEE TER ST JOHN FOR REF.
MYSTIC "EYE" OVER PEACE SIGN AS HIS EMBLEM.

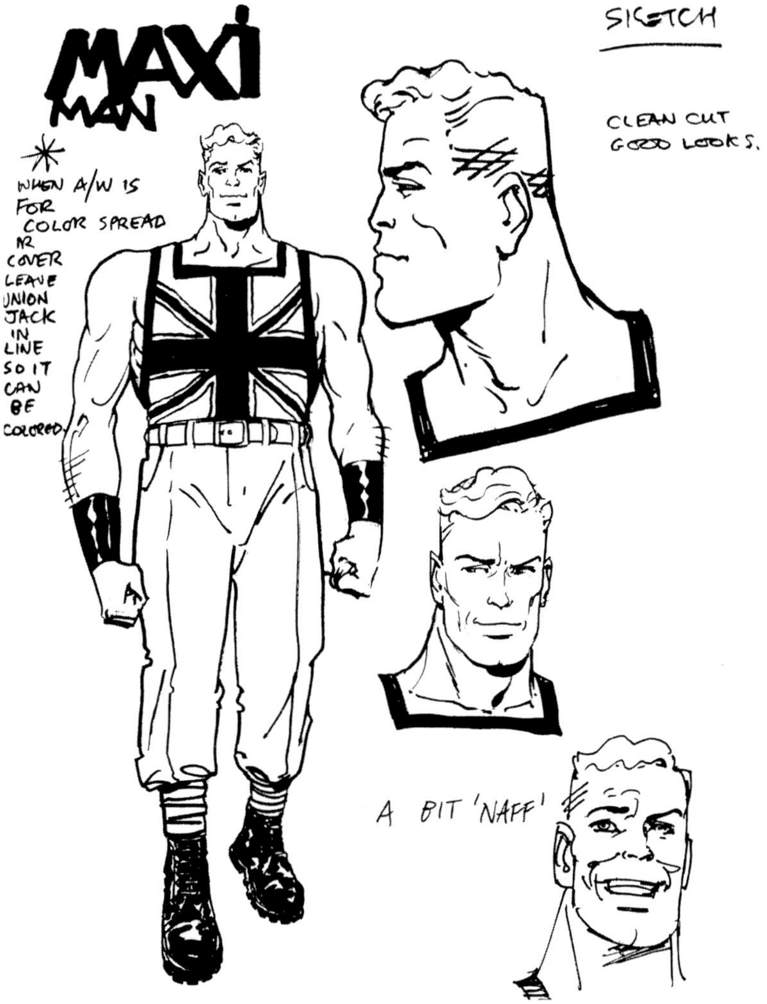
SKETCH
MAXI MAN
WHEN A/W IS FOR COLOR SPREAD OR COVER LEAVE UNION JACK IN LINE SO IT CAN BE COLORED.
CLEAN CUT GOOD LOOKS.
A BIT 'NAFF'

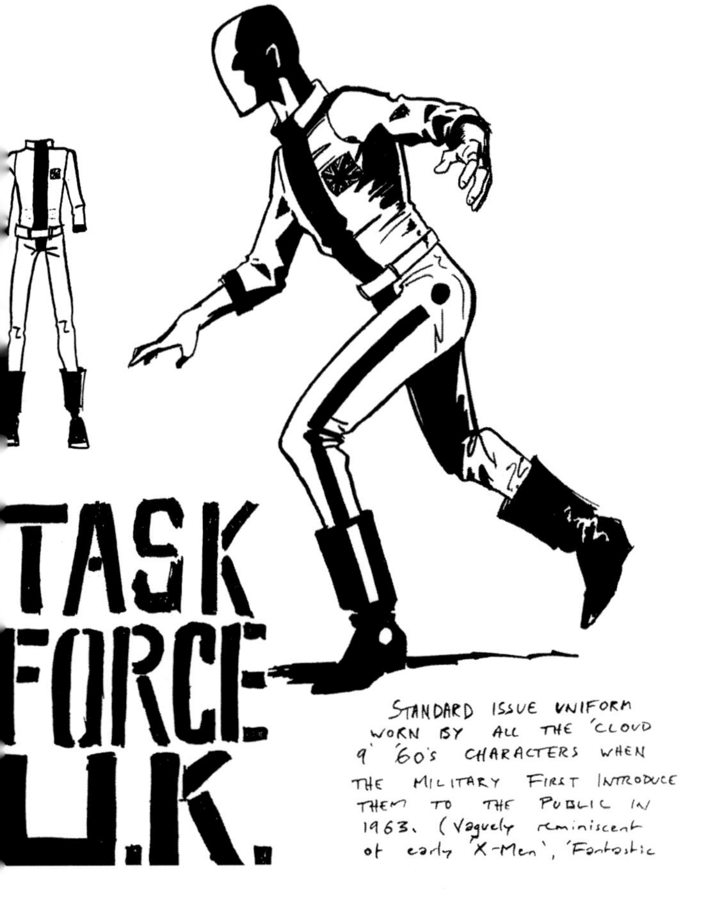
TASK FORCE U.K.
STANDARD ISSUE UNIFORM WORN BY ALL THE 'CLOUD 9' '60's CHARACTERS WHEN THE MILITARY FIRST INTRODUCE THEM TO THE PUBLIC IN 1963. (Vaguely reminiscent of early 'X-Men', 'Fantastic

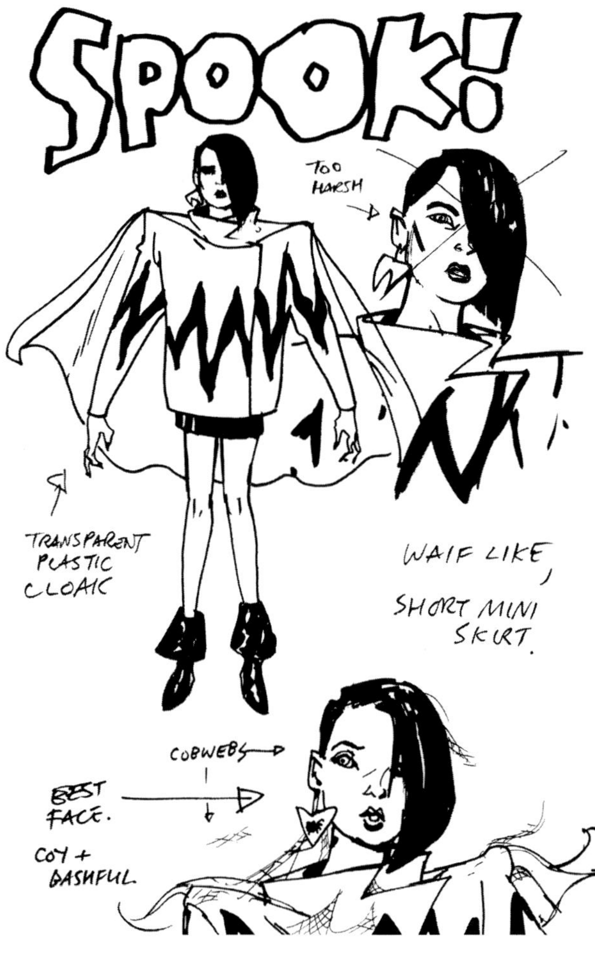
SPOOK!
TOO HARSH
TRANSPARENT PLASTIC CLOAK
WAIF LIKE, SHORT MINI SKIRT.
COBWEBS
BEST FACE.
COY + BASHFUL.

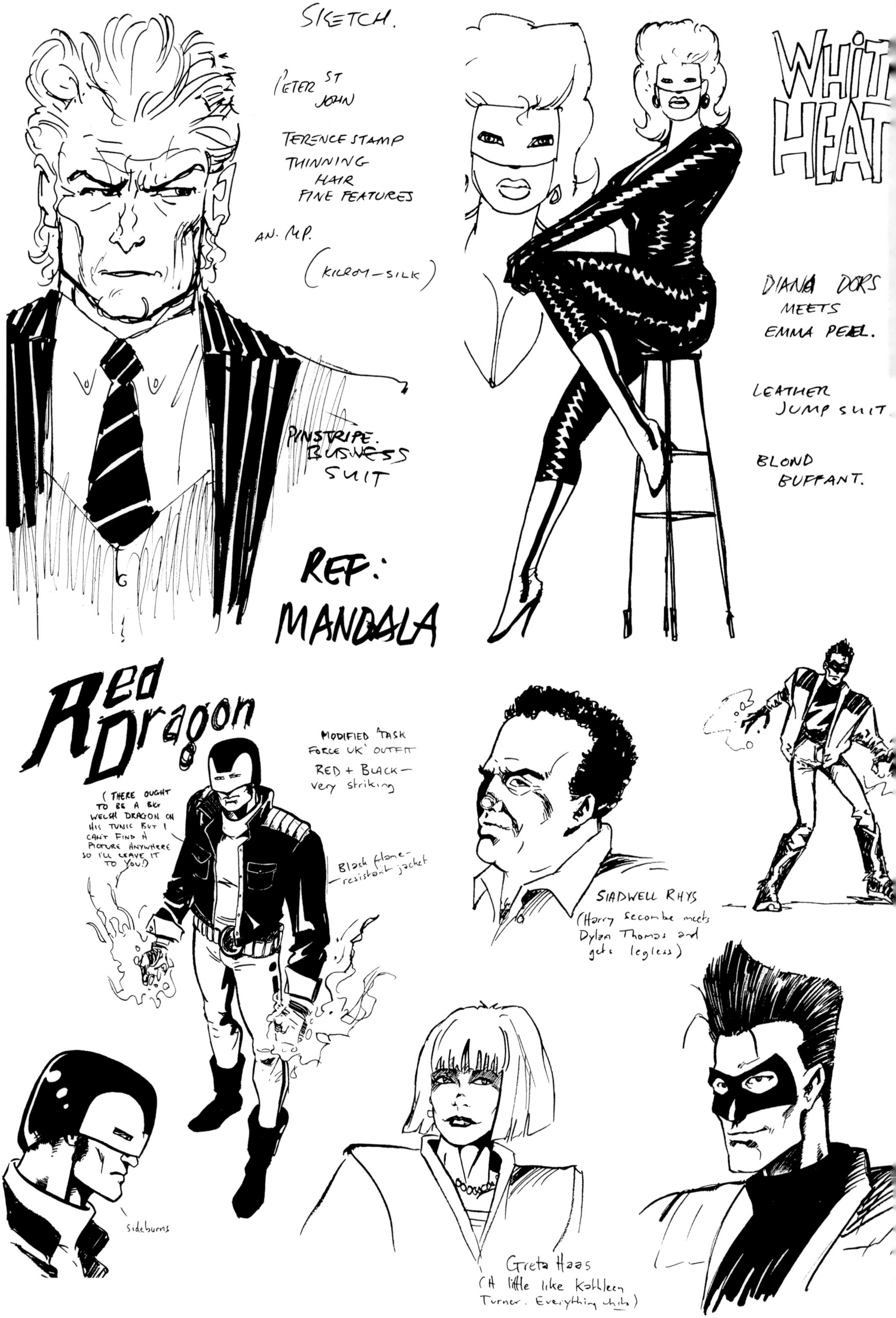
SKETCH.
PETER ST JOHN
TERENCE STAMP
THINNING HAIR
FINE FEATURES
AN. MP.
(KILROY—SILK)
PINSTRIPE. BUSINESS SUIT
REF: MANDALA
WHITE HEAT
DIANA DORS MEETS EMMA PEEL.
LEATHER JUMP SUIT.
BLOND BUFFANT.
Red Dragon
MODIFIED 'TASK FORCE UK' OUTFIT
RED + BLACK— very striking
(THERE OUGHT TO BE A BIG WELSH DRAGON ON HIS TUNIC BUT I CAN'T FIND A PICTURE ANYWHERE SO I'LL LEAVE IT TO YOU!)
Black flame-resistant jacket
SIADWELL RHYS
(Harry Secombe meets Dylan Thomas and gets legless)
sideburns
Greta Haas
(A little like Kathleen Turner. Everything white)

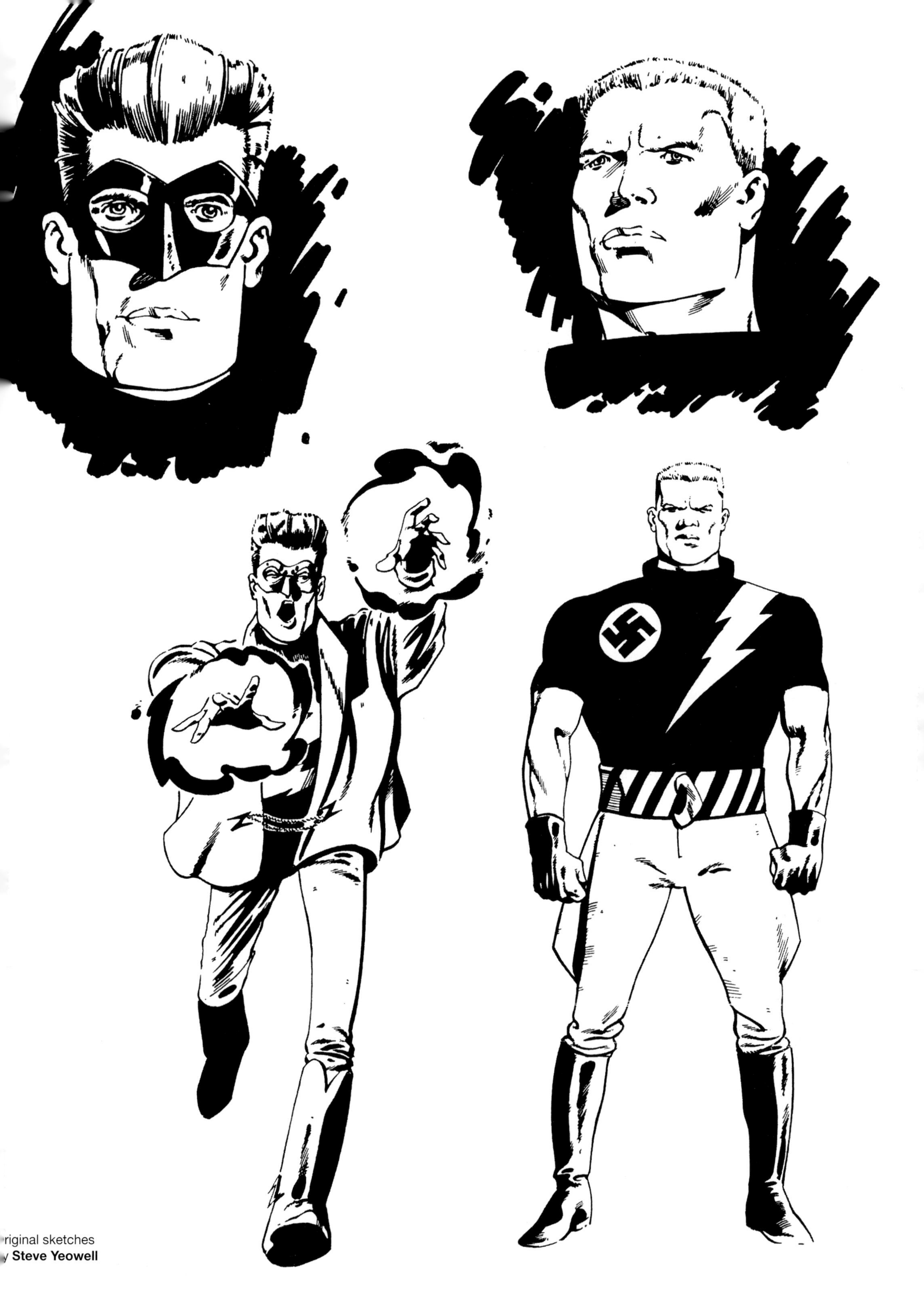

riginal sketches
y **Steve Yeowell**

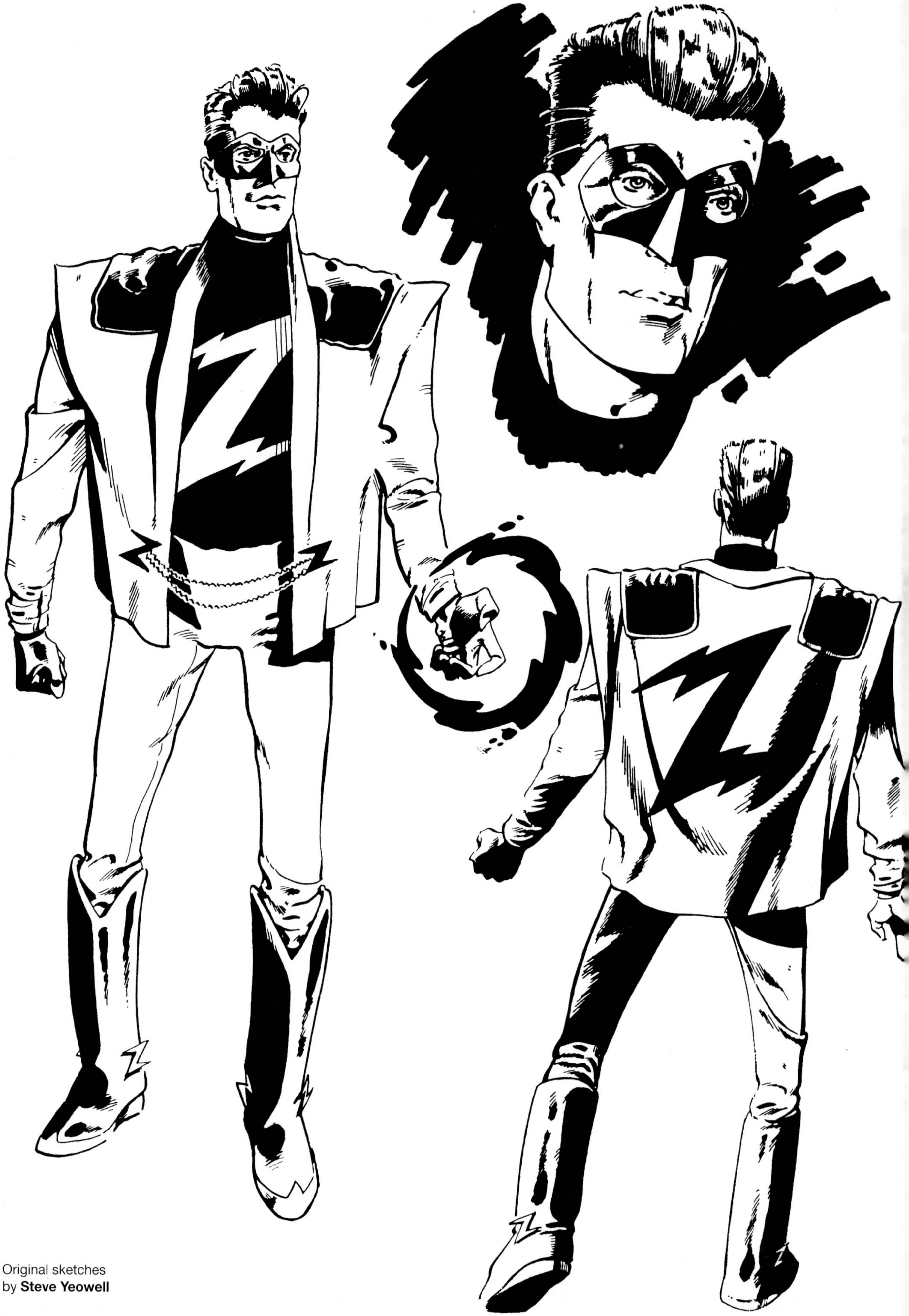

Original sketches
by **Steve Yeowell**

GRANT MORRISON

Grant Morrison is one of the most successful ex-*2000 AD* writers, with a host of critical awards and a huge following. He began his career on Marvel UK's *Zoids* before coming to the Galaxy's Greatest Comic, where his strip *Zenith* became a fan-favourite. At first a prolific writer of 'mature readers' comics, including the award-winning *Animal Man, Batman: Arkham Asylum, Doom Patrol, The Invisibles* and *The Filth* for Vertigo, he has gone on to write successful runs on the *X-Men* and *Batman* and won numerous awards for his work on *All-Star Superman.*

STEVE YEOWELL

Steve Yeowell has been a massively popular *2000 AD* artist, since his debut as artist of the classic *Zenith*. He is also co-creator of *Maniac 5, Red Fang, Red Razors* and *The Red Seas*, and has pencilled *Armitage, Black Light, DeMarco, Devlin Waugh, Future Shocks, Judge Dredd, A Life Less Ordinary, Nikolai Dante, Pussyfoot 5, The Scarlet Apocrypha, Sinister Dexter, Tharg the Mighty, Vector 13* and *Black Shuck*.

His work outside the Galaxy's Greatest Comic includes *Batman, Doom Patrol, The Invisibles, Sebastian O, Skrull Kill Krew, Starman* and *X-Men*.

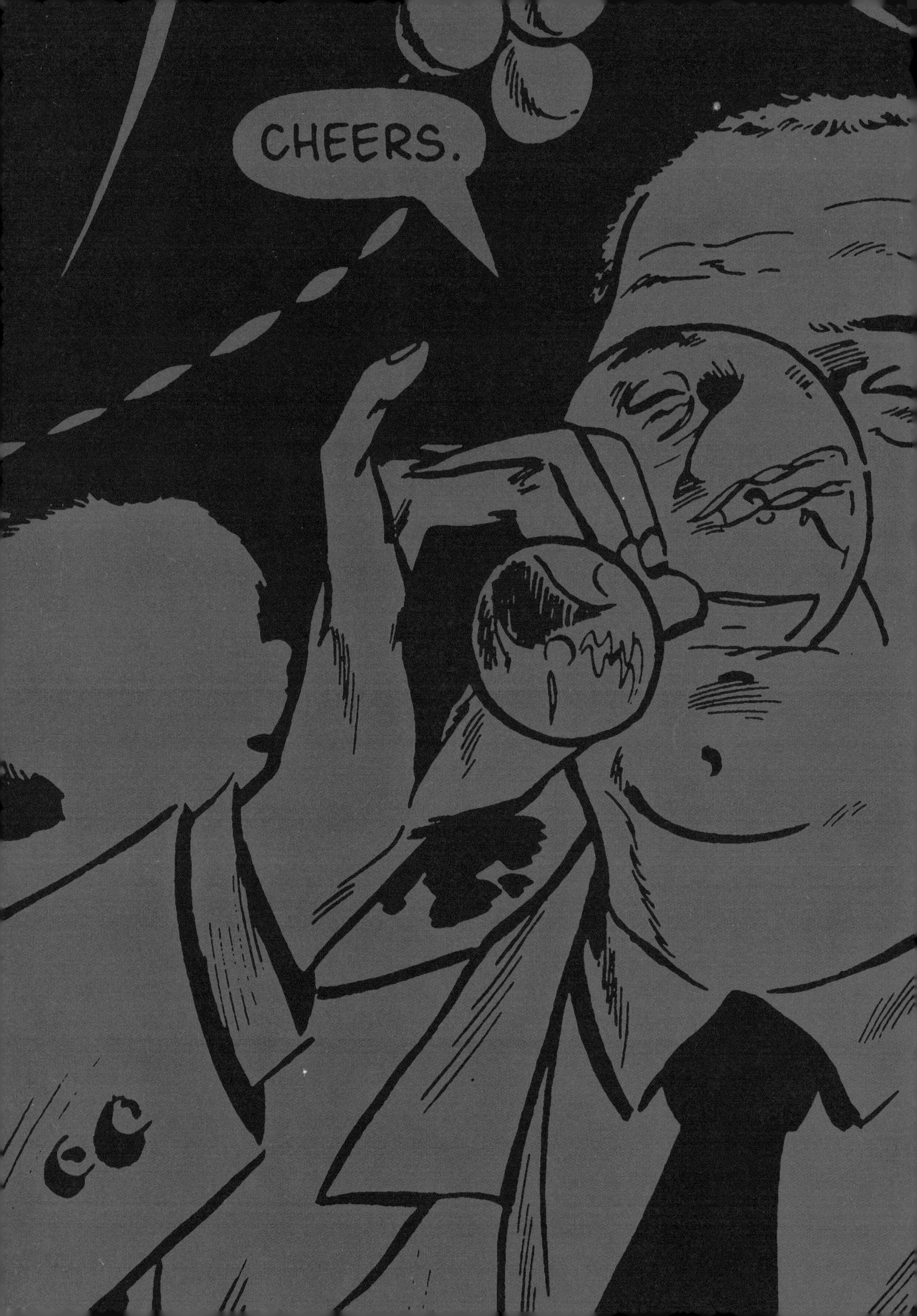
CHEERS.